Seeing Through the Visible World

ALSO BY JUNE SINGER

Boundaries of the Soul: The Practice of Jung's Psychology

*The Unholy Bible: Blake, Jung, and the
Collective Unconscious*

Androgyny: The Opposites Within

Love's Energies

Seeing Through the Visible World

JUNG, GNOSIS, AND CHAOS

June Singer

1817

HARPER & ROW, PUBLISHERS, SAN FRANCISCO

*New York, Grand Rapids, Philadelphia, St. Louis
London, Singapore, Sydney, Tokyo, Toronto*

Library of Congress Cataloging-in-Publication Data
Singer, June.
    Seeing through the visible world: Jung, Gnosis, and Chaos
      / June Singer.—1st ed.
      p. cm.
    Includes bibliographical references.
    ISBN 0-06-250780-X
    1. Psychoanalysis and religion. 2. Subconsciousness.
  3. Gnosticism. 4. Jung, C. G. (Carl Gustav), 1875–1961. I. Title.
BF175.4.R44S55 1990
150.19'54—dc20   89-45988
                                            CIP

90 91 92 93 94 RRD(H) 10 9 8 7 6 5 4 3 2 1

This edition is printed on acid-free paper that meets the American
National Standards Institute Z39.48 Standard.

For Irving—
the Sunshine in my life.

Art does not reproduce the visible.
It renders visible.

Paul Klee, 1919

Contents

Preface

The Parable of the Ant

The little girl watched intently as a large black ant walked slowly across the wooden floorboards of the back porch, crawled up along the edge of the doorjamb, and began to climb the vertical plane of the door. The ant strayed in its path, now to the right and then again slightly to the left, but it seemed to the girl that the ant was heading for the doorknob. The ascent would be long and arduous, and eventually, when the ant arrived at that destination, it would have no possible way to open the door and enter the house. But I, the girl thought, can easily get up from where I am sitting, turn the knob, open the door, and walk in. The ant would have no idea how I managed this marvelous feat, because an ant could never do such a thing, much less figure out how I did it.

The girl, who could not have been more than seven or eight, thought about this long and hard: I am so much more than this ant. What I can do, the ant cannot even imagine. If the ant observed me as I got up and walked over to the door, put my hand on the doorknob, opened the door and stepped inside, it would surely wonder at my marvelous powers. From the ant's point of view I would be accomplishing a miracle!

Then a great realization struck the child. The way the ant is in relation to me, must be the way I am in relation to God. Just as my acts are great mysteries to the ant, even so are God's acts great mysteries to me. As the ant doesn't have the ability to understand what I do, much less why, so I don't have the ability to understand what God does, much less why.

I was that little girl. The incident I have described was the first spiritual experience I can remember. Although I had heard about God from my parents and my religious school, and had been taught to pray, I was always troubled by a healthy skepticism about anything I could not see for myself. That moment on the back porch was the first time I realized that what was a mystery to me was mysterious only because of my own limitations. There might be more beyond the familiar world than I had thought, only I could not see it. This idea tantalized and challenged me. I must have determined then and there to try to expand my ability to see—not that I expected to see as God sees, but I wanted with all my heart to penetrate as far as I could into the interstellar spaces of the invisible world.

■

Stories from the Bible made up most of the subject matter of my Sunday School classes over the next several years. My parents belonged to a Reform Jewish congregation that based its teachings more on contemporary interpretations of the Jewish faith than on strict adherence to the traditional laws and customs. In those days, before the rise of Hitler, Reform Judaism was the denomination of choice for Jews who desired to maintain a minimal identity with the religion of their ancestors while at the same time assimilating most comfortably into the general culture. In public school and in my home I was used to hearing about all sorts of religious customs and holidays, from strict Orthodox Jewish practices to those of Roman Catholicism (my mother had spent her early teens in a Catholic boarding school). My parents had decided—rightly, I think—that it was important for their children to have some religious identity and religious background. That way, if we should choose at some later time to follow a different religious tradition, or none at all, we would at least know from what we were departing.

My Sunday School teachers presented the Bible stories to the younger students as the record of events that happened to the Jewish people. For three or four years, I thoroughly enjoyed hearing these exciting adventures of a brave and God-fearing lineage. However, before long I found myself wondering whether the tales were really absolutely true. It had already been impressed upon me that it was a good thing to tell "the truth." I could accept the *idea* of the miraculous, and when I *saw* something I could not understand, I was willing to believe the miraculous; but how could I be sure these things really happened—like the sea parting before the wand of Moses—just on someone else's word? So I asked aloud in class, "Did this *really* happen just the way you told us?" The teacher, taken aback, replied, "Yes, indeed, just the way I told you." Not to be put off, I continued, "How do you know?" "That's enough, June. We'll have no more questions," came the reply.

From that time on, I became increasingly resistant to attending religious school. I continued only because of the insistence of my parents. I entered the confirmation class at the age of fourteen with high expectations, because the rabbi himself was coming to give us instruction. On the first day he confided to us, with great solemnity, that certain events in the Bible may not have happened exactly as they had been represented to us. He said that they could have been records of people's beliefs in those days, or that they were probably the best explanations those people could find for happenings they did not understand. I did not hear whatever else he may have said, because I was so angry at having been duped. I had known all along that they were not telling me the truth! They thought I was too simple to understand! Well then, I decided, I would find out for myself what was true and what was story.

■

Myself when young did eagerly frequent
Doctor and Saint, and heard great Argument
About it and about, but evermore
Came out by the same Door as in I went.
Rubaiyat of Omar Khayyam, FITZGERALD TRANS.

During the next few months I "went for a walk" every Sunday morning. What I actually did was to visit a different church in my neighborhood each week. Some were of stately gothic design, with stained glass windows. Others were simple wooden structures with little decoration. One had painted statues of saints, another was adorned only with a simple brass crucifix. One priest chanted in a language I did not understand, another offered a moralizing sermon. They all had one thing in common, though, and that was that the clergymen all seemed to know what God was like, what he did, and exactly how he expected people to behave. Still, in my mind persisted the questions: How do they know all this? How can they be so certain? My confusion was compounded by the fact that although each clergyman professed to imparting "the truth" to his congregation, these "truths" often differed in marked degree.

There was little room in those churches for me, stumbling toward God, to find my own way. If I'd wanted to talk to Him there were plenty of ministers and priests who would have told me just what to say. I could not have put my feelings into words at that time, but now, in retrospect, I see that I had begun to realize that religion often stands in the way of spiritual experience, and that spiritual experience often stands in the way of religion. I use the word *religion* here in the sense of a belief system handed down through a line of authority and supported by an institution designed to preserve that system. By *spiritual experience* I mean an individual's direct, original glimpse into the divine mystery.

I began to become aware of the relationship between psychology and spirituality when I was in my middle teens. I recall the day in the public library near my home when I discovered a whole section of books locked behind glass doors. My natural curiosity aroused, I peered through the leaded panes and read such intriguing titles as *The Mind That Found Itself* and *The Psychology of the Unconscious*. I asked the librarian whether I could take out some of those books. She replied, "You'll have to bring me written permission from your mother." Mother wrote the note that released to me the books that propelled me toward what was to become my life's work—exploring the mysteries of the mind. That must have been about 1933.

I have now passed the age of seventy and am still engaged in the work of directing that slender beam of light called consciousness into the vast realms of darkness, the invisible world. I have come to understand that the only aspects of the interstellar spaces that I am likely to see lie within the universe of the mind, because nothing that exists in fact or fantasy has any reality except as filtered through the mysterious complexity of the brain, and the mind or psyche that interprets what the brain makes perceptible.

I recall now what Schopenhauer wrote a century ago in his essay "The Ages of Life" (1891): "The first forty years of life furnish the text, while the remaining thirty supply the commentary: without the commentary we are unable to understand aright the true sense and coherence of the text, together with the moral it contains" (p. 113). For me, the first four decades were occupied in constructing a life for myself that conformed essentially to the standards that my early conditioning and later my role as wife, mother, and professional woman had led me to regard as "appropriate." The word still makes me cringe! *Appropriate* means "fitting" in the eyes of the world, a world that in reality is only the tiny fragment of humanity to which, by virtue of birth or circumstance, one belongs. Toward the end of that period I began to study psychology in a university, and though I earned a graduate degree, I did not practice as a psychologist. My academic work had not brought me to that deep understanding of the boundless realms of the psyche that I had imagined I would find when I first read the books on the forbidden shelves of the library. Yet all the while I was adding to the "text" of my life. It was only when I began my personal Jungian analysis, and later when I went into training to become an analyst at the C. G. Jung Institute in Zurich, that the "commentary" began to take form.

A Century of Psychology

When I was a teenager, I thought that psychology was about the psyche. The word *psychology* comes from the Greek word *psyche*, meaning life, spirit, soul, self, and is akin to *psychein*, to breathe or blow. It is the vital principle of corporeal matter that is a distinct mental or spiritual entity coextensive with but independent of the body or soma. I knew that Psyche in Graeco-Roman mythology was a beautiful maiden personifying the soul who was loved by the god of love, Eros. I am certain that the earliest psychologists knew this too, but this knowledge was apparently lost when psychology aspired to become a science.

A young woman who is working toward her doctorate in psychology is in analysis with me. Recently she brought me a fragment of a dream, consisting of the following single statement: *Schools of psychology are not psychology, the minuet is not the dance, the clothes are not the person.* Something in her knew that learning about a subject is different from experiencing it, and that appearances should not be confused with essence. How many individuals enter into the field of psychology hoping to gain an understanding of the subtle and mysterious workings of the human mind, only to find themselves embroiled in the observations of minute portions of behavior of mice and men, not to mention the tasks of sorting these all out with the aid of tests and measurements and computers, and a language that no one except a fellow student or professional in the field could begin to understand! It was not always like this.

Psychology as a modern science began only at the turn of the century. Sigmund Freud published his most important early work, *The Interpretation of Dreams* (*Traumdeutung*), in 1900. Actually, it was completed in 1899, but sensing the importance of the centenary as a time of new beginnings, Freud requested that his seminal book be dated 1900. That same year the behaviorist John B. Watson received the first doctorate in psychology given by the University of Chicago with a ground-breaking dissertation on maze learning in rats; C. G. Jung was completing his doctoral thesis in Zurich, "On the Psychology and Pathology of So-Called Occult Phenomena" ("Zur Psychologie und Psychopathologie sogennante occulter Phaenomene"); and William James was preparing his controversial lectures on "The Varieties of Religious Experience," to be delivered in Edinburgh the following year. Every one of these pioneers in the scientific study of the mind was concerned at least as much with the mysteries that lie behind the thought processes and behaviors of human beings as they were with documenting specific events that occurred in the outer, or visible, world. The passion with which these early psychologists pursued the unknown was well illustrated by William James in one of his lectures, when he said, "That unsharable feeling which each one of us has of the pinch of his individual destiny as he privately feels it rolling out on fortune's wheel may be disparaged for its egotism, may be sneered at as unscientific, but it is the one thing that fills up the measure of our concrete actuality, and any would-be existent that should lack such a feeling, or its analogue, would be a piece of reality only half made up" (1928, p. 499).

Psychology Becomes a Science

Since those days, psychology has strayed far from the vision of the early seekers. In its effort to gain respectability among the sciences, it has turned to examining what can be weighed and measured, counted and verified. But psyche, which is supposed to be the subject matter of the field of psychology, resists mightily all efforts to contain and control it. The science of psychology is further complicated by the fact that the entity that considers the human psyche is the human psyche itself—hardly a disinterested observer. Yet "scientific method" seeks to reduce, or better yet, eliminate, the effects of subjectivity in its experiments. The consequence of scientific attempts to achieve objectivity is that traditional academic psychology has limited itself mostly to the study of discrete samples of behavior and to extrapolations derived from that study. The visible world of the mind has been reduced to elementary particles, and the resulting minutiae have been laid out— to be named and categorized. But the soul, that aspect of the human being that refuses containment in the visible world, is turned away by this approach. Two centuries ago William Blake, poet, painter, and philosopher, might have been predicting the calcification of "scientific psychology" (an oxymoron if there ever was one) when he wrote in his long narrative poem *The Four Zoas,*

Why wilt thou examine every little fibre of my soul,
Spreading them out before the sun like stalks of flax to dry?
 . . . naught shalt thou find in it
But Death, Despair, & Everlasting brooding Melancholy.
Thou wilt go mad with horror if thou dost examine thus
Every moment of my secret hours.

(1957, p. 265)

Plumbing the Depths of Psyche

I believe that the depth psychology of Freud, Jung, and their followers (in contradistinction to academic psychology, to which it has never wholeheartedly subscribed) survives and will continue to exist because it takes into account the whole person: conscious, unconscious, and the flow between them; body, mind, and spirit; known, unknown, and unknowable. I write in the spirit of inquiry into those unconscious depths of the human spirit, and into the ways those depths are projected upon the outer world—where they may be seen as aspects of the "interstellar spaces." Today, when so much is being reported from the field of high-energy physics and other rapidly advancing sciences about the quest for a universal field theory, I cannot help but wonder whether there might someday be a universal field theory of mind as well as of matter and energy. Much of what I explore in this book are the efforts of people who seem to me to be wise, and who have directly or indirectly come to this same hope. If there is wholeness and integrity in this world, and among all its interlocking systems, then surely we are part of this integrity; and mind, the organ of consciousness, is part of the whole as well, and functions as an element of the system. For whatever is observed to be outside of ourselves has first to come through the boundaries of our skin, into the eye or the ear or the highly disciplined scientific mind, or the mind of the ordinary individual. Nothing can be seen or heard or understood unless there is first someone to perceive it. Over and above the complex scientific machinery that helps theorists discover the wider reaches of the world we live in, is the complex human being, the person, who interprets the data that the machinery spews forth. Every fact, every theory, every assumption, every belief, must be screened through the filter of human consciousness, sifted, sorted, and arranged by the mind so that people can make sense out of observations or data. The task of the mind, the human intellect, is not only to see through or see beyond what is apparent. It is to make the apparent transparent.

When I began my studies at the Jung Institute in Zurich in 1960, I was given very little guidance as to what to read, how to sort out and arrange Jung's ideas, how to apply them to my own experience. Only a small portion of Jung's *Collected Works* had been translated into English, and it was necessary to rely on the translations and interpretations of the instructors and the personal analysts. For the first few months I sat in class understanding only a small bit of what I was hearing. When I did understand something, it was as if brightly colored jewels appeared all of a sudden in the night sky, a few to remain and the rest to be reabsorbed quickly by the darkness. Ever so gradually the jewels began to link together into constellations, and then I began to see patterns and interrelationships. Eventually I was able to perceive a fairly coherent system and to apply the insights gleaned from it to my own life and work. It was a slow, laborious, and agonizing process. I often thought, Why doesn't someone arrange this body of knowledge in a sequence from the simple basic elements to the more complex concepts, and illustrate every concept with the actual experience of a real person?

I took up my courage and asked this question of my analyst. Immediately her back stiffened. "How could you imagine," she said, "that these strange and mysterious workings of the psyche could ever be explained to a novice in purely intellectual terms? One has to go through the experience of analysis to understand this. I don't think it's possible to do what you want to do." I believed that it *was* possible, but recognized that I was ill-prepared at that time to undertake such a task; still, I resolved that somehow, someday, I would do it.

After I had completed my studies, received my diploma in analytical psychology (the term Jung used to differentiate his work from Freud's psychoanalysis), and had been in practice as an analyst in Chicago for nearly a decade, I decided to write the book I had conceived while at the Jung Institute. I took my title from the words of the Greek philosopher Heraclitus: "You would not find out the boundaries of the soul, even by travelling every path, so deep a measure does it have." (Bakewell 1907, p. 31) My objective with this book was to organize and systematize Jung's basic concepts having to do with the nature and function of the psyche. I would describe each concept in general and then illustrate how it functions in human lives, especially in the lives of men and women of our own time in the United States, using examples from cases I had encountered in my own analytic practice. It was the only way I knew whereby the reader might be given insight into how the Jungian analytic process is experienced by individuals, and how the mysteries of the unconscious are revealed to them through observation of their dreams and behavior, and reflection upon these observations.

In the process of writing *Boundaries of the Soul* (1972), I saw early on that it would be important, if not essential, to draw upon the experiences and insights of clients with whom I worked in analysis. I hesitate to say "Jungian analysis" because I have often departed from the classical Jungian form of therapy, choosing to follow my inner guidance in preference to any preconceived theory, no matter how valuable. But since my way of working has been informed and inspired by the teachings of C. G. Jung, I must acknowledge that what I do, though not done in imitation of Jung, is nevertheless basically in the spirit of Jung. Since Jung himself never imitated anyone, I believe I am on safe ground in saying this.

I used a great deal of case material in *Boundaries* in attempting to describe the practice of Jung's psychology. When I began to write, I explained to my analysand-clients that I wanted to portray the events and experiences of the analytic process as realistically as possible, and I requested their permission to use some details from their personal lives and from their dreams. Of course, I would be careful to disguise their identity, I assured them. Without exception, all the people I asked agreed to the use of their material. I took their affirmative statements at face value.

I recall that I had some uneasy feelings at the time, knowing that I was using something that did not belong to me, even if the "owners" were willing to allow me to use it. Now I am writing again, and I know that unless the material comes out of living experience, it does not live. However, with the passing years I have come to realize that using case material responsibly is not a simple matter of requesting and receiving "informed consent." I feel a need now to examine some of the questions of which I was only dimly aware at the time but did not explore with the analysands. The questions have not gone away. Following are some of them:

Did these analysands give their consent with open hearts and true willingness? Or was the transference operative—that is, were they unconsciously "transferring" some feelings associated with their earlier experiences into the analytic relationship? For example, were they eager to please me, to do something for me—as they had done previously with their parents and teachers to gain approval—even if that something were not consonant with their personal feelings?

Would they attempt to push the unconscious into supplying the sort of material they thought I wanted? Would they only bring "meaningful" dreams, for instance?

Would they discuss matters that they knew were of interest to me, even though these might not be at the top of their own priority lists?

Would they consciously or unconsciously feel exploited? I was acutely aware that, after all, they had not come into the sacred space of the analytical relationship to have their personal material published.

Would they think that I was more interested in their material for my book than for what it meant to them?

Would they feel obliged to bring me material I would find useful in my writing, and feel inadequate if the material they had to present might be dull and uninteresting?

Would their knowledge that I might use their material have the effect of turning a positive transference relationship into a negative one?

As I write this nearly twenty years after beginning *Boundaries of the Soul*, I realize that I did not make all these issues sufficiently conscious while I was working on the earlier book. I preferred not to think about them. Doubts and hesitations did arise in the course of the writing, but I managed to push them aside without fully exploring them. After all, the analysands had said yes. It was only now, as I was facing the prospect of using case material again, and with many more years of experience as an analyst behind me, that the doubts and fears not made sufficiently conscious before came flooding into my awareness. I swore to myself that this time I would handle it differently.

My first impulse was to not use case material at all in *Seeing Through the Visible World*. The world of the unconscious is a secret world. The darker powers, what some call "the archons," lie hidden in the deepest inner recesses of the psyche beyond the range of discrimination and judgment. No serious or consequential writing about deeply personal matters comes from an abstract process of cognition in a vacuum, or from material written down in the past; it comes out of the flesh-and-blood experience of living day by day. To write truly, and not simply to paraphrase material that has been passed down and repeated time after time, it is necessary to observe keenly what is happening in the world and in the psyche. A writer needs to *see* and then to attempt to draw meaning out of what is seen, meaning that is not always visible but that may belong to the invisible world. I felt the need to work with the real soul-substance, knowing that if I did not do so my work would be counterfeit.

There have been other books since *Boundaries*, and they have had a life of their own. *Boundaries* left certain questions unanswered, and if the years between have not answered them, they have surely added dimension and depth to their exploration. The last chapter in *Boundaries* dealt with an elderly man who had striven to live a conscious inner life. He had experienced the meeting of the opposites in many ways; for example, he had come to terms with his feeling side as well as his intellectual side. Over the long years, Eros (the god who presides over loving relationships) had come to rest at the side of Logos (the principle of truth as sought through reason) so that what the ancients called the *hieros gamos*, or sacred inner marriage, had occurred in him. At the end of his life, he dreamed that his dearly beloved child had died in his arms, and he had to let go of her. In his dream, he grieved inconsolably that he must give her up. As I talked with him about the dream, the meaning of the child emerged. In the end everyone must lose what is most precious, that to which one's whole life has been devoted. That precious treasure is consciousness. It is the final sacrifice of the ego, which must be offered up before the ultimate moment when one merges with the unconscious and stands before the *Mysterium Tremendum*. In the dream the old man fell on his knees and prayed to God to give him back his child. The book ends with the statement: "It is the prayer that may or may not be answered. It belongs to the unknowable."

Seeing Through the Visible World

Where *Boundaries of the Soul* ended, *Seeing Through the Visible World* begins. It begins with "the unknowable." The theme of this book is the recognition that there is much in life that is unknowable through the mechanisms of ordinary human awareness. There is a "visible world" and there is an "invisible world." Both are real, although they are real in different ways. Both need to be recognized and experienced, and ways can and must be found to move between the two in response to the demands that life places upon us as human beings.

I conceive of the *visible world* as finite and limited, and the *invisible world* as infinite and unbounded. The mind is a function of the brain, which is part of our physical bodies. Mind depends upon brain for its functioning; hence its primary concern is for the survival of the body, the structure that enables it to exist. Thus, our minds belong mainly to the visible world, for the human mind has its limitations and its boundaries. Yet the mind is more than this. It reaches out beyond itself. When we speak of "pushing our edges" we mean that we are pushing back those boundaries ever farther into the invisible. But the paradox is that as soon as we discover, or rediscover, something that *was* invisible, it is no longer invisible but has become a part of the visible world.

Another term for the visible world is *consciousness*. The invisible or the unconscious is still out there, forever beyond our reach, because it has no limits. A more visual way of conceptualizing this is to imagine yourself at the center of a small spiral drawn on a sheet of paper. As you move outward along the line in spiral fashion, the spiral rolls out ahead of you encompassing an ever-increasing area. As you move along the spiral defining the visible world, the space around the spiral that is tangential to it becomes correspondingly larger. As you continue to wind in the same direction, the spiral increases in size and the area outside the spiral expands exponentially. If you were to continue until the spiral rolled out beyond your paper, beyond your room, beyond your house and beyond your city, the boundary between the spiral of the visible world and the infinite expanse of the invisible would become ever greater. The more you encompass of the visible world with the knowing of the *mind*, the more aware you may become of the expanse of the unknowable.

But there is another way of knowing: the way of the *soul*. This kind of knowing has been called *gnosis* since ancient times, to distinguish it from the kind of knowledge that comes from intellect and reason alone. *Psyche* is the Greek term for *soul*, and it is in this sense that I use it. Soul, or psyche, is that aspect of the individual that is composed of both the conscious and unconscious aspects: ways of knowing of which we are primarily aware (such as thinking, feeling, and sensation), and ways of knowing that seem to be mobilized primarily in realms of the unconscious (for example, intuition, speculation, imagination, and dreaming). All these ways of knowing belong to the realm of the psyche, or soul. Mind is included in the psyche, but the psyche is not limited to the exercise of the mental processes. The soul bridges the gap between what can be learned through the mind, through the senses, through the intellect, and through the exercise of scientific observation—and the intuitive awareness of a deep, abiding, mysterious space that may be penetrated by consciousness but can never be encompassed by it.

My first primitive realization that there are different levels of consciousness and that there are natural limitations to understanding came about when as a small child I watched the ant inching up my back door. Recently, I was reminded of my earlier experience while I watched with fascination a National Geographic Society television documentary on the life of insects. Close-ups of ants in well-organized colonies, scurrying about as they carried out their "duties," demonstrated clearly that the ant—who to me had appeared quite stupid in comparison with my sense of my own superior intellect—does not appear stupid at all when viewed from another perspective. I saw that this tiny six-legged creature holds an active membership in an extremely well-developed social order where everyone has a place, where each member cooperates by doing useful work to contribute to a society that sustains the needs of all, and that the ant has adapted in a way that suggests it will survive at least as long as the human species. I had then to add to my original insight that those who are lower in the hierarchical *levels* of consciousness, are lower only from the perspective of those who consider themselves higher. I had also to add that there are different *orders* of consciousness, based upon differing needs, differing assumptions, and the differing capacities of individuals. This realization supplemented the kit of tools I have been collecting for my forays into the invisible world. The adventure is the subject of this book: how it is possible to discover the invisible world, and to traverse the boundaries between the known and the unknown, and between the unknown and the unknowable.

About This Book

Seeing Through the Visible World is divided into three parts. Part I reminds us that an awareness of an invisible world that exists alongside the world we know through our senses is not a new insight. As individuals, we have always known of both worlds, but due to many circumstances, we tend to forget about the existence of the invisible aspects of reality. Nevertheless, the invisible world forces itself upon us from time to time, and inevitably we find it necessary to confront it, whether we wish to do so or not.

Part II explores some of the ways in which society has tried to explore or explain the invisible world and its effects upon humankind.

Science, and particularly the physical sciences, have attempted to describe "the way things are." In the eighteenth and nineteenth centuries, scientists relied on sensory perception and objective observation to provide a picture of a world that was known or could be known eventually, given sufficient data. Whatever did not fit into the confines of this assumption was deemed to be outside the province of science and hence not to be a fit subject for scientific inquiry. But the twentieth century has produced a wave of "new scientists" who are asking questions that cannot be answered with facts and figures only: What is the nature of the universe? How did it come into being? What, if any, is its purpose? What role does humanity have in the process of evolution? We will see how the new scientists respond to those questions in Part II.

Religion, also, has attempted to explore and explain phenomena on the edge of the unknowable. Two diametrically opposed methods of approach have been used here; the first is based upon faith in traditional belief systems and acceptance of the doctrines put forth by the theological authorities, while the second arises out of gnosis, an experience of inner knowing based upon a direct perception of the divine mystery that cannot be named. Religious approaches to the essential questions have been both pessimistic, as expressed by those apocalyptists who foresee an end to this visible world along with all its negative qualities; and optimistic, setting forth the hope of a Messiah or Redeemer or a Messianic Age when we will have learned how to bring the resources of the invisible world into the world we know, and thereby to forestall the cataclysmic end.

The third approach investigated in Part II is that of contemporary psychology, and in particular the psychology of the unconscious. Much of what we think and do is motivated by ideas that we believe to be our own, but that may have been imposed upon us from outside ourselves and may be contrary to our own best interests. I will describe how societies create their own worlds, or world views, and then institute the fiction that these views represent "normalcy." We will see the necessity for discriminating the ways in which social, scientific, and political institutions may use psychological means to manipulate the psyches of their members.

Part III is about discovering and using the best of both worlds. It begins with a survey of the tools and methods that we can cultivate in order to make contact with the invisible world, which is not very far away. The marvelous can be found in the mundane if we learn how to recognize it when it emerges into view. With a receptive attitude and the development of certain practices that will be described, we can experience within ourselves the unfolding of the invisible world. Some warnings are in order, however. The invisible world can be a dangerous place if approached improperly, without the necessary preparation and commitment to the process. Those who embark on this quest will be tested to see if they have the necessary fortitude to pull away the veil between the visible and the invisible. Striving toward this goal will bring about some surprising consequences, not the least of which is the recognition that the process by which we come to this level of consciousness is far more important than any specific knowledge we may have gained along the way.

■

I wish to touch on one more matter before moving into the main body of this book. It has to do with the necessity I feel for dealing with my subject from the perspective of individual experience. I cannot talk about seeing through the visible world without recognizing that there is someone who sees through, and without knowing who that someone is and something about that person. To a depth psychologist, nothing is real until it has been processed through the human psyche. So to make my points, I find that if I am to come near to telling the truth I must be free to draw from the personal experiences of real human beings and the insights that derive from them. My personal insights flow mainly from three sources: from my readings; from what is revealed to me by others in the course of the analytic process; and from what comes up in me from my own depths—my experiences, observations, and dreams. I am deeply indebted to those people in analysis who have shared with me the twists and turns of their own journeys between the visible and invisible worlds and have allowed me to recount some of their adventures on the way. I can do no less than they, by sharing with the reader some of the highlights of my own journey.

PART I

Astride Two Worlds

The visible world and the invisible world exist for each person, but they are not the same for everyone. Each of us gives these worlds a unique imprint, because we see them through the lens of our own psyche, a lens colored by our own conditioning. That the worlds are viewed from a great variety of perspectives is not to deny that they have their objective reality. They have. We do not see everything that exists, nor is everything that exists perceptible. One of the attributes of humankind is an insatiable desire to see more, to know more, about both worlds. This book is one more effort among many to speak to that desire.

The visible world is the world in which we live day in and day out. It is the world of the familiar, a world in which all of our assumptions seem true to us. In the visible world we perceive and accept everyday consensual reality as a matter of course. This world coheres around the concept of who we are, what we need, what goals we feel motivated to achieve, and how we proceed as we seek those goals. The personal ego dominates this world, giving rise to ambitions and drives, and seeking practical solutions to pressing problems. The visible world of the here and now stands solidly between the vanished past and the still unformed future.

The invisible world is stranger and, to some, a greater challenge. This second world is more fundamental and at the same time more elusive than the first. The invisible world is smaller than the smallest particle it is possible to imagine, and it is also larger than the whole universe. It stretches back in time to the timeless past before the "big bang" that supposedly started it all, and goes forward into the infinite future when all we can ever conceive of today will have come and gone. This world encompasses everything in between these extremes of time and space, connecting it all with an invisible web, with a center called the eternal present. The spider who spins it all is named Consciousness.

To see through the visible world and into the invisible requires a different kind of perception from the one we are accustomed to using as we go about our daily business. Whether or not we address ourselves to the second world, it affects us profoundly through subliminal messages, feeling tones, unconscious impulses and reactions, hopes and dreams, fears and specters, and glimpses into the sometimes frightening, sometimes glorious realms of possibilities. The invisible world is also the one from which inspiration comes, in which new connections may be seen, and where we can sense the relatedness of all that appears to be separate and distinct in the visible world.

You may say in response, "Of course, I know all that," and you will be right. This is just the point. We do know a great deal about the world that lies just beyond the visible world. But in our daily lives, most of us behave as though we do not know about it or that it does not matter. Often we push away the images and manifestations of the invisible world when they intrude into the forefront of consciousness. We tend to rationalize our perceptions of the second world, saying that it is too idiosyncratic, too far from the mainstream, too impractical, too odd; that it is unproved, unsubstantiated, illogical, superstitious, disreputable, and that to attend to it would distract us from the business at hand. In exchange for the promise of security, many people put a barrier between themselves and the adventures in consciousness that could put a whole new light on their personal lives and, extrapolated, on the society in which we live.

A stormy relationship has existed between the visible world and the invisible world ever since the late Middle Ages, when these worlds existed in relative harmony under a church-state liaison. Since then, Western Europe and later the United States have lived through periods when the two worlds scarcely took note of one another, and through episodes of outspoken strife and overt rebellion. In our own times, there are once again signs of movement toward the possibility of a new rapprochement. This will be strengthened when large numbers of people rediscover and develop their capacities to see *through* the first world, the visible world, and into the second.

Jung, gnosis, and chaos all converge when we start to explore the invisible world. C. G. Jung explored the farther reaches of the invisible world in ways in which no other psychiatrist had done before him. He regarded the archetypal foundations of the unconscious as the basis of a creative, expanding consciousness. He drew upon ancient gnostic texts for a symbol system that touched upon issues in ways that religious orthodoxies resisted. He found in the old gnostic texts explanations for evil in the world, for the harshness of the Old Testament deity, and for the apparent chaos in the phenomenal world. He discovered that what seems like randomness and chaos in the human mind may be part of an as yet unrecognized system. That there may be a hidden order underlying what we call chaos is today also the subject of much speculation in the world of high-energy physics.

Over the last decade, a new science called chaos has emerged as physicists, biologists, astronomers, and economists have created new ways of understanding the growth of complexity in nature. In his survey of their research, Gleick (1987) says, "Now that science is looking, chaos seems to be everywhere. A rising column of cigarette smoke breaks into wild swirls. A flag snaps back and forth in the wind. A dripping faucet goes from a steady pattern to a random one. . . . No matter what the medium, the behavior obeys the same newly discovered laws" (p. 5). Since human beings are a part of nature, it is little wonder that we, too, experience puzzlement and aberration when we venture beyond the surfaces of things or when we sink into the depths of our own psyches.

1

Two Worlds: One Visible, One Invisible

How do you know but ev'ry Bird that cuts the airy way
Is an immense world of delight, clos'd by your senses five?
WILLIAM BLAKE, *The Marriage of Heaven and Hell*

The Known, the Unknown, and the Unknowable

We have always known that we live in two different worlds that in some mysterious way are connected, but we have forgotten it. Although the evidence is all around us, we often fail to notice it. For example, when we look at a house, are we aware that it gives evidence of a blueprint that provided the basis for its construction? The blueprint is implicit, and the house is the explicit expression of it. How many of us can *see* the blueprint, however, when we look at the house? In the ceiling we can observe the lighting fixtures, each shedding its separate glow on its immediate surroundings. We could believe, if we depended upon appearances only, that each one is an independent, autonomous source of light. Yet as we recognize the flowing order behind what is manifestly separate, we can *see* that all the fixtures are connected, though invisibly. The actuality of their being connected is what makes them work, what enables them to spread their light. It is not only that each one is connected with the others; there is a switch somewhere. Switching on and off the mysterious power we call energy, and that we have learned to transform into electricity, is a necessity foreseen by the architect who designed the house. We infer by observing the switching mechanism that while energy itself is virtually unlimited in supply, the amount of electricity that we can use productively is finite or limited.

We can imagine that the invisible blueprint indicates a point where the wires in the house are connected to an external source. The local electrical system connects each house on the street with all the others and with a series of connections and transformers, back to the power-generating plant. All these complex arrangements are well known to the architect, and to the person who sees the plan behind the constructed house. But look further. The electrical power comes in from a distant source, perhaps a dam somewhere that controls a great river, with locks and turbines and machinery built to utilize the force engendered by the release of pent-up waters. All this depends in turn upon an infraplan—a cycle of water rising as mist, falling as rain, refreshing and sustaining Earth and her creatures, and eventually, inexorably, running down the hills in streams to the sea again. The house is the *known*; the architect's plan is implicit, but unknown to the person who sees only the house. The greater plan, or order, upon which the architect's plan depends is finally an archetypal plan, a function of the unknowable Arch-architect, the designer of our dwelling place, the universe.

We can extend this metaphor beyond the house with its lighting system and its heating system and its plumbing system to everything human-made or existing from nature. Nothing stands entirely on its own, although in our ordinary perception we see individual objects and individual events. All are, in a deeper sense, intertwined, interconnected, interdependent. When we know this, all things assume their correct proportion as part of a whole, and we realize that what exists is what must be. Theoretical physicist Paul Davies recognizes this in the title of his book, *The Cosmic Blueprint* (1988), in which he points out that the major conflict in the physical sciences is between holism and reductionism, as it has been from the time of Plato and Aristotle down to today.

■

> Whose immortal hand or eye
> Dare frame thy fearful symmetry?
>   BLAKE, "The Tyger"

The first world, the visible world, is the world of everyday consensual reality that we perceive and accept as a matter of course. The second world, the invisible world, is more fundamental and, at the same time, more elusive than the first. To the second world belongs the blueprint, the plan and the infrastructure that give form and meaning to our lives and that have been a source of conjecture for people of all lands and all ages. Every culture has its myths and legends that tell its people how the world they know came into being from a place or a world they do not know. Our own culture has its myths as well, only we are less willing to call them myths. "Mysteries" suits some people better. For others, "unsolved problems" is an even more acceptable expression. It is as though there were many veils between the world we know and the one we do not know. Every time we pull away one veil hoping to reveal the answers to our questions, we find only another veil, another question. And yet we continue to seek. What draws us? What makes us believe that there are answers? What possesses us to continue to explore on the boundaries of consciousness, confident that if we probe only a little longer, only a little deeper, we will uncover what we are looking for?

I assert that we know more than we believe we know, that we have always known far more than what exists in our consciousness at any given moment. Consciousness is like the moment of awakening from a deep dream: we remember only fragments and feelings, but know with serene certainty that there was more that we have forgotten.

How the Soul Found Its Place

An old Jewish legend speaks to this knowing and forgetting that we know. It is told that when the soul of Adam was created, the souls of all the generations were created and stored in a promptuary in the seventh heaven. When a child is conceived, God decrees what manner of human being it shall become—male or female, strong or weak, beautiful or ugly, short or tall, fat or thin. Piety and wickedness alone are left to the determination of the person. Then God calls upon the angel appointed to souls, to fetch a certain soul that is hidden in the seventh heaven and carry it to the womb of its mother. The angel goes to the seventh heaven as he is bidden and invites the soul to come along to the world below. The soul opens her mouth and pleads, "Do not take me from this place. I am well pleased with where I am." The angel replies, "The world to which I will bring you is better than this one, and besides, it is for this purpose that God created you." So the soul is dragged away and forcibly placed in the womb of the mother. Two angels are set to watch that the soul does not escape.

In the morning, the first angel returns and takes the soul on a trip to Paradise, and shows her the righteous who sit there in glory with crowns upon their heads. "Do you know who these are?" the angel asks. When the soul replies that she does not, the angel says, "These were formed like you in the wombs of their mothers, and when they came into the world they observed God's commandments. When they departed that world they became partakers in the happiness that you now see. Know that you, too, if you observe God's commandments, will be found worthy of sitting among these when your life on earth is over. But if you do not, you will be doomed to the other place." So saying, he returns the soul to the mother's womb. The next morning the angel comes again, and this time he takes the soul to Hell, and points out the sinners who are being smitten with fiery scourges by the angels of destruction, and who cry, "Woe, woe is me!" The angel tells the soul that these, too, were created like herself, but that when they were put into the world they did not observe God's commandments, and for that reason they came to this sorry state. "Know then that your destiny is also to depart the world. Be just therefore, and not wicked, that you may not come to such an end as this." On the third day, the angel returns and carries the soul around and shows her where she will live and where she will die, whom she will marry and where she will be buried, and many other things. Then he replaces the soul in the womb, to remain there for nine months.

When it is time for the child to emerge from the womb, the angel returns and tells the soul, "The time has come for you to go forth into the world." The soul objects strenuously, saying, "No, I like it here. Why should I go forth into the world?" The angel replies, "As you were formed against your will, so you shall be born against your will and you shall die against your will." The soul continues to resist mightily, until the angel strikes the babe on the nose, extinguishes the light at its head, and brings it into the world against its will. Immediately the child forgets all it has learned and comes into the world kicking and screaming.

This is a tale told by a people to its children when they, perhaps vaguely remembering that there is another place or having dreamed another place, ask their parents, "Where did I come from?" It is archetypal in nature, being an attempt to give life and substance to an age-old and profound question that is asked in every part of the world and in every generation. A literal answer may be given to such a question, and it may be true enough. But, as with so many literal answers, it is not the whole truth, and somehow, somewhere, we always know it.

The secrets of the psyche are closely held by individuals. Often children feel that they see something other people do not see. Or perhaps they understand unspoken meanings in tones of voice that no one else seems to perceive. They also know, somehow, that they are not to tell anyone that they are aware of these secret things. They think:

Nobody else speaks about things you cannot see—Perhaps nobody else sees them—Maybe there is something wrong with me that I can see what other people don't talk about—I guess I am the only one who sees them. If the child is naive enough, he does speak, and usually gets punished for his trouble. Such a child was William Blake, according to his earliest biographer Alexander Gilchrist (1863), who wrote of him, "On Peckham Rye it is, as he will in after years relate, that while quite a child, of eight or ten perhaps, he has his 'first vision.' Sauntering along, the boy looks up and sees a tree filled with angels, bright angelic wings bespangling every bough like stars. Returned home he relates the incident, and only through his mother's intercession escapes a thrashing from his honest father, for telling a lie" (p. 7).

I was luckier than most, in that I had a mother who believed in cultivating the imagination. I was poignantly aware of this as I was disposing of her possessions after her death. I came upon a set of books I had loved in childhood, called *Journeys Through Bookland*. I opened the first volume, the pages nearly crumbling and the edges worn thin from many turnings so long ago. There I came upon a poem that she must have read to me before I was able to read and that probably was my introduction to the writings of William Blake, who has served me as inspiration and spiritual teacher these many years. It was "Infant Joy" from his *Songs of Innocence:*

"I have no name:
I am but two days old."
What shall I call thee?
"Joy is my name."
Sweet joy befall thee!
            (1957, p. 118)

■

It was only on my recent rereading that I realized the deeper meaning of this apparently simple verse. The newborn infant *knows* its name! Its name says what it is here for. Only later does it forget! Sometimes it takes many years for a person to come to such a remembrance, and many people are never able to call back to mind that secret knowledge.

■

The Tiger Under the Table

I also remembered that at an early age I knew I was a tiger, but I somehow sensed that this information would not be properly appreciated by my parents. Such knowing in a child is not so rare. We have all but expunged such ideas from our "civilized" consciousness, but in earlier times, and today among some people who live close to the land in tribal societies, it is not unusual for people to invest an unseen part of themselves in a totem animal. In our modern setting, people have pets whom they treat as friends and companions, and who, if the truth be told, are so close to them that they seem to be almost a part of them. Adults, of course, make the distinction between *affection* for a particular animal and *identification* with that animal, but young children can "be" that animal in the same way so-called primitive societies can live in a *participation mystique* with animals and other aspects of nature.

A member of a primitive tribe can put on a bearskin and dance around a ceremonial fire growling like a bear, but as a child I could not do exactly that. I could only crouch in the space under the dining room table or in my den under the baby grand piano, occasionally growling at anyone who passed by. My parents took little note of this. One evening they were giving a dinner party and I was supposed to be in bed. Before the guests sat down to eat I sneaked into the dining room and settled down in my lair under the table. I waited until just the right moment, and then bit one of the ladies on the ankle. She reacted with a wild scream and accidentally overturned her wine glass. When I was discovered my mother scolded me and promptly sent me off to bed.

Not many days after this incident, my mother took me to a child psychoanalyst because of my "strange behavior." Of course, she did not know I was a tiger. The kindly old gentleman, Dr. Huebsch by name (the name means pretty in German), took me up onto his lap and asked me to tell him about the dinner party. He was so warm and had such a twinkle in his eye, like Santa Claus, that I was sure he would understand. I told him that I was really a tiger, but that nobody knew it, and I wished he wouldn't tell. He did understand, and he didn't tell anyone. As Mother explained some years later, what he did tell her was that my imagination was running far ahead of my ability to express myself verbally. He suggested that I learn to draw, so that I could find ways of bringing out whatever was inside of me. Soon after my visit to Dr. Huebsch, a student from the local school of art began coming to my house twice a week to give me art lessons. She bore the lovely name of Miss Diamond. I shall never forget how she would let me scribble on a page and then I would look into the scribble and see what mysterious picture might be hidden in it. I would then paint in the shapes outlined by my scribbles and this would reveal the picture I had seen. The scribbled drawings released the flow of energy, unhampered by shoulds and should-nots. I could look at them with a fresh "beginner's mind," and re-member the disparate pieces into images of dancing girls or fantastic animals. So I was saved from the necessity of abandoning my secret world, and I had the privilege of keeping to myself the secret knowledge I had concerning my tiger while at the same time bringing forth what lurked inside of me.

■

> [Jesus said:] If you bring forth that within yourselves, that which you have will save you. If you do not have that within yourselves, that which you do not have within you will kill you.
>
> *The Gospel According to Thomas*

■

The secrets of the psyche come to light in metaphor, myth, and ritual. This is because they have to do with the invisible world, where nothing is objectively real or objectively true, but where anything can be subjectively real and subjectively true. Metaphor is the word, myth is the story, and ritual is the enactment of the story that is built up of the words. Objective truth and reality refer to a world in which things are supposed to exist as they are, independent of what anyone happens to think about them. In this world, there is a "correct" way to look at things, and there is a reasonable and rational way to talk about them. Literal language is that in which words correspond exactly to objects, and the meaning conveyed by the words reflects this one-to-one correspondence. But in the subjective world, literal meaning in this sense is senseless. The psyche's response to events is often nonverbal. The individual or subjective view of reality is slightly different for each person. The particular, idiosyncratic way we experience a world, our world view, may be invisible to someone else. If we try to explain it in literal terms, we may get into trouble when no obvious correspondence exists between our own experience and that of someone else.

Metaphor, then, is a method of substituting one word for another to convey a meaning that is not literal but that carries the feelings evoked by the implied word. To say "I am a tiger" is not a literal statement but a metaphorical one. Such a statement is an attempt to express a self-image that corresponds to my feelings about a tiger. *Tiger* suggests, at least to me, a creature who is strong and lithe, who loves hunting in the forests of the night (another metaphor—this one for the unconscious), one who can be fiercely independent, yet is passionately protective of her cubs, who has a tawny beauty, and whose amber eyes pierce the darkness.

Metaphor is the stuff of which myth is made. It is the language of the imagination. Using it, we fashion individual myths and collective mythologies. Much of the Jungian analytical process consists in finding out a person's individual myth and then unraveling all the associations and feelings attached to it until one comes at last to the root metaphor or guiding principle. The individual myth finds expression in all of us through dreams and fantasies, hopes and fears, and all the other non-rational experiences that evoke an intensity of feeling that reason can-not counter.

Myths in every culture, including our own, are enacted through collective nonrational practices in the form of ritual. These stir masses of people in an endless variety of ways—from the national obsession with covertly using drugs that promise a taste of paradise in a hellish world, to traveling halfway around the earth to view an athletic contest that reenacts an Olympiad that took place in ancient times on the plain of Elis in the northwestern Peloponnesus.

The Human Animal as Pathfinder

The search for that something more, that other that just eludes con-sciousness, is a preoccupation that distinguishes the human animal from other animals. Characteristic of the human species is a particular kind of consciousness that is inquisitive, reflective, and synthesizing. The search takes many paths. One path pursues the line of reason, of cause and effect, and proceeds in logical steps. It begins with what is known on the basis of earlier investigations and accumulates additional information, all the while adapting its original formulations to concur with the new constructs that have come into awareness. *This is the path of science.*

Another way is based on tradition, on holding onto treasured ex-planations from the past and reading newer meanings into them to make them congruent with our lives in the present. *This is the path of religion and mythology* (remembering that one person's religion is an-other's mythology).

A third way is through personal experiences in which one is able to glimpse what lies behind the many veils, or at least behind some of them. These excursions into the invisible world can be accomplished through various means, including dreams and fantasies, meditations, or sudden insights that come unbidden. Sometimes seekers on this path find the invisible world fearful, sometimes awe-inspiring, sometimes consoling. We call this way *the path of the spirit.*

A fourth approach is through *the path of psyche.* Much has been said and written about the world we know and the world we do not know. Some people speak with authority and some offer tentative hypotheses hedged about with qualifications. All of it is potentially meaningful, but until we consider what is behind the knowing process itself, by which I mean psyche, the meanings we fasten upon must be lacking an important constituent. How does psyche come to know what it knows? This question haunts me night and day. I have gone to and must continue to go to the psyche to ask the questions. I could not write about the visible world and the invisible world and the space between them without asking myself and asking others how these questions arise, and how answers come.

All of the paths I have mentioned are valid routes for moving toward the invisible world, and there must be many more that are equally valid. From my perspective, the way of psyche elucidates all the others. As we begin to move on to the threshold between the visible and invisible worlds, we will call upon bits and pieces of knowledge and information discovered along every path. But most particularly, we will refer to the psyche as a primary source of information. The path of the psyche is the one with which I am most familiar, the one I walk most often, and the one that seems to me the crucial one.

Logos and Eros

The worlds reveal themselves to the psyche in different ways, depending upon the individual and his or her manner of receiving knowledge. Two diametrically opposed ways of viewing the world and responding to it may be characterized by the terms *Logos* and *Eros*:

■

In the beginning was the Word [Logos], and the Word was with God, and *the Word was God.* He was in the beginning with God; all things were made through him, and without him was not anything made that was made. In him was life and the life was the light of men. The light shines in the darkness and the darkness has not overcome it. (John 1:1–5, RSV; my italics)

Beloved, let us love one another; for love [Eros] is of God, and he who loves is born of God and knows God. He who does not love does not know God; for *God is love.* (1 John 4:7–8, RSV; my italics)

■

The person in whom Logos is a guiding principle tends to view the world through logical, rational processes. Such an individual tends to be highly verbal, often intellectual, and needs to have a reason or an explanation before accepting something as valid or true. If this person is convinced of the rightness of a position, no effort will be spared in putting it forth and standing up for it. Because this person's own self-esteem depends largely on being correct or accurate, on seeking the truth in whatever form it may be found, and on expressing that truth in the most cogent forms possible, he or she does not feel a great need for the approval of others. Consequently, Logos people often find themselves in isolated postures, and they may be loners or have only a very few intimate and supportive friends.

Eros-oriented people, on the other hand, are quite at home with human relationships, and, in fact, desperately need them. Such people will go to almost any length to avoid causing pain to another person—not so much out of generosity as out of the fear of being abandoned. They are compassionate and thoughtful, and find it tempting to put aside their personal needs or beliefs in favor of being loved by another. For the Eros-oriented person, the world of Logos seems nearly inaccessible.

I have chosen two analysands to illustrate how very different the process of seeing through the visible world can be for individuals of the Logos and the Eros inclinations. These women portray two distinct pathways toward the realization of the two worlds within and without themselves. While these women may seem to be extreme, it is important to stress that none of us is all Logos or all Eros; we each have qualities of both. Although I have selected two women to follow through their process, I could just as well have selected a man and a woman, or two men, for the issues with which I will deal here are not specifically feminine issues or specifically masculine issues, but are human issues that transcend gender. It appears to me on the basis of my work as an analyst that in both men and women, either Eros or Logos may be dominant. By choosing two persons of the same sex, it seemed to me that the differences between a Logos-dominated person and one who is Eros-dominated would be unlikely to be confused with gender differences.

When I considered writing about the two women and their encounters with the visible and invisible worlds, I was prepared to talk with them about my intention and to request their permission to include in my book some of the analytic material they had shared with me. I was not as naive as I had been nearly two decades earlier when I wrote *Boundaries of the Soul*. I knew that a simple yes response, if given, could cover some unexpressed feelings they might have. This time I would not take their answers at face value, but would be open to exploring more deeply the meaning of my having chosen them and their having been willing to enter into this "covenant" with me. Naturally, as I assured them, I would not use their real names and I would avoid any material that could cause them to be identified. Furthermore, I would not stick precisely to their material but would alter it to make a point or to illustrate an idea. In any case, I told myself, in approaching these women I would be as attentive as I could be to their feelings on every level.

Ruby

I chose to speak to the woman I shall call Ruby first. Her sparkling brown eyes and ruddy complexion give the impression of vitality and enthusiasm. She is a warm, loving person with a capacity for relationship, and I supposed it likely that she might be more willing than some of my other clients to say yes. In Ruby we meet a woman whose primary attitude is characterized by Eros. She is strongly directed toward, and dependent upon, her relationships with the many and varied people in her life. When she came to me, Ruby's world was filled with demands on her time and energy that frequently seemed too strong to withstand. To develop the ability to extricate herself from the tight grip of some of her relationships was a major task for her. She needed to discover that far from being overwhelmed, she could maintain her own center of strength in small ways, simple acts of care and tenderness, and especially in her attention to nature and the natural processes taking place all around her.

I told Ruby I was writing a book, what the name of it was, and what I would be trying to do. I told her I was in a dilemma, that I would like to use case material—such as what she brought to me—but that I had many reservations about doing so. I did not go into all my reservations with her, but stressed my feeling that she as an analysand might feel exploited, or that knowing of my special interest in her process might affect the sort of material she would bring to me. Ruby reacted with a thoughtful silence. Then she said she wanted to give the matter some thought. I had the impression that she was somewhat favorably disposed toward allowing the use of her material. I did not press her for an immediate answer because I wanted to see what a little time and some ripening on an unconscious level might bring, so we left the matter unsettled. Perhaps the reason she could not give me an immediate answer was that she had an inner resistance to granting me permission, but hesitated to say so for fear of incurring my displeasure.

Laurel

The woman I am calling Laurel, a tall, slender blonde with piercing blue eyes, had issues about relationships that were quite the opposite of Ruby's. Far from being inclined to rely on other people for her validation, Laurel was skeptical of the opinions of others. Long ago, in her childhood, she had become convinced that hardly anyone either understood her or trusted her. She had learned to rely on her own judgment and what she called "my knowing place" to guide her toward what was right and true and meaningful. Consequently, in her adult life she rarely sought the ongoing feedback from other people that might have kept her grounded and feeling secure. There was a certain advantage in this, in that as a young child she had allowed her ideas to take flight and soar; but as an adult, she had had a hard struggle translating what was transparent to her into language that would be readily understood and appreciated by others. In her profession, she was involved in scientific research, and here she was able to communicate her ideas to fellow professionals. As a Logos-oriented person, she relied on carefully considered data to support her statements so that she could defend her work against criticism. Knowing this, and even though I was particularly eager to use the material she had been bringing to analysis, I found myself hesitating to speak to her about her participation. Laurel had a kind of sixth sense, an intuition that often seemed to correspond to my own. She trusted material that comes from the unconscious. I felt that the right time would present itself and that I would be given some indication when to talk with her about allowing her material to be shared with others.

Several weeks after I had spoken with Ruby, Laurel brought in the following dream:

> I go to my analyst's house for my analytic hour. She lives in a tall, very old building. Each floor has a vaulted roof with beautiful paintings, rather like the Sistine Chapel.
> She is very reflective when I show up and she begins to talk to me in a slightly troubled voice. It is as if she is seeking a way to be with

me, a place to stand with me that is new, and is not clear about how to go about it. She talks haltingly about her feelings and appears very vulnerable. I have never seen her this way before, and find myself wanting to rescue her, but I still am not certain where all this is headed.

At one point we go for a walk. During the walk we enter an old library full of ancient leather-bound books. We are both happy to be there. As we walk through I notice a genial old man reading a large magnificent book to a small group of children who are clustered around him. I stop to listen and turn in amazement to my analyst and say to her, "He is reading Brothers Karamazov *to them!" I can't believe that the children understand what he is saying, but they appear to be enthralled.*

As we continue to walk, my analyst tells me that she feels a deep connection with me that she has not felt before. I impulsively squeeze her hand and the mutual empathy is acknowledged.

After we return to her apartment I suggest that this deep connection is based on a task that we need to complete. We will either be helpful (actually, we are necessary) to each other's research or will accomplish something jointly. It is a major task that has been set for us and is part of our destiny.

I then place my hands on her head and "read" her energies, seeking any evidence of ill health. I find nothing and I bless her, sending her messages of my caring and commitment to both our journeys.

I was struck by the synchronicity of this dream, especially with its statement that Laurel and I had a deep connection based on a task that we needed to complete together. (*Synchronicity* is the term Jung used to denote a meaningful coincidence that is acausal by nature—that is, one event has not "caused" another, but seems to have an uncanny correspondence to it.) I began to explore the dream with her.

The house in which I lived in the dream was very grand, a work of genius. This suggested that Laurel had a very high opinion of me; she overvalued me. I needed to be aware that her positive transference was not realistic and that such an exalted view was inevitably accompanied by overly high expectations. If I did not meet these, there was a strong likelihood that in her disappointment she would experience a sudden reversal to an equally unrealistic low opinion of me and my role in her life. I took this as a warning to be careful in proceeding.

Laurel had intuitively picked up the fact that I was troubled about something, but she did not know what it was. She wanted to connect with the vulnerable part of me. She had fantasies about rescuing me, but was hesitant to indulge them because she had her own needs and did not wish to be distracted by mine. This was what I had both expected and feared, and was one of the reasons I had hesitated to tell her about my project.

The library of ancient books symbolized the sacred space in which we found ourselves together. Our shared interest in certain arcane literature called forth this kind of scene, a room filled with musty leather-bound volumes that were of great interest to us both. The genial story-teller was the proverbial wise old man who knows the simple but profound truths and lives by them. Reading this book to children implied that even the naive are capable of understanding mysteries and profundities if they are allowed to hear about them and to receive them at whatever level they are able. I suspected that Laurel was concerned that the process in which we were engaged was not something that could be shared with people who, like the children in this dream, have not been "initiated." But the children were enthralled—the importance of what was being said did reach them at some level; it excited them and penetrated their minds. So it seemed to me the dream was saying, do not be afraid that what you have to tell may not be understood by everyone. If a hundred people read it and only ten understand it and of those ten, only two are deeply moved by it, your work will not have been useless. In fact, those two may keep it from sinking into oblivion. They could be "the saving remnant."

The dream spoke to Laurel's own situation at the time as well as to my own. It was, after all, *her* dream. She was working currently on a research project, and she feared that some of its implications would not be understood, just as I feared that she would not see the value of letting me use her dream because not everyone would understand it. This was a curious parallel, of the sort that often arises in the analytic process where two people are connected on an unconscious level as well as a conscious one. The dream gave Laurel permission to recognize that we were in this process together; we were both searching, though independently of each other. At the same time, we were in a mutually interacting, mutually influencing system. It is this process of finding a mutually harmonious path that makes analysis work.

In the dream, the unconscious gave permission for Laurel to help me as I helped her. The wisdom of the unconscious rightly directed her to "read" my energies—that is, to see if they were "healthy." I understood this to mean that she was to discern whether I was psychologically open and honest, or whether I was attempting to impose something of my own upon her. I would need to make clear to her that I wished to explore with her any possible unconscious motives she might have for agreeing to participate in my endeavor, as well as her possible unconscious resistance to doing so. In any case, the dream suggested a willingness on the part of the unconscious to make a "commitment to both our journeys."

This was the state of the unconscious portrayed by Laurel's dream, *before* I told her about the book I planned to write. On the basis of this dream, I told her what I had in mind—an acknowledgment of the two worlds and an exploration of how we come to know the invisible world. I could now speak of my hope that she would allow me to draw upon her analytic material to show how some of the issues with which I expected to deal are experienced in the process of analysis. I let her know that I was aware of the depth of some of her experiences, that I valued them, and that I would treat them with respect.

Her response was slow and thoughtful. "You're asking me if I can share some things that are sacred. I'm not sure. I feel that these inner experiences that give me an aperture into the invisible world are not really mine to give. I don't want to misrepresent what comes to me. I have opted for the position that what I have experienced cannot be communicated."

I replied that there is always the possibility that what we communicate may be misunderstood, even if it is not misrepresented. We have no guarantee that even if we say something correctly, people will understand it. This is a painful experience for everyone who writes or teaches. Many people will misunderstand, but there is also the potentiality that some people will understand. That prospect alone makes the effort worthwhile.

Laurel suggested that her dream might also be saying that perhaps her life purpose did not lie in presenting her ideas exclusively to intellectuals, professionals in her field; perhaps she was meant to address herself to people who do not "know," like the children to whom the old man was reading Dostoevski. "Life is so full of paradox!" Laurel exclaimed. "I'm always occupied with it! I'm constantly probing on the edge of what is known to discover what is unknown. I have to use the methods of science to go beyond science. My aim is to understand, and as if that were not difficult enough, now you tell me that I have to communicate. I have to turn inward to reflect and I have to turn outward to communicate. Somehow it doesn't make sense."

I reminded her that she had once said that people who are Logos-oriented believe that "life is a dichotomous variable." They must dis-

cover the ordering principle behind paradox, because they find chaos
impossible to deal with. Clearly, Laurel identified herself as a Logos
woman.

Our discussion turned to the subject of paradox, one of the major
problems with which Laurel was dealing. I, too, was occupied with it,
for the coexistence of a visible and an invisible world is surely a paradox. A related paradox that Laurel and I had often talked about is
that of the coexistence of Logos and Eros. When we speak of Logos
we mean the intellect, the word, the logical mind, the discriminating
function. Eros, we understand to mean warmth, compassion, the relationship function.

Laurel said, "When I talk about paradox from a Logos perspective,
it feels incomplete. My abstract perception of paradox is only partial.
To complete it I must introduce Eros; this brings the richness and the
fullness. But my way of thinking is bound to be misunderstood."

I wondered if she might feel this way because the Logos-oriented
person doesn't really trust Eros, and the Eros-oriented person trusts
Logos even less. So a wide gulf, an abyss, opens between Logos and
Eros. Eros-oriented people believe there is a primary unity in the universe, that everything is essentially one. The relationship principle exists for them but only within its own parameters, which is to say that
it excludes the Logos orientation. Laurel's frustration was evident. "I
get into a quandary when I write about paradox in my diary. I get so
preposterous, so far out. Few people would understand what I am
talking about. So then I close my diary and clean my house."

"Don't do that!" I told her. "Don't be afraid to express the spontaneous thought that streams out from the invisible source within you.
It is the most precious thing you have. Let it flow out until it has its
say. Later you can sit in judgment upon it and decide who, if anyone,
shall read it. But write it down. *Then* you can go and clean house."

∎

Awareness of the visible world and the invisible world is an exercise
in paradox. What is true in one world is not necessarily true in the
other, and vice versa. Eros tries to heal the breach between them, while
Logos tries to clarify the differences. But the paradox, or *irony* if you
will, is that where the person's conscious orientation tends toward one
perspective or the other, a compensating orientation of the unconscious
presents the opposite point of view by way of dreams and fantasies,
speculations, and sudden uncalled-for illuminations. It is through our

ability to accept and live with these paradoxes and tolerate the ambiguities that go along with them, that we take the first step toward gaining access to the invisible world.

2

Limitations of the Visible World

Across the doorsill the breeze at dawn
        has secrets to tell you.
Don't go back to sleep!
You must ask for what you really want.
Don't go back to sleep!
People are going back and forth across the
        doorsill where the two worlds touch.
The door is round and open.
Don't go back to sleep!

RUMI

The belief that there is only the visible world can be disheartening to the point of despair. It feeds a sense of hopelessness—this is what the world is and no one can do much about it. One must live for today, and only for today. But in the end, living only for today ends in disaster. So finally, one must ask, Is this all there is? It is a question many of us come to when we reflect on the meaning of life, and especially on the meaning of our own lives.

In the field of psychology, Freud made his most important break with the traditional attitudes of the infant science by stating clearly and unequivocally that the ego, that sense of "I-ness," does not account for the entire psyche—that there is more, and that what we can see, observe, quantify, predict, and evaluate in psychological terms is clearly not the whole story. The unconscious, a concept that everyone takes for granted these days, was inadmissible to the new science of psychology before Freud. But experience told a different story. Freud knew the monsters of the depths, as we all know them. He knew what every child knows who fears the dark and what may be lurking in the closet: that there is more to the world than meets the eye. The primitive and destructive aspects of the "more" have been explained away by the religious as manifestations of negative or evil forces called by many names, and by the rational-minded as figments of the imagination. It is to Freud's eternal credit that he was willing to submit to the eye of critical examination the darkness and the dreads, as well as the fantasies and hopes, of the emotionally disturbed people who came to him for help.

Freud posited the field of the unconscious as standing in opposition to the ego, confronting it at every turn through projection, metaphor, and symbol, demonstrating that the ego or "I" is not all there is. Nor, in his view, is the visible world that is accessible to the ego, all there is. The invisible world that Freud saw is the repository of two kinds of matter or data. (I use the words *matter* and *data* metaphorically, since the contents of the unconscious cannot be material or factual.) The first kind is the givens that are part of the human condition, the primary drives and instincts present in all of us that motivate us in ways we are unaware of, to act as we do. The second kind is the flotsam and jetsam of our personal lives: all that has been rejected because it was incompatible with our self-image or our comfort, all that has been forgotten, and all that has simply not been noted in consciousness because our attention was elsewhere. This unconscious material remains in the psyche's invisible world, poised to break into consciousness unannounced and uninvited, and often at the most inconvenient times. It may cause untold trouble; yet, when we begin to understand it we find that it possesses the capacity to enlarge consciousness immeasurably by its presence. The following is an example of such a break-in from the unconscious.

In the case of an analysand whom I will call Dolores, a dream signaled the limitations of her visible world. Dolores had recently walked away from her marriage. She was feeling tired and dispirited, and was suffering from various aches and pains for which no physiological basis could be found. She had been experiencing much tension, when she had this dream of letting go:

> I drive onto a lonely beach and park my car head down into the ocean. I put my old blanket on the hood of the car and climb up onto it. I slowly slide into the sea and drown. There is no panic, I simply let go.

The car Dolores drove was a very expensive one that her husband had bought for her when they married. She regarded it as her security blanket. Now she had gone back to work because, among other factors, she wanted to be economically self-sufficient. Instead of feeling free and independent as she had expected, she was weighted down by the responsibilities of a job that was secure but joyless.

I suggested a possible message of the dream: "When your body is dragging your soul to so many places it does not want to go, it gets very tired. It uses up all the available energy—and then you become vulnerable to a host of stress-induced illnesses." She was experiencing them all, including headache, insomnia, stomach distress, loss of sexual desire. One of the ways she became aware of the invisible world was through her body.

But even as she was living entirely in the visible world, she dreamed of letting go, letting go of her need for security, and slipping into the sea. Water, and particularly the ocean—being murky, teeming with unseen organisms, and infinitely extensive—is a metaphor par excellence for the unconscious.

The visible world in this dream was the only world this woman knew. Her body, her automobile, and her security blanket were part of it. But something in her knew another place, symbolized by the sea, and called her to enter it. She could only become aware that she was stuck in the visible world when she got an inkling that there was something beyond what she could see.

The Four Functions of Cognition[1]

The visible world is the familiar world. One way of coming to know this world is through the four functions of cognition: *sensation*, *feeling*, *thinking*, and *intuition*, as they were first defined by C. G. Jung. Everyone uses all four functions, but most people prefer one or two and use them more frequently, leaving the other functions relatively undeveloped. *Sensation* is the most direct way of knowing, because our senses provide an easy access to knowledge: we see, hear, smell, taste, or touch what is around us, and think we know it. Today we must extend the sensation function to include the process of cognition through the use of all the prosthetic devices that expand the range of our senses, such as radio, telephone, computers, satellite communications, microscopes, telescopes, X rays, and all the other technical inventions we look upon as extensions of ourselves. The data of sensation consist of a collection of details, and sensation-oriented people are good at gathering facts and figures without prejudging them.

1. For a fuller description of Jung's theory of psychological types, see Singer, *Boundaries of the Soul*, chapter 7.

We also know this world through an immediate *feeling* response to people, events, and ideas—that is, by our spontaneous reactions. A person in whom feeling predominates will have a strong sense of values. When something is important to this person, nothing will stand in the way of doing this thing. Individuals who have feeling as their most highly developed function desire an organized world. They want to belong within a family, a group, an organization that is in harmony with their value systems.

A third way of coming to know the visible world is through the *thinking* function, which proceeds step by step to take what we perceive and construct some sort of order out of it. People in whom thinking is predominant like to arrange facts or ideas in a meaningful sequence or in a hierarchy of values. Thinking is a problem-solving function. It is concerned with cause-and-effect relationships. It weighs the pros and cons and rationally determines the outcome. When thinking gets its data or information from the senses or from concrete facts, it functions primarily in the visible world. But sometimes thinking is abstract and speculative. At such times, thinking may serve as a way of approaching the territory of the invisible.

The fourth function, *intuition*, allows us to gain knowledge from inner images or ideas that we grasp in a holistic way. Intuition relies for its data largely on the invisible world. Intuition helps us to establish a self-image, because we cannot really *see* ourselves in our totality. We have never even seen our own face directly; but based on mirror reflections or the feedback we receive from other people, we *think* we know what it is like. Having a self-image, we tend to believe that we are that person, the one who was born at such and such a time, had a series of experiences, looks and behaves in a certain way, subscribes to certain beliefs, and professes certain values. Intuition, however, goes beyond the boundaries of beliefs. It is open to sudden awareness, to speculation, to imagination, and to wandering about on invisible pathways.

How people typically select among and use these four functions determines to a large extent how they form their unique picture of the visible world. Different degrees of reliance on each of these four functions make for individual differences in perception and in the way information is processed. We see from our own particular perspective, so that what appears to us to be "real" will appear quite different to those who see from a different perspective.

Perceptions of the visible world are also colored by our conditioning, deriving from what we are told by our parents and other early caretakers, from what we observe ourselves as young children, and later from the spoken and unspoken messages that we pick up from the particular environment in which we live. Thus, our visible world will hold many contradictions. What we see will not always be confirmed by what we are told, and what brings rewards may not correspond with either of those sources of information. We have to learn either to close our eyes to dissonance or to coexist with ambiguity and paradox, and even to enjoy the prickly stimulation these provide.

The "I" and the "Other"

One characteristic of the visible world is that it appears to be solid and complete. If we tend to find validation for ourselves in the inner life, what we discover by way of our own perceptions and experiences seems totally real to us. We know within ourselves what is right and proper, and we structure our relationships to support our inner convictions. If our self-esteem is more responsive to the validation of ourselves that comes from others, we trust what people say of us and we develop effective means of gaining respect and approval. Either way, we commit ourselves to the world we see and that nurtures us, with the strong conviction that we are right in doing so. We become possessive about our opinions—we "own" them, so to speak. We believe that we know who we are.

This is expressed by psychologists in the phrase "having a strong ego." The "I," which is the core meaning of the term *ego*,[2] is the coherent, stable, and enduring aspect of us with which we are familiar. It exists in the here and now. This ego, this "I," has its limitations. For one thing, its duration is limited by birth and death. If anything survives us after physical death, it is not our ego. It has other limitations. Sometimes our neat self-concept becomes too narrow, too restrictive for our comfort.

Laurel suffered from such restrictions, although she had not articulated this fact in her analytical work. The following dream brought the matter to her attention:

> *There is a big aquarium in the home of some very ordinary people, and also a small aquarium that has some defect in it. It is necessary*

---

2. Neither Freud nor Jung used the word *ego*. They used the German *das Ich*, which translates simply as "the I," but which has been jargonized into psychology as *ego*, a foreign and esoteric-sounding word that was never intended by the founders of depth psychology.

to transfer the fish from the small to the large aquarium, or else they
will die because the small aquarium is gradually losing water. The big
aquarium is self-sustaining, as it has a system that aerates and filters
the water and plants and there are secluded places in it for the fish
to breed in.

I asked Laurel what her associations were to the small aquarium. She said that it was as though the small world of the small aquarium were gradually running down. The space was too limited. Everything was sliding toward disorganization—the way people lose energy when they get old. She was reminded of the second law of thermodynamics in physics, which says that there is an inescapable loss of energy in the universe, leading to entropy.[3]

"And what about the big aquarium?"

Laurel responded, "It's really large and there are parts of it you can't see into. It will sustain the fish. They can grow and rear their future generations there."

We saw that the small aquarium served as a metaphor for the visible world. The large aquarium could represent the self-perpetuating, adaptive cosmos, the farthest reaches of which are part of the invisible world. The small aquarium was a closed system. Nothing came in from the outside to replenish it. Nothing escaped its confines. The large aquarium was an open system, admitting fresh air from the outside. Laurel had been feeling much like the fish in the small aquarium. She understood the parallel in classical physics[4] to her own situation.

Laurel needed encouragement to take her ideas out of the realm of restrictive thinking, to dare to risk transferring them to a place of wider vistas. The dream pointed the way to this other place, as symbolized by the larger aquarium. It would be a place to begin, an intermediate place, where she would not need to feel intellectually and emotionally

---

3. "I like to think of entropy as a quantity that expresses the most certain property of our present Universe: its tendency to run down, to burn out. Others see it as the direction of time's arrow, a progression inevitably from birth to death" (Lovelock 1988, p. 22).

4. "The famous Second Law of Thermodynamics affirmed that for any given system conceived as a closed—in fact, isolated—unit of matter and energy, differences and gradients in concentration and temperature tend to disappear, to be replaced by uniformity and randomness. The universe, at least its material components, moves from a more organized and energetic state toward states of growing homogeneity and randomness. It ultimately reaches the state of perfect heat distribution in which no irreversible processes can any longer occur: there are no hotter and colder bodies to create a flow of energy. The arrow of time is thus given by the probability that closed systems run down, that they move *toward* equilibrium rather than *away* from it." (Laszlo 1987, pp. 15–16).

cramped and confined. It was not possible for her to change her perspective all at once. The initial step was to emerge from the situation that was threatening her with suffocation. She recognized this, and said that she would need to take the risk of exposing her ideas to people who could not be counted on to respond favorably to them.

Society and Chaos

As a child, you were required to become humanized by the discipline of the society in which you lived. Even at a very early age, you needed to learn to restrain your impulses and to recognize the rights of others in order to be socially acceptable. As you grew older, you practiced using society's rules, because these were functional and necessary. Abiding by the rules, in general, enables people to live "normal" lives, raise their families, and achieve a measure of "success" in the world. You grow old and finally you die, and maybe it has been a good enough life. But do you come to the end like Sinclair Lewis's Babbitt, the archetypal small-town small man, who reflects in his old age, "I never did a thing I wanted to do in my life!"? Or do you finally loosen your hold on the rules and follow the inner purpose that you know is yours, the direction for which you were born, the path that is your own and that makes you truly joyful?

Laurel was facing a dilemma in her life. Breaking through the restrictions, finding a "bigger aquarium" in this world of fish-eat-fish, takes courage and faith. She was facing this dilemma in her life. She had been a good student and had learned her lessons well. She had at her command all the technical tools that she required. But in her imagination she had gone far beyond the conventional methods of her field of expertise. One of the issues that had brought her into analysis was her concern about some of her ideas that she characterized as "decidedly unconventional and grandiose." If she followed where they led, she would be entering into unknown territory. She would be doing it alone, and she would have to throw away the rules. But for her, as the dream suggested, the visible world was defective and leaking. The dream seemed to be telling her that she would need to enter another space, and she would need to be exceedingly careful how she made the transfer.

The process as Laurel envisioned it would not prove easy for her. The visible world in which she was embedded continued to make demands upon her. One cannot simply pick up and leave the visible world even if, at times, it seems limited. Laurel continued to work at her job and to conform to what was necessary in that setting. For the most part, she had the freedom to pursue her own special activities, and her interaction with her co-workers was generally cordial, if not intimate, within the work situation. Then came the time for the "annual retreat," a weekend of boisterous activities in which Laurel had no interest, to put it mildly.

I asked her why she was so resistant, since she felt obligated to go. She replied that it took too much of her energy to protect herself from "discordant vibes" in people. By "discordant vibes" she meant a whole system of values that were foreign to her own, a kind of cavalier attitude toward fellow human beings, a concern with things in which she had no interest, much superficial talk about inconsequential minutiae, and so on. But it wasn't any one thing or combination of these things, actually, she explained, but a sort of vibration that she experienced in the presence of these people, and that made her uncomfortable and irritable.

I asked her how she protected herself from what she called discordant vibes.

"I need filters. Someone with discordant vibes comes into the room. The energy is like acid rock at a very high volume. I have a series of filters: the first one cuts it by 50 percent, the next one cuts it by 25 percent, and maybe 20 percent is what gets in."

I was not sure that filters were what she needed. Perhaps a better metaphor would have been a shield. Filters let a certain amount of the noxious stuff through. A shield protects against the noxious substance. But Laurel rejected the idea of a shield. She thought it sounded like trying to escape from something that she had to face.

I told her a story from the gnostic tradition that deals with the issue of facing or not facing the darker elements in the world and in the psyche. In this tradition, Sophia, the feminine aspect of God, was also the First Eve, fashioned before the visible world came into being. She was a sort of archetypal heavenly Eve. She descended to the lower world to ease some of the pain she had observed as she looked down from heaven on the people below. But the worldly powers, called the archons, engulfed her in their density and rendered her blind. The narrative goes on to explain that it was not really her, but her likeness, that was blinded, for the essential Sophia had left her body and gone up into the Tree of Knowledge (that is, of gnosis) leaving only her visible likeness below where it could be defiled.

Laurel asked, "Does this mean that one is supposed to save oneself by putting oneself above and beyond 'normal' worldly concerns?"

It emerged in our discussion that the key was that discordant vibes exist on different levels. She had always thought that they didn't have a place, that it was aberrant to be so sensitive. What she saw, and what bothered her so much when those people behaved in the chaotic way they did, occurred only on the superficial level of her awareness. Then there was another level. When she was able to shift her perspective on these discordant vibes she could see that they represented part of the ordering principle—they enabled people to let off the steam created in their workplace in a socially sanctioned way. She understood that she had to use the "filters" for two reasons: first, they enabled her to maintain relationships with people; second, they gave her the opportunity to stay centered on who she was and what was her life's course.

I could not help thinking that this was the natural response of a Logos woman, always asking why, always seeking to understand, to figure out the reasons, and to discover how to put her knowledge to good use.

Society and the Place Where You Live

In the wonderful way the world provides compensatory experiences to help us keep in balance, the next person to come into my office after Laurel was Ruby, her eyes blazing. "I'm very angry today," she said. I waited to hear what it was about but Ruby wouldn't talk to me. She found the clay statue of an ugly old Mexican woman, with big ears and eyes wide open and lips slightly parted as if paying close attention, that sits on the floor of my room.

Ruby addressed the old woman vehemently. "You don't know how hard it is for me to keep my own sense of who I am when I am with other people! It's like being pulled out of myself. My self gets lost and I am wandering about, unattached. I am so influenced by what other people want, what they expect. I can't find me. I'm so angry that they do this to me! But I'm like a little child, always trying to please, trying to be nicey-nice." Then Ruby turned to me as if just noticing that I was present and said, "Tell me what I should do."

I pointed to the clay figure and told Ruby to ask *her*. Ruby asked the old woman. She listened for the old woman's answer. "She says, 'Go home!' " Ruby told me. She repeated this in a commanding tone. Then she said, speaking to the old woman: "Home! You don't really mean that I should leave here. You mean 'home,' " and here she put her hand over her heart. "I have to be where *I* live, not where other people want me. I have to be able to say no to always being nice."

This is the dilemma of an Eros woman, who is pulled this way and that by the people in her life because relationships are so important to her. Perhaps this is why she is such a fine actress—she can engage people in a way that holds them fast and involves them emotionally in the show. People make demands on her that are all out of proportion sometimes, and yet it is just this attention that makes her feel important. When she is simply being herself, she feels that people don't like it.

"My husband, my sons, expect certain things from me. My husband expects to have food on the table when he comes home, clothes put away, a made-up bed to sleep in, and my boys expect me to be there for them. Last week my youngest forgot to take his lunchbox to school and called me and wanted me to bring it to the school for him. He expected me to drop what I was doing and come to school, and I resent it. I don't want all those responsibilities. If only I could unload these burdens one by one that have been accumulating on my back. My shoulders hurt. They ache. I feel all cramped up like a little child."

Ruby was sitting on the floor with her knees pulled up and her arms wrapped around them as if to protect her vital organs from attack. She continued to lament, "I need to stretch out, to be free of all this, to breathe openly. But I can't."

This was a mature woman who had been living in her well-developed Eros function to such an extreme degree that she was in danger of losing her balance. Eros was the function she used by preference in the visible world, and it would have worked well enough if something beyond her line of vision had not been calling out to her—the "I," the individual who was capable of independent functioning. Ruby secretly longed to be able to live out this aspect.

"Why can't you breathe free, Ruby?" I had to put my question this way because it was not natural for her to ask *why*. Her questions tended to begin with, *how*? "What's stopping you?"

Ruby howled in anger, "My husband! My mother! Meeeee!" But the anger dissolved into a jest and I caught the twinkle in her eye. A bit of theater.

I told her that if she wanted to be free she couldn't do it piecemeal. She couldn't continue to drag the past around with her. "You mean let it all go?" she cried. "All? Now? I would just run wild. Crazy. You know how long it took me to learn how to manage my household tasks. It was only because you showed me how to handle the everyday responsibilities that were always such a burden to me. You got me organized so I could accomplish them fairly quickly. I learned that, but now I'm so compulsive about it. I go buzzing off to work like a house-keeping robot."

I was thinking, there's the undeveloped Logos speaking. It was important that I let her see this too, and so I took the voice of this small Logos: "It's efficient, Ruby, isn't it? Isn't that what you wanted? Before you had your system, there was never any end to the household responsibilities. Now, at least, you get through them."

Ruby responded, "But now it's so—so soulless." She had come to the edge of her visible world. "If only I could get the two parts of me together. If I could let the real me penetrate into the compulsive part. Or let the part that tries to make order protect the demanding creative part by providing boundaries."

Ruby's experience demonstrates how people limit the development of their full potential by blockading themselves in the fragile house of ego. To avoid the pain of conflict and possible failure, they repress the very parts of themselves that would bring them a free exercise of their talents and the fulfillment of living in accordance with their natural gifts.

Freud was one of the first to see how traumas of all kinds threaten to break this fragile house apart, requiring tremendous amounts of energy to shore up its defenses. When the defenses eventually start to crumble, individuals may begin to feel that they are nothing. It seems to them that they are only that which moves through them: their fears, their anxieties, their suspicions, their unrealized desires. Freud devised the techniques of psychoanalysis for the purpose of bringing unconscious material into consciousness. It was his work that pointed out the task for us as for so many before us: to explore the boundaries of the visible world. There is a further exploration to which we now address ourselves, and that is to discover how we can move toward bringing some of the contents of the invisible world into the realm of the visible.

3

Opening to the Invisible World

What is essential is invisible to the eye.
ANTOINE DE SAINT-EXUPÉRY

How can I go into eternity if I am imprisoned in form?
The Gospel of Joseph of Arimathea

I assert for My Self that I do not behold the outward Creation & that
to me it is hindrance and not Action; it is as the Dirt upon my feet,
No part of Me. "What," it will be Questioned, "When the sun rises do
you not see a round disk of fire somewhat like a Guinea?" O no, no,
I see an Innumerable company of the Heavenly host crying, 'Holy,
Holy, Holy is the Lord God Almighty.' I question not my Corporeal or
Vegetative eye any more than I would question a Window concerning
a Sight. I look thro' it & not with it.
BLAKE, "A Vision of the Last Judgment"

When I write of *seeing* through the visible world, I am using seeing
as a metaphor. Our experience of seeing evokes another metaphor, the
metaphor of the eye. The way in which we experience the eye, in
seeing or not seeing, in being blind or being sighted, shows us in a
deep inner way how it is to apprehend the difference between the
everyday visible world and the secret, mystical, unknown world that
lies under its surface (another metaphor). This difference was brought
home (another metaphor) to me in a stunning way when I had cataract
surgery. I, who have always taken my vision for granted, was not prepared for the experience, an experience I will recount presently.

We will also see in this chapter how Laurel experienced an opening
to the invisible world in a shocking way, and will reflect on the implications of her ordeal. We will then consider how Jung differed from
Freud in his understanding of the process of confronting the invisible.
But first, I will begin with my own recent episode.

It had only been one day since the cataract surgery and the implantation of a new plastic lens when the physician took the bandage off my left eye. In that single day I had gone from a reasonably self-confident and independent person to a woman who moved about in a world of fog and distortion, unsure of every step she took. It wasn't so much that one eye was bandaged and covered with a big bulky patch. It was the other eye, the "good" eye, which had been corrected with glasses. The patch made it impossible for me to wear my glasses, so I could not see at all out of the operated eye and very little out of the "good" eye.

Because I did not know how I would feel after the bandage was removed, I decided to stop at the grocery store with my husband on the way to the doctor. I tried to shop, but I could not read any of the labels or any of the signs or any of the prices. I could only see that the meat was red and the chicken came in flat plastic packages. Fortunately, I knew how the store was laid out and where to find things, and that low-fat milk came in a different-colored carton from regular milk. I had to be led around. I found out what it was like to be nearly blind. I felt very sad because I could no longer enjoy the beauty of the world.

With great apprehension I entered the doctor's office. She removed the bandage and told me to put on my glasses. Suddenly I could see again. I experienced a moment of the most painful joy! The light in her office was unbearably bright. She gave me dark glasses to wear over my regular ones because my new eye would be sensitive to ultraviolet light for some time. At home, I stretched out on my bed, still wearing the dark glasses. The bedroom opens out onto a patio shaded by hanging plants and vines. I took off the dark glasses and the other glasses and lay there with my eyes closed for a long time. Then gradually I began to open them. Again, the brightness assailed me. I opened only narrow slits at first and for a short time, and then little by little I let in the daylight and the sunlight as it filtered through the leaves. I had to protect myself against the brilliance of the colors by taking in only small glances, resting my eyes between these glances. I was a soldier, raising my head above the battlements and swiftly lowering it before the arrows of sunlight could fly toward me. I played this little game until I felt more secure and certain that indeed, I could see again.

And then I looked out through the leaves. What strange color was that, that intense blue, vibrating with the clarity of a million jewels?

Surely something was wrong—that could not be the sky, not this glim-mering, shimmering airiness, this living, breathing, sparkling purity of azure that now danced before me. I saw a sky I had never seen before. Or had I seen it and then forgotten it? I walked to the window. The colors! Oh my God, the colors! The green of the grass was not a color as in a painting, it was emerald! The flowers in the garden were flu-orescent! But there was something odd about these colors. I covered up my old eye and saw with the new. The colors were dazzling. Then I covered up my new eye and saw with the old. The colors were or-dinary. They were clouded over by a yellowish film, as when you look through a dirty windshield. I switched from one eye to the other. Through the new eye I could see that the blouse I was wearing was the most delicate shade of lilac. Through the old eye my blouse was gray with just a hint of lavender, an ugly shade compared to the new eye's view. The color had faded; except that it was not the color but my perception that had faded. The film caused by my cataracts had cast a pall over my whole world.

Gradually I came to understand certain things, like my mother's smearing the brightest possible lipstick over her lips and wearing garish clothing in her old age. She must have wanted to compensate for the going of the light by adding as much luminosity to her world as she could. And I never knew it!

■

If the doors of perception were cleansed
Everything would appear as it is—infinite.
                        BLAKE, *The Marriage of Heaven and Hell*

Individuals are led in many different ways to confront the invisible world. It is all around us, just beyond our line of vision. If we are not open to it—if we are not receptive to the ways in which it affects our lives—the invisible world will find its own ways of intruding into our everyday affairs and drawing us into its orbit. When this happens, it is time to take notice.

A physical change, like that of my surgery, is only one of the ways the invisible world might intrude. I might have asked concerning my cataract operation, What am I not seeing as clearly as I might? How can I remove the obstacles that stand between me and the possibilities of seeing that I did not suspect were mine?

Extended physical illness can become another opening. We often hear about radical changes brought about by insights that come when a person is forced to inactivity and is given an opportunity to turn inward and contemplate what is overlooked most of the time. It may begin with the question, What is the meaning of this illness? Or, better still, What can I learn from this illness? Illness can then be reframed as metaphor—Why this particular change in circumstances? Or illness may offer an opportunity to indulge in fantasy and allow the thoughts and feelings to range where they will, without attempting to exercise control over them. This is giving permission for the wellsprings of the unconscious to gush forth into consciousness. They are always present *in potentia*, but active people do not always give themselves time and space to reflect on what these wellsprings bring.

Those who make a place for meditation in their lives create a quiet empty space through which the invisible can enter. In periods of stillness, the turbulence of ordinary activities ceases and the deeper structures of the psyche can then appear with a new clarity.

It is not only in solitude that we discover the invisible world. Relationships can be thoroughfares to it, if only we do not take the relationships at face value. No matter what may occur in a relationship, it is always possible to ask ourselves, What is behind this word, this action? To do this requires humility and compassion; otherwise, it becomes an exercise in presumed superiority. But if we seriously ask, What is behind this? and then continue to ask the same question on deeper and deeper levels, we may be given the grace to understand.

Science is another avenue through which the invisible may reveal itself. The discipline of scientific investigation requires a person to be aware of what has been learned in the past and yet to regard all preconceived notions as provisional, rather than absolute. Received knowledge belongs within the realm of the visible. The new scientist stands at the far edge of this knowledge and gazes into the expanse of the unknowable.

Music and art also serve as gatekeepers to the invisible world. By releasing the individual from the strictures of words, they allow the imagination to play with sound and image. When play is unstructured it provides many openings for the unplanned and the unexpected. Poetry falls into this group also, as do some forms of fiction and drama. When these are more evocative than descriptive, they invite us into the mysteries.

On the darker side, death and grief bring us to speculation about our own mortality, and about what lies beyond that. They shake us out of complacency and remind us that nothing is permanent in this world, the visible world. All we can count on for certain, outside of death and taxes, is change. But in an existence beyond time and space, it may all be different. And there is such an existence—for time only takes its meaning by contrast with timelessness or eternity, and space only takes its meaning in terms of what is nonspatial, or infinite.

Of course, we can change our consciousness through the ingestion of substances that promise visionary experiences. The question in my mind when we alter consciousness through the use of psychoactive substances, is whether we are seeing what is there, in the invisible world, or are merely seeing distortions of what is here, in the visible world. I am not sure what the answer is, but so many natural ways to move into the invisible world are available that I am reluctant to suggest methods that may be contaminated by foreign substances of questionable value and potential harm.

Individuals experience the world at the edge of consciousness in differing ways, depending upon their own nature or typology. This is to be expected, because people of differing types have type-specific value systems. When these values are threatened, people feel they have nowhere to turn. Logos people are the most amazed when the bottom drops out of their solid system of human supports. Unlike Eros-oriented people, who can handle relationships with ease and comfort for the most part, Logos people take a long time to cultivate significant relationships, and they set a very high value upon those they do establish. When the image of themselves that they have carefully crafted in order to impress the important people in their world is shattered—through the loss of a position, a lover, or someone upon whom they have depended, or through some discovery of bad judgment or gross error that puts them to shame—they are suddenly hard put to function in the visible world. Their self-concept falls apart and they are devastated. Jung (1928/1966) describes this situation well:

A collapse of the conscious attitude is no small matter. It always feels like the end of the world, as though everything had tumbled back into original chaos. One feels delivered up, disoriented, like a rudderless ship that is abandoned to the moods of the elements. So at least it seems. In reality, however, one has fallen back upon the collective unconscious, which now takes over the leadership. We could multiply examples of cases where, at the critical moment, a "saving" thought, a vision, an "inner voice," came with irresistible power and gave life a new direction. (par. 254)

A Glimpse of the Greatness

Laurel was in danger of losing the respect of her colleagues when she ran into their objections about her research findings. What she was

so strongly convinced of was being challenged and actually negated by
the people who had authority over her. She took off a day to "get away
from it all," and was motoring along the coast with a friend at the
wheel, when she had a strange and shattering experience. She described it to me in her analytic hour.

> We were driving along and I was looking at the very beautiful coun-
> tryside, when I suddenly felt this tugging at my skirt. I looked down
> to see this trap door open, and when I looked to see what might be
> down there I was amazed to see this incredible Greatness. I cannot
> possibly describe it; it was so full, so rich, so bright, so overpowering!

I understood the trap door of Laurel's vision as a gap, a hole in her
ego identity, making it possible for her to see through into something
beyond ego, something we could call *transpersonal*. It was so frightening
to her because her ego, frustrated in the visible world, needed and
wanted to come into contact with something Other. She sensed a tremendous source of power, but did not feel, in her words, "that I am
able to contain it. I'm not a strong enough vessel."

I was certain (and she later confirmed it) that her image of the not-
strong-enough vessel came from the creation myth that is found in the
works of the sixteenth-century Kabbalist Isaac Luria, who wrote in
Safed in upper Galilee. Laurel's interest in Western mysticism had led
her to read about the Lurianic doctrines in Scholem's *Major Trends in
Jewish Mysticism* (1954). She was familiar with the concept of the emanations of the divine mind, called *En Sof*, as the divine light that per-
vaded the fullness that preceded all creation, and that exists in all that
is. According to this doctrine, says Scholem, the first being to emanate
from the light was Adam Kadmon, the primordial man. He was the
first and highest form in which the divinity began to manifest itself
after the original light. From Adam Kadmon's eyes, mouth, ears, and
nose the lights burst forth. At first these lights coalesced, so they did
not require any vessel to hold them. With the beginnings of creation,
however, it was necessary to isolate and capture the lights that were
to play the central role in fashioning a world. The vessels that had
been prepared to capture and hold this light ruptured under its weight,
causing the light to explode into millions of particles. These resulted
in the birth of evil in the world. The light symbolized the divine power
of the Self, and the vessels stood as instruments within which change
and transformation might take place.

I suggested to Laurel that the light, which she called the Greatness and which Jung referred to as the Self, was not at risk. It was only her ego that was at risk. I asked her whether she was afraid because of this. She said that she did not feel threatened, because the Self was not making demands on her. It was as though the Self had said, it is time for you to *see* this Greatness, but you can't handle it yet.

I wondered if Laurel was imagining that she possessed more power than she actually did. If so, this could be a sign that her ego was inflated, that she had a grandiose idea of her own importance. She insisted that she did not. What she said was, "The vessels broke when there was too much light. If anything, such a catastrophe would demolish the ego, not inflate it, because the ego's demonstrations are so petty. I, my ego, is somewhat troubled by this whole experience. My ego says, 'Laurel, you're just misinterpreting it.' Then my observing eye says to my ego, 'But you were there.' "

I related what Laurel called the observing eye, the eye that watched the interaction between her ego and the invisible world, to what Jung called the transcendent function. He said that the transcendent function mediates the relations between the conscious ego and the unconscious part of the psyche, because it can transcend both of them. It can be cultivated as a guide, a companion, or a mentor. I asked Laurel whether it might have been the transcendent function as mediator that was responsible for the tugging at her skirt and for showing her the way to the trap door.

"If that is true," she answered, "then the transcendent function has a wry sense of humor. It is close to my tendency to sense the paradox. Perhaps that is what makes me able to see both sides, the absurdities. It's been around my whole life—when I'd feel sorry for myself the mediator would say, 'All right, enough!' Then I'd stop. Sometimes it has a faculty for harnessing my inner wisdom. The problem when it speaks through my inner wisdom is that it comes through in cryptic one-liners that I can spend years trying to figure out—like Zen koans. The mediator also makes more practical statements. It tells me where the boundaries are, and when I transgress them it says, 'enough already!' In situations of heightened emotions the transcendent function is there like an internal regulator to warn me if I go to the limits of sadness, anxiety, boredom, or depression. When I ignore it I pay a heavy price. It's not my buddy. It does not have my ego's interest at heart: it has wholeness at heart. I mean the whole psyche, both the ego and the unconscious aspects of it. The mediator or transcendent function helps to keep the whole in balance. What closes the trap door is my ego. It says, 'No way. I cannot contain that.' "

I saw that closing the trap door could either be a good thing for her, or else it could represent denial or escape. I did not believe that Laurel was trying—consciously or unconsciously—to avoid the invisible world. For her, there was wisdom in closing the door. She did not feel that she was ready for it yet. She did not feel prepared to contain what might be revealed to her. It frightened her, and brought her to the edge of inflation. She knew that this Greatness does not manifest very often. She feared that if she could not contain it, it could destroy her. The slow and patient "working through" of the analytic process can be like a series of initiation rites through which the ego or conscious personality gains strength so as to deal with powerful unconscious material like that symbolized by the Greatness. It is important that the ego become strong, because without the ego there is no vessel, no instrument for the individuation process. This process, I explained to Laurel, is oriented toward wholeness. This is why in analysis we must deal with the practical problems of everyday life. It is absolutely necessary to learn to manage one's outer life, or else the inner quest will continually go awry because practical necessities will interfere with the person's ability to reflect quietly and thoughtfully upon his or her place in the larger scheme of things.

Laurel was afraid. Her biggest fears were the knowledge that she had been chosen for an unusual experience and the fear that she could not measure up to it. She worried about the possibility of inflation. She was also concerned that she might be crazy. This led her to ask if she was being arrogant in suggesting that her tendency for inflation was worse than anyone else's tendency for inflation.

I said to her, "The inflation you are afraid of comes from the necessity you feel to 'contain' this Greatness. Like a balloon that has to take in this unlimited unfathomable substance, you want to make space within yourself for the ineffable. Fearing that you might be crazy could be your way of saying that you feel you are unlike anyone else, that you are so special. That may be where your fear of arrogance is coming from. You suffer from what creative people often have to endure, the sense that there is something incredibly wonderful to which they have access and that they must do something about—surrender to or close off. If you surrender you could be annihilated by its power. If you shut it off, you yourself will be forever diminished."

When she responded that it seemed hopeless, I suggested that there were other possibilities. She needed to recognize that she was not alone in her dilemma. She was one of a company of creative people who have lived in every age, people who have been able to see through the obvious, through the dogmas and designs of the past, into something more—something beyond, something potential that has not yet taken form. It can be found in painting, in architecture, in music, in physics, or in the imaginative rearing of children. The task of these people is not to enlighten the world, but to push against the boundaries in the particular area that calls out to them—to enlarge the knowledge that they find there, to the degree they are capable of. If these people can begin by following the dictate of hatha yoga, "stretch but don't strain," they will increase and extend their limits without harming themselves, without shattering their ego boundaries. Later, perhaps, they will be able to extend those boundaries a little bit further.

The meaning of the trap door became clear: it works something like a dam. To a certain degree, one can regulate the flow of unconscious material. Another way to say it is that one can allow portions of the infinitely extensible invisible world to permeate, or filter into, the visible world.

The Analytic Dialogue

The analytic dialogue between Laurel and myself demonstrates how ego consciousness and the unconscious can converse when an individual confronts the invisible world. The process just described is an active one in which the analyst and the analysand participate together. My role as analyst is to help the analysand bring to awareness material that emerges spontaneously from the unconscious. I work from a Jungian perspective, based on Jung's view of the unconscious.

It is important to clarify how Jung's view of this process differs from that of Freud, inasmuch as Jung's perspective is an underlying theme in my work. Jung "discovered" the unconscious at almost the same time as Freud did, but the two men came to their insights by traveling different paths. Freud, a Jew in a Vienna that, to say the least, was not very hospitable to Jews, was deeply concerned with the factors in the external world that one had to come to terms with in order to exist. This context of life, coupled with his naturally extraverted personality type, created a desire in him to learn how to make his peace with the outer world and to have an important effect upon it. His patients would be cured of their neuroses when they could live productively in the world and have normal relationships with other people.

Jung, the son of a small-town pastor in introverted Switzerland, from early childhood found a well-defined place for himself in the society in which his family moved. What fascinated Jung was the inner life, the trials and mysteries of the spirit that he could not discuss with anyone he knew because they did not conform to the religious dogma that was served to him with his daily bread. The challenge of the outer world was minimal for Jung. The really important focus of his energy was the life of the spirit; in our terms, the invisible world.

For Freud, the ego had to be empowered so that it could deal constructively with the conflicts it must face with the unconscious. Eventually, if one worked hard enough at it, the ego could assimilate enough unconscious material so that it could exert a certain amount of control over the unconscious rather than being at its mercy. This hope did not seem impossible to realize, given Freud's concept of the unconscious. Jung, on the other hand, saw the unconscious as far wider and less comprehensible than Freud had suggested. Not that Jung disagreed with Freud about the contents of the unconscious: he accepted everything Freud said was present as probably correct, but he saw Freud's unconscious as far too limited. Jung referred to Freud's concept of the unconscious as the *personal* unconscious, to denote that it was related to a particular person. He said that we all have unconscious material that is related to personal history and the events of our own lives, but that there is also a *collective* unconscious in which all people participate and share. Laurel's look into the Greatness had nothing to do with specific events in her own life, according to Jung's viewpoint, but rather it was *ein Augenblick*[5] into the collective unconscious, an experience of the magnificence and terror and awe that must mark anyone who has glanced into those depths.

For Jung, the collective unconscious is the counterpoint to culture, just as the personal unconscious is the counterpoint to the ego. Culture is the container of what has been cultivated by a particular society. It encompasses the rules and mores, the rituals and practices, the values and kinds of behavior that the society allows, espouses, and approves. The ego, as a general rule, strives to find a place for itself within the context of its culture. The collective unconscious is directly related to a society's culture, in that it contains all of what is unconscious by reason of its having been rejected by the culture's standards and/or practices. This is, however, only the smallest part of the collective unconscious. Whatever has not yet come to consciousness in a cultural

---

5. A word Jung often used to denote "the blink of an eye."

sense, remains unconscious to that culture—hence a part of the collective unconscious. This includes all the knowledge that is yet to be discovered and that may or may not be the subject of that society's exploration. This yet-to-be-discovered aspect of the collective unconscious rests on the threshold between the visible and the invisible worlds. On the far side is the unknowable—that is, unknowable by any rational means. If it can be known at all, it has to be through a process of subjective knowing. That means that it comes to one person at a time, in a way unique to that person, and that it cannot be validated by any of the methods that are culturally approved in the rational, visible world.

Toward the end of his life, Jung summed up his reflections on the importance of acknowledging the invisible world. In his autobiography, *Memories, Dreams, Reflections* (1961), he wrote, "The decisive question for man is, is he related to something infinite or not? That is the telling question of his life. Only if we know that the thing that truly matters is the infinite can we avoid fixing our attention upon futilities and upon all kinds of goals which are not of real importance. . . . In the final analysis we count for something only because of the essential we embody, and if we do not embody that, life is wasted" (p. 325).

In part II, I shall deal with people who have dedicated their lives to the pursuit of Jung's question: Are we related to something infinite or not? They are people who know that the thing that really matters is the infinite, and they seek in various ways to discover what is truly essential.

PART II

Touching the
Mysteries

I have heard it said that if we desire to understand the world, we must first understand ourselves; and if we want to heal the world, we must first heal ourselves. I think there is some truth in this, but I must take issue with the word *first*. In my years of working with the human psyche—my own and that of others—I have observed that understanding and healing are ongoing processes. Understanding pushes us farther and farther into the limitless realms of the unknowable, and healing strengthens our ability to pursue the quest. But if we must wait until we fully understand ourselves and until we are fully healed from the fragmentation that is a quality of our humanness, then the world will have to wait a long, long time for people to give their attention to it.

One alternative is to forget about the inner work and simply address ourselves to the world and its problems. But then we open ourselves up to the destructive forces of the worldly powers that the Gnostics called the archons—personal ambition, dishonesty, subversive machinations, and greed being only a few members of that legion—and we render ourselves blind to what is really motivating us and others in all we do and coloring the results of our endeavors. It is insufficient to rest with the task of perfecting ourselves, for even if this task could be accomplished (and it can't), we would still find ourselves in an imperfect and intrusive world that would contaminate our hard-won purity

I remember hearing early in my analytic training that Jung had once said in a lecture, "Ladies and gentlemen, remember that the unconscious is also on the outside!" This was both shocking and affirming to me, for I was even then a bit skeptical of the idea that every problem could be resolved by adopting a different attitude toward it. And so I was pleased to hear that "the old man" had said quite firmly that real issues, real problems, and real mysteries really do exist outside of ourselves and outside of the psyche—even though the psyche may be involved to the extent that there is where we notice them.

The mysteries, then, exist outside of this bag of skin in which we reside, as well as within it. Part II of this book is devoted to the ways in which people have explored the outer realities and mysteries, often with an eye toward the inner as well. This part consists of six chapters, in which I will paint a broad canvas, moving among many different areas that are related by the common task of pressing forward into the apparent chaos of the invisible world. In every field, people are exploring uncharted territory, seeking in some way to discover whether human existence might have some purpose, or whether we, and all of life, are the result of some fortuitous accident that occurred beyond the beginning of time as we know it.

The first two chapters in part II deal with the physical sciences. Chapter 4 shows how some scientists have been able to break through the limitations of their own traditions, their own axioms, to find that what applies in the visible, palpable world is not necessarily true in the world of subatomic particles and the farther reaches of the universe. They have had to overcome psychological hurdles to do this, and the hurdles may not be altogether unlike those we all must jump if we are to change our attitudes to embrace a larger world view. Chapter 5 looks at how the "new scientists," having freed themselves from strict adherence to the old shibboleths, have found themselves face-to-face with the eternal questions of all time: Where did the universe come from? Where is it going? Chapter 6 deals with similar questions as the Gnostics of two thousand years ago saw them, and indicates remarkable similarities with the present investigation. Following Gnosticism, chapter 7 explores old and new images of the apocalypse, predictions of how the world we know will come to its end as a result of human error, ignorance, or sinfulness. Always in conjunction with the despair of apocalyptism comes the renewed hope of messianism, the expectation of a world that holds the possibilities of an unbelievably fruitful future. In more contemporary terms, the apocalypse is seen today in the forces threatening the well-being of the planet, including the perils of war, the implications of environmental destruction, and the challenges to the social conditions of humans throughout the world. The image of messianism, in today's world, is translated into the incredible potential for assessing and distributing the earth's resources and for attaining a level of human awareness of self and other that can lead to peace and plenty for all the inhabitants of the planet. Chapter 8 relates a personal experience of my own in an artificially constructed "promised land," the "Kingdom of the Spirit," if you will. Here we will see how messianism gone awry and turning into a human obsession with perfection can bring about disastrous results. And finally, in chapter 9 we return to the psyche and see how the infinite expanse of the universe affects the inner world as much as or more than inner processes affect the cosmic order.

We see in part II how Jung, gnosis, and chaos are interwoven. Chaos is the *prima materia*, as the alchemists would say, the elemental stuff out of which order emerges. It is also the condition into which order tends to collapse over time. Jung, of all psychologists, has recognized the eternal flux, from chaos to order and back to chaos again, seeing this as an ever-recurring movement characteristic of life and growth. Gnosis, as first enunciated two millennia ago by heretical sects who refused to be bound by institutionalized "truths," was understood by Jung as a spirit of inquiry that is independent of dogma and that requires confirmation through personal experience and reflection. Gnosis today still supports the knowledge that either comes from within or that is found in the world and is confirmed by an inner sense of correspondence with one's own experience.

4

Frontiers of
Science

This is an exciting age, perhaps the most exciting in the history of
humanity. We live at the precise moment when we are simultaneously
becoming aware of the processes that evolve our societies and acquiring
mastery of the technologies that determine how they evolve. We live
at the conjunction of knowledge and power. Whether we also live at
the moment of emerging wisdom remains to be seen.

LASZLO, *Evolution: The Grand Synthesis*

For the physical scientist, the abyss of power and wonder is outside
the psyche, in the farthest reaches of the universe and in the smallest
particles of matter. During the past thirty years, human beings have
penetrated more deeply into these mysteries than over many preceding
centuries. I wondered what the state of theoretical physics was just
before the computer revolution made possible the dazzling break-
throughs that could never have been imagined as recently as three
decades ago. I looked for some answers to this question in March and
Freeman's *New World of Physics*, based on an essay by Arthur March,
late professor of theoretical physics at Innsbruck, Austria, and first
published in a German encyclopedia in 1957. The book reminded me
of something I had nearly forgotten: that the ancient Greeks knew that
a world existed beyond the world we could see, and that it was a world
of atoms. The philosopher Democritus was apparently the first to conceive of *atoms*, the name he gave to the ultimate indivisible particles
of matter. *Atom* means, literally, not capable of being divided. Democritus' statement "Nothing exists except atoms and the void. Everything
else is conjecture" made so deep an impression on science in antiquity
that its danger was not noticed. While it did indeed represent a useful
maxim that led to important knowledge in physics, at the same time
it led to the absurd idea that such things as mind and spirit consist

only of matter in motion. This atomism became the basis for a mater-
ialistic-mechanistic world view. It was a strictly deterministic view:
nothing happens by chance, and given like conditions, the same thing
always follows. As March pointed out, "In reality, this proposition is
applicable only to the material world—and then only with certain limitations. . . . All affairs of the mind, such as thought, emotion, perception, and volition, have nothing to do with atoms but form a world
of their own."

Even back in the fifth century B.C., scientists (who were then called
philosophers) argued about whether all events in the physical world
are strictly determined. Still, this concept of nature as being strictly
determined constituted a firm basis for classical physics until the second half of the present century, when March's book was written. It is
interesting to note that Democritus' ideas did not meet with general
acceptance even in his own time, since Aristotle and his followers rejected them. Aristotle claimed that Democritus had overlooked the necessary existence of a *first cause*, which Aristotle regarded as being
supremely important because it was only through first causes that
events acquired any meaning.

This is exactly where the *mechanistic* and the *teleological* views of
nature came into conflict. Democritus' notion of a strict determinism
is mechanistic. Aristotle's teleological view, ascribing design and purpose to nature, remained in force from late Hellenic times to the Renaissance in the fifteenth and sixteenth centuries. It cannot be said that
one view is true and the other is false, but the first view proved useful
for physics while the second did not. Whatever one might think to be
the task of physics, it cannot be denied that its purpose includes predictions about the future based on experimental data.

In the early beginnings of civilization, around 3500 B.C., societies
exhibited the same basic structures and characteristics, no matter where
they evolved. These were agriculturally based communities centered
around hierarchically organized cities and towns that were eventually
united into larger entities. They developed written languages, and they
founded religions whose purposes were political at least as much as
spiritual. They trained armies and they developed modest sciences and
technologies. The ancient world was dominated by four or five empires
that continued these basic structures for millennia. Europe in the Middle Ages saw a destabilization of this kind of society, fostered by the
particular challenges brought about by barbarian invaders. Further destabilization came about through such technical innovations as gun-
powder, the compass, and the sturdy sailing ship. These extended the

horizons of medieval Europe, and the voyages of discovery that followed brought about political and economic expansion.

Europe in transition became a force that moved much of the rest of the world out of its classic stability toward the modern age. Propelled by the experiments of such scientists as Copernicus, Galileo, Bruno, Kepler, and then Newton, whose aim was to "wrench the secrets of nature from her womb," modern science—with its insistence on observation and experiment—came into being.

We live in a culture where the greatest portion of intellectual and scientific thought continues to be dominated by scientific method. This particular perspective is the fruit of a paradigm rooted in the so-called Enlightenment of the seventeenth and eighteenth centuries, when Descartes made a conceptual separation between the visible and the invisible worlds acceptable to the European intellectual community. Before this time, institutionalized religion in the Western world had maintained its strong role in determining what was and was not the province of science, and had exercised its authority to decide what would be legitimate subjects for scientific exploration. The basis for this domination of science by the Church was its view of God's design and purpose for the world, for nature, and for human beings. Thus, areas approved for investigation included both the material and the spiritual domains, with the reservation that the Church must approve the findings wherever they occurred. Galileo challenged that authority. He based his theories on the results of his own observations instead of the knowledge passed down in the form of authorized revelation. In so doing, he put into motion the transition from medieval scholastic physics to classical physics.

The Enlightenment philosophers who followed Galileo were able to extricate the intellectual and scientific disciplines from control by the Church and from preconceptions based on its dogma. Severing the ties between the visible and invisible worlds, ties that had become ragged and frayed over the centuries and could barely hold together anyway, the newer intellectual tradition rendered unto science the things that were science's and unto God the things that were God's. Even though some of the Enlightenment's leading scientific minds held strong religious beliefs, these people managed to compartmentalize their religious feelings and commitments so that their faith would not intrude to affect the soundness of their rational thinking processes. The latter assumed primacy with Descartes' announcement *Cogito, ergo sum*. The separation of "this world" from "that world" meant that a mechanistic world view could exist in science and a teleological world view could exist with respect to religion. Inspired by the late seventeenth-century work of Isaac Newton, classical physics discovered the laws of motion and gravity. It viewed the universe as a gigantic clockwork mechanism set in motion at the beginning of time and allowed to run on undisturbed. These physicists believed with Democritus that given all the necessary data, the entire material creation from its largest to its smallest motion behaves in a way that can be predicted with absolute accuracy, and further, that the events of the past can be inferred on the basis of observable data in the present. Everything by its very nature is predetermined. Nothing is left to chance. The task of science, then, was to continue to discover and refine those laws and principles that would enable it to predict physical events in our world. The determinism that characterized the paradigm of classical physics influenced other disciplines as well. People believed that if they could somehow accumulate all the factual knowledge about a given problem, eventually the answers or solutions could be found.

When it proved impossible to deal with a relatively large field of knowledge in this way because new data were always being discovered that would not necessarily narrow the problem but often expanded it, a tendency developed to specialize in one branch of science. If one could break down a science into narrow specializations, or break down a problem into a small discrete and finite area, perhaps then all the facts about that area could be discovered. As the saying goes, people began to know more and more about less and less. Scientific fields became more and more separate from one another and cross-disciplinary efforts became increasingly rare. Despite Herculean efforts, the number of problems with which science was dealing multiplied, and the dream of understanding fully the workings of the clockwork universe diminished. The only hopeful solution, or so it seemed, lay in breaking down the problems into small and simple constituents, and dealing with these within closed systems in which the initial conditions and most of the variables could be strictly controlled. For a long time this approach seemed to work fairly well. But as complexity piled upon complexity, trying to solve one single aspect of a complex problem came to be like trying to behead the Hydra.

In Greek mythology, the Hydra was a weird creature with a prodigious doglike body and eight or nine snaky heads, one of them immortal. It was so venomous that its very breath or the smell of its tracks could destroy life. Heracles forced the Hydra to emerge from his lair beneath a plane tree at the source of the river Amymone by pelting it with burning arrows, and then held his breath while he caught hold of it. The monster twined around his feet in an endeavor to trip him up. In vain did Heracles batter at the Hydra's heads with his clubs: no sooner was one head crushed than two or three more appeared in its place. Heracles shouted to his charioteer Iolaus for help. Iolaus set one corner of the grove alight and then to prevent the Hydra from sprouting new heads, seared their roots with blazing branches; thus the flow of blood was checked. Now, using a sword, Heracles severed the immortal head, part of which was gold, and buried it, still hissing, under a heavy rock beside the road to Elaeus (Graves 1955, Hamilton 1969).

The many heads of the Hydra represent all the closed systems with which we try to cope in a mechanistic-materialistic world. From a closed-system perspective, each problem is seen as separate and distinct; yet when one of them is resolved, two more arise in its place. Closed systems are subject to entropy, losing energy as they move toward equilibrium. The single golden head of the Hydra, which is immortal, suggests an open system that is continually exchanging its resources with other systems outside itself, hence is able to maintain itself in response to the challenge of the environment. So this immortal head represents aspects of reality that go beyond the limited realm of the visible. Even though there may be attempts to bury it—that is, to repress these sometimes discomfiting aspects of reality—the head goes on hissing.

Seeing Through Belief Systems

Until the momentous times at the beginning of the twentieth century, the sharp demarcation remained between the provinces of science on the one hand, and religion and the humanities on the other. The two-hundred-year split between the sciences and the humanities, as described by C. P. Snow in *The Two Cultures* (1959), was based upon the incompatibility between the Newtonian deterministic paradigm and the paradox that living beings do not conform to it. But with the advent of better instruments and freed from some of the restrictions of an earlier era, scientists in this century have proceeded to explore the invisible worlds that formerly were inaccessible to research: the microworld of subatomic particles and the regions of the macrocosm beyond the reach of the most powerful telescopes. As a consequence, our understanding of the nature of this planet has expanded with dizzying rapidity as physical and biological scientists have discovered more and more of what was not even imagined in the past.

   While these profound changes have been affecting the way our culture perceives the external world, you and I have not been able to avoid
becoming aware of a subtle shift in our own ways of separating the
visible world of everyday reality from the invisible world of tentative
speculation. While we might not be able to delineate our images of
these differing worlds, we probably would recognize certain words as
belonging to one category or the other. When I tried to think what
some of those words might be, they seemed to fall into two groups:
words that are descriptive of perspectives and words that are descriptive of values. These were some of the words that came to mind:

CHARACTERISTICS OF THE TWO WORLDS

The Visible World	The Invisible World
Perspectives	*Perspectives*
Order and stability	Chaos and flux
Earth	Sky
Matter	Energy
Form	Formative
Items	Systems
Goals, ends	Pathways, process
Belief, disbelief	Suspension of disbelief
Places	Contexts
Definite	Indefinite
Finite	Infinite
Fixed in time	Evolving
Spatial	Non-local
Ethnic/racial	Human/animal
Ego coherence	Ego permeability
Self as ideal	Self as experience
Religion	Spirituality
Values	*Values*
Knowledge (factual)	Gnosis (inner knowledge)
Achievement of goals	Becoming conscious
Worldly success	Inner harmony
Improving lifestyle	Spiritual practice
Competition	Cooperation
Knowledge about God	God as Mystery

The perspectives and values of the visible world—whether they refer to cultural mores or to scientific discoveries—are undergoing critical examination. Increasingly, they are seen to be inadequate to explain certain of our experiences or some of the discoveries that scientists have made. It is as though the subjective vessels of consciousness and the objective vessels of information are filled to overflowing and cannot contain any more. Yet the questions keep coming, and the searchers keep searching. What they discover is more and more evidence of the invisible world, much of it incompatible with the classical world view. Either we must close our eyes to our new awareness and pretend it does not exist, or we must create a larger vessel.

Thomas A. Kuhn in his 1962 classic work *The Structure of Scientific Revolutions* analyzed the nature, causes, and consequences of revolutions in basic scientific concepts in an effort to explain how such a "larger vessel" comes into existence. Kuhn uses the term *paradigm shift* in reference to the upheaval in the sciences that has been taking place in our own century. A paradigm is what the members of a scientific community share, and conversely, a scientific community consists of people who share a paradigm. Kuhn explains why paradigms are so persistent within a scientific discipline:

> The study of paradigms . . . is what mainly prepares the student for membership in the particular scientific community with which he will later practice. Because he there joins men who learned the bases of their field from the same concrete models, his subsequent practice will seldom evoke overt disagreement over fundamentals. Men whose research is based on shared paradigms are committed to the same rules and standards for scientific practice. That commitment and the apparent consensus it produces are prerequisites for the genesis and continuation of a particular research tradition. (pp. 10–11)

In the normal progression of scientific inquiry, problems are solved and the scope of and precision of scientific enterprise increase in a highly cumulative enterprise. This is the usual image of scientific work. Normal science does not seek novelties of fact or theory. Nevertheless, new and unsuspected phenomena crop up again and again, and radical theories are invented by scientists to try to explain them. Or it sometimes happens that a scientist looks at familiar phenomena in a new way and sees something unexpected that has not been noticed before and that does not seem to fit into the categories of normal science. Discovery begins with the recognition of anomaly that makes it appear as if nature has somehow violated the paradigm that governs normal science. The scientist has moved away from the old paradigm and entered a liminal area, beyond which a new paradigm may be waiting to be born. But the scientist can only do this when he or she is not emotionally identified with the work, but sees it rather as one endeavor in a long chain of investigation. Melvin Schwartz exemplified this spirit well when upon being notified that he had just won the Nobel Prize in physics, he said in a newspaper article, "The research has no practical significance other than very long term. If you understand something better, sooner or later it will be practical."

The scientific method is not designed primarily to produce novelty. It supplies a highly disciplined set of procedures that require sufficient knowledge and skill on the part of the scientist to be able to predict with some degree of accuracy what can be expected to occur in the course of an experiment. Only a person who can anticipate what should happen is able to discern when something does not fit within the constraints of the paradigm. Such a discovery is usually met with rebuff and denial. This resistance to the novelty serves a useful purpose; it demands that the proponent of the novel concept exercise extreme care in checking and rechecking the findings so that any human error in the research process can be discovered and eliminated, or the accuracy of the observation can be verified. As more such discoveries are made, tensions between the old paradigm and the new findings increase.

Around 1925, in the months before Heisenberg's paper on matrix mechanics pointed the way to a new quantum theory, Wolfgang Pauli wrote to a friend, "At the moment physics is again terribly confused. In any case it is too difficult for me, and I wish I had been a movie comedian or something of that sort and had never heard of physics." That testimony was particularly impressive when contrasted with Pauli's words less than five months later: "Heisenberg's type of mechanics has again given me hope and joy in life. To be sure it does not supply the solution to the riddle, but I believe it is again possible to march forward" (Kronig 1960, pp. 22, 25–26).

The Birth of a New Paradigm

A new paradigm is often present in embryo before the old paradigm is seen to be at risk—that is, before a crisis develops. The first blurring of the rules for normal science may bring about a vague sense of unrest in the scientific community; then a sort of random searching takes place. This turns out to be a series of extraordinary experiments based on highly speculative theories without a clear expectation of what the outcome will be. The new data thus acquired loosen the hold of the old paradigm; hints of the possibility of a new structure keep scientists awake at night. It is apparent that a crisis exists.

Kuhn tells us how, in 1962 or thereabouts, he saw the resolution of the paradigmatic crisis taking place:

What the nature of that final stage is—how an individual invents (or finds he has invented) a new way of giving order to the data now all assembled—must here remain inscrutable and may be permanently so. Almost always the men who achieve these fundamental inventions of a new paradigm have been either very young or very new to the field whose paradigm they change. . . . These are men who, being little committed by prior practice to the traditional rules of normal science, are particularly likely to see that those rules no longer define a playable game and to conceive another set that can replace them. (pp. 89–90)

Now, more than a quarter of a century after Kuhn suggested that we live in a time of paradigm shift, we find ourselves in a second Industrial Revolution, based upon communication and rapid transportation and characterized by increasing complexity. With the advent of the computer, we can travel where we have never been and where we can never go without its aid. Scientists can "talk" to each other across the globe, from the air to the ground, from outer space to under the sea. No longer do lonely individuals work out their theories in isolation, as did Galileo and Einstein. Today, most research and development is the product of efforts in which many people participate, either linked physically in university or corporate research centers or linked through computer networks and electronic conferencing.

A growing number of the "new scientists" are multidisciplinary evolutionary thinkers who specialize in being generalists in the study and synthesis of various fields and realms of evolution. They tend to find each other quickly in this information age, and even if they have been trained in different disciplines they lend support to one another by affirming the necessity of bringing forth new ideas—whether or not these conform to the assumptions and theories of the past. A time comes when the weight of their arguments cannot be disregarded, and little by little the "old scientists" begin to take note of the novel perspectives. Still, members of the old guard usually tend to feel threatened because the work to which they have devoted their lives has built up a body of knowledge and techniques designed for further research based upon the cumulative knowledge of the past. They may find it difficult to relinquish the reliable supports they have worked so long and hard to acquire. What tends to happen is that the new paradigm slowly emerges nevertheless, while at the same time the old paradigm clings like dry oak leaves to the branch in winter. The dying paradigm and the paradigm being born exist side by side for a while, but in the course of time the old one loses in strength and the new one gains in adherents. There comes a time when the old patterns can no longer accommodate the new data, and then the situation is ripe for a scientific revolution.

Darwin, in a particularly perceptive passage at the end of his *The Origin of Species* (1889), wrote: "Although I am fully convinced of the truth of views given in this volume . . . , I by no means expect to convince experienced naturalists whose minds are stocked with a multitude of facts all viewed, during a long course of years, from a point of view directly opposite to mine. . . . But I look with confidence to the future—to young rising naturalists, who will be able to view both sides of the question with impartiality" (p. 240).

Since Darwin wrote this, his theory has not only been fully accepted, but also some paleobiologists have gone beyond him to attack the now-classic conception that natural selection, acting on individuals, is gradual and continuous. Some now believe that nature progresses by sudden leaps and transformations rather than through piecemeal adjustments. In 1972, over one hundred years after the original publication of *The Origin of Species*, Niles Eldredge and Stephen Jay Gould came out with the study "Punctuated Equilibria: An Alternative to Phylogenetic Gradualism," which initiated the leap into neo-Darwinian biology.

Kuhn reminds us that Max Planck, surveying his own career in *Scientific Autobiography* (1949), sadly remarked that "a new scientific truth does not triumph by convincing its opponents and making them see the light, but rather because its opponents eventually die, and a new generation grows up that is familiar with it" (p. 33–34).

Planck and Einstein and the other scientific revolutionaries whose radical insights startled the scientific community at the turn of the century and in the few years that immediately followed are now dead, as are most of their students. Their work, once incomprehensible or at the least unacceptable to their peers, now rests securely between the covers of textbooks. The work has become normative science. When Planck first formulated quantum theory in 1900, it was not clear that a clean break with Newtonian physics was inevitable. Between 1900 and 1926, attempts were made to reconcile classical physics with quantum theory.

Physicist Heinz Pagels said of Einstein: "Einstein was present at the birth of twentieth-century physics. One might say he fathered it"

(p. 18). Ironically, Einstein, who had opened the door to quantum physics, was unable to see the implications of quantum theory and to recognize its possibilities, because he could not accept the idea that the foundation of reality could be governed by chance and randomness.

Most of the new breed of scientists who have come to the fore were adolescents or undergraduate students during the tumultuous consciousness-raising sixties, and then went on to serious study and creative scientific work in the seventies. By now they have passed through their first early bursts of creativity and have deepened their insights. Somewhere in the process, they have been able to make the shift whereby they can see the world of normative science as just that, and not as it was seen in former times as *the truth*. They can recognize normative science, textbook facts, as the accumulated knowledge of the past, with all the value and all the limitations that implies. They can see that it belongs to what I have called the visible world, the world of validated data and consensus reality. Understanding the process by which a paradigm shift or a scientific revolution takes place, they have also recognized that beyond all the given facts and knowledge of the visible world, an invisible world contains innumerable resources. The shift is far more than a scientific revolution; it is a revolution in consciousness. When this takes place in an individual, the entire approach to problems changes. The goal is no longer merely the solution of problems, but the movement through one problem into the wider world that the investigation of the problem reveals. Goals become less important than the processes by which they are attained, for the person who can see through the visible world into the invisible—even a little way—knows that every new insight brings with it the possibility of conceiving more insights. The deeper one can penetrate into the vast invisible world, the more rapidly the realm of the unknowable recedes beyond the knowable.

The "Coming Out" of the Scientists

What is different today, it seems to me, is that the work of some of the world's most creative scientists is no longer hidden behind the closed doors of the research laboratories. There is a hunger in our society for some light to be shed on the eternal questions: Who are we? Where do we come from? How did our world begin? What is happening to it? How will it all end? Will we survive? Is there reason for hope? Today, as soon as an interesting discovery is announced in a technical journal, it is swiftly reported in the public press. Television takes it up and the public broadcasting networks produce programs that describe, explain, illustrate, and animate the details of the research. Scientists and lay people comment for the media on the implications of the discovery. Subjects that until recently were incomprehensible to all but the specialists in the field have now become topics for family dinner table conversation, albeit in greatly oversimplified terms. The nonfiction best-seller list in the *New York Times Book Review* regularly includes books by first-rate theorists in the fields of physics, chemistry, and biology, explaining the work they are doing in terms the intelligent nonscientific reader will understand. The scientist has come down from the ivory tower to talk to the man and woman in the street, and the people in the street are listening. The information age has made the mysteries of science less exclusive. The informed public now can find out what problems are of greatest concern to theoretical scientists, and what they have been working on.

It is beyond the scope of this book and my abilities to discuss the specifics of the problems that occupy theoreticians in the sciences today. What is most interesting in terms of our investigation is the shift in *attitude* among the new scientists. I am not referring to those who are working primarily on applications of theory to practical problems in the visible world, although these people are by no means immune to the new syndrome, but my attention is attracted to the speculations of the new theorists. If the old scientists, the inheritors of classical physics, were characterized by the word *determinism*, then the new scientists might be characterized by words like *uncertainty, probability, indeterminism, open systems, paradox,* and, above all, *chaos. Chaos* was the word most dreaded by the physicist of the past, because it represents that which exists not only beyond the known but also beyond the knowable. But it is just here, in the area of seeming randomness, that questions arise for which the answers appear to lie beyond the scope of human understanding. Sooner or later the new scientists find that their concern is with cosmology, which is nothing more or less than the attempt to explain the generation of matter in space-time.

Whether scientists direct their attention primarily to the smallest conceivable quantum of matter or to the infinitely large dimension of the universe, eventually they must arrive at the most fundamental questions, which they cannot answer using the logic and the techniques of their trade. They come to a stone wall, a barrier, a separation between the visible and the invisible worlds. They face the abyss, the darkness and the mystery of chaos. It is not a mystery that can be resolved by more knowledge, by shedding more light. The truly invisible, not just the temporarily obscured but the truly invisible, is best approached through the intuitive mode. And we find, indeed, that the scientist, whose work depends so much on sensation (accuracy of perception) and thinking (the ability to draw logical conclusions from data), must at times make space for a kind of quiet speculative dreaming that invokes something fundamental—not the hundred heads of the Hydra, but the one immortal golden head that, though buried, is still hissing. That hissing sound—is it also related to the serpent of Apollo residing in the fissure in the earth in the sacred place at Delphi where the priestess of the oracle always speaks the truth, but often in words whose meaning is far from clear?

5

In the Beginning There Was Chaos

In the beginning there was chaos, instability, inflation, and radiation. Within an almost infinitesimal fraction of a second the first microparticles evolved. After half a million years stable atoms evolved—matter in the nonionized state—appeared. Within five million years the galaxies began to take shape and the stars. In the last three billion years life emerged on earth. For the last quarter of a million years or so, hominid creatures with conscious minds roamed this planet. And for the past several thousand years we sapiens have wondered: Where have we come from—and where are we going? Today, some 20 billion years since the origins of the universe, we may be nearing the approach to an answer.

LASZLO, *Evolution: The Grand Synthesis*

One of the reasons that the psychology of Jung appealed to me was that it was one science that took chaos seriously. Jung treated schizophrenics in a time when there were no psychotropic drugs and psychotics were allowed to babble away at will, constructing what their therapists would refer to as "word salad." Most mental health professionals shrugged off these ramblings as nonsense, but Jung tried to understand the contents of these confused and disordered verbal productions. He discerned that underneath the apparent gibberish was an attempt on the part of the disturbed person to make some sense out of an experience that could not be fitted into the conventional categories of experiences of people in a particular milieu. The schizophrenic person received data from the environment and also from the unconscious that did not conform to consensual reality. Having no apparent structure, these data were perceived as chaotic by the patient, who then might devise elaborate delusional systems to impose an order upon them. Jung's first published work, his doctoral dissertation "On the Psychology and Pathology of So-Called Occult Phenomena" (1902), presented the case history of a woman who in a "semi-somnambulistic state" produced a sort of "mystic science" in which the forces in the known world and beyond were revealed to her "by the spirits" as different forms of energy arranged in seven concentric circles. Jung described the visions related to him by the patient, S.W., thus: "With the sixth circle the visible world begins; this appears to be so sharply divided from the Beyond only because of the imperfections of our organs of sense. In reality the transition is a very gradual one, and there are people who live on a higher plane of cosmic knowledge because their perceptions and sensations are finer than those of other human beings. Such 'seers' are able to see manifestations of forces where ordinary people can see nothing" (1902/1970, pars. 65–70).

From the beginning of the first chapter of Genesis to the annals of contemporary physics, sane people, too, have been addressing the question, What lies beyond the scope of human knowledge? It seems to me that the essential difference between the sane and the not-sane person who faces this question is that the not-sane person has no context in consensual reality for exploring its implications, while the rest of us have a sense of the boundaries of the known, the unknown, and possibly even the unknowable. We are not adrift in a world of our own construction. We have some anchors in the knowledge we have gained through science and through history. The answer to the question of what lies beyond comes down to the same principle, however, no matter how it is expressed. There is knowledge, there is the knowable, and there is chaos.

Chaos stands for all that the human mind has not been able to fit into some kind of order or some set of rules or propositions that assure us that nature is systematic and predictable. Everyone has to deal with chaos in life, in the form of the incomprehensible, the unpredictable, the irrational, the confused aspects of personal and natural existence. Most of us find ways to avoid the essential question. One of the most common ways is to retreat behind the cover of what we know and deal with that, leaving the Big Question to the theologians or the scientists. Others look to the popular prophets of the day, who offer easy answers based on specious authority or disguised as personal revelation.

The more difficult way is to face the reality of chaos and to ask of disorder in nature the same question that Jung asked concerning the minds of disturbed people: Can some kind of order be hidden deep within chaotic systems? James Gleick writes in the prologue to his book *Chaos* (1987), "Where chaos begins, classical science stops. For as long as the world has had physicists inquiring into the laws of nature, it has suffered a special ignorance about disorder in the atmosphere, in the turbulent sea, in the fluctuations of wildlife populations, in the oscillations of the heart and brain. The irregular side of nature, the discontinuous and erratic side—these have been puzzles to science, or worse, monstrosities" (p. 3).

I was excited when I read those words. They suggested to me that as contemporary scientists probe ever more deeply into the abyss of chaos, they might discover a common ground between the physical sciences and the human sciences. I found myself drawn to the writings of those I have called the new scientists in the hope that some of the metaphysical questions that had led me in my adolescence to visit nearly every church in my neighborhood, and later to study depth psychology, might now be considered on another level and from the viewpoint of another discipline.

Henry Miller once said that since Thomas Aquinas there has been no metaphysics. He was wrong—the new scientists have opened the door to a metaphysics far beyond the range of Aquinas. The new breed of theoreticians may or may not limit themselves to a narrow field of specialization, but in their world view they roam far and wide. They range from botanist and biochemist Rupert Sheldrake, to astrophysicist Steven Weinberg, to theoretical physicists David Bohm, Stephen Hawking, and Paul Davies, to systems theorist Erwin Laszlo—to name only a few. None of these individuals has limited his horizon to the confines of his scientific field, but each in his own way has transcended the boundaries of the discipline to speculate and explore the very edges of knowledge and beyond. Often these explorations have encountered the spiritual dimensions of the invisible world.

Where Have We Come From?

One of my first exposures to a contemporary scientist who was exploring the possible source of all that is manifested in the visible world came about when I read David Bohm's 1980 book *Wholeness and the Implicate Order*. Bohm, a professor of theoretical physics at Birbeck College, London, is one of the new breed of scientists whose physics has moved closer to philosophy. Bohm develops a theory of quantum physics that treats the totality of existence, including matter and consciousness, as an unbroken whole. This is the same man who wrote the classic text in quantum mechanics *Causality and Chance in Modern Physics* (1957) a quarter of a century earlier.

When Bohm came to the edge of his understanding of the physical world and needed to make the leap into the unknown, he turned to the wisdom of the East, and especially of India. There he found a tradition in which people viewed the world as fundamentally whole rather than fragmented. Guided by the Indian sage and mystic Krishnamurti, Bohm learned that while Western science and technology rely mainly on measure, the East sees primary reality as immeasurable. Krishnamurti said that measure was an insight created by people. He believed that a reality that is beyond the person and prior to the person cannot depend upon such insight. Bohm sees the commonly accepted world view of our day as fragmented—beset by fragmentary problems, fragmentary thinking, fragmentary content, and fragmentary process— and he is dismayed. The central underlying theme of *Wholeness and the Implicate Order* is "the unbroken wholeness of the totality of existence as an undivided flowing movement without borders" (p. 172). He conceives of an *implicate order* within which the totality of existence is enfolded. The implicate order is invisible; it can only be inferred through observing its manifestations. The implicate order "unfolds" into the world of manifestation. Then, what has been *en*folded in the implicate order, is *un*folded in the *explicate order* (what I have called the visible world). We experience the explicate order when we perceive realities with our senses. What we normally perceive, in this commonsense everyday dimension of reality, are separate objects being pushed around by various kinds of forces, interacting with each other and influencing each other in various ways. When we look at a single organism, what we see is an entity with several systems operating within it, as well as upon it—a circulatory system, a respiratory system, a reproductive system, and so on. We "have" a body, but we do not necessarily feel that we "are" that body. We also "have" a psyche (we speak of "my psyche"); we "have" an ego, which is not the entirety of the psyche, but only a part—and there are other parts as well. In this explicate world of things and thoughts, we can hope to integrate the various disparate parts. Wholeness appears to us as an ideal state of being, but few in the Western world would lay claim to having achieved it. Furthermore, we consider our individual lives in terms of coherence and continuity from birth—or possibly from conception—to death.

We can compare Bohm's view with that of Jung, who, to his credit, did not limit the notion of consciousness or of the unconscious to the life span of the individual. He saw these as emerging from, and at the end of one's lifetime surrendering to, the matrix of the collective unconscious. For Jung, the collective unconscious was the fundamental reality, with human consciousness deriving from it.

In a similar way, Bohm sees the implicate order as the fundamental reality, with the explicate order and all its manifestations as derivative. To illustrate his view he uses the image of a turbulent mass of vortices in a stream. He says that the structure and distribution of vortices, which constitute a sort of content of the description of the movement, are not separate from the formative activity of the flowing stream, which creates, maintains, and ultimately dissolves the totality of vortex structures. So to try to eliminate the vortices without changing the formative activity of the stream would evidently be absurd. He then moves into the psychological dimension of the problem:

Once our perception is guided by the proper insight into the significance of the whole movement, we will evidently not be disposed to try such a futile approach. Rather, we will look at the whole situation, and be attentive and alert to learn about it, and discover what really is an appropriate action to the whole, for bringing the turbulent structure of vortices to an end. Similarly, when we really grasp the truth of the one-ness of the thinking process that we are actually carrying out, and the content of thought that is the product of this process, then such insight will enable us to observe, to look, to learn about the whole movement of thought and thus discover an action relevant to the whole, that will end the "turbulence" of movement which is the essence of fragmentation in every phase of life. (1980, pp. 18–19)

How Did the Various Forms of Life Come to Be as They Are?

Closely allied to the question, Where have we come from? is another question: How did the many and various forms of life come to be as they are? This question has been a major preoccupation of another of the new scientists, Rupert Sheldrake, who studied philosophy and the history of science at Harvard, then returned to Cambridge and took a Ph.D. in biochemistry. He worked on the physiology of tropical crops in India, where he met Father Bede Griffiths, a philosopher-priest who has brought together the harmonious principles underlying both Christianity and Hinduism.

I first met Rupert Sheldrake when he addressed the International Transpersonal Association in Bombay, India, in 1982, at a conference with the theme of "East and West: Ancient Wisdom and Modern Science." At that time Sheldrake was relatively unknown, although Dr. Stanislav Grof, the convener of the conference, had the foresight to recognize that the ideas being put forth by this new scientist would electrify the audience.

Sheldrake's book *A New Science of Life* (1981), had just been published, and I was one of the few at that conference who had read it. Sheldrake had written most of it while living at a Christian ashram in India headed by Father Griffiths. In this book, he presented for the first time in public his "hypothesis of formative causation." When his book appeared in 1981, Rupert Sheldrake was called "the most controversial scientist since Galileo." I found in the book's approach to biology a concept similar to that of Jung's archetypes and the collective unconscious, and I was eager to hear Sheldrake and to discover whether he indeed knew Jung's work, or whether he had come upon his own discoveries totally independently of Jung.

Sheldrake's appearance at the conference was postponed several times, apparently because of transportation difficulties. I assured my fellow conference attenders that they would find Sheldrake eminently worth waiting for, and indeed he was. A tall, lanky young Englishman, he arrived, somewhat breathlessly if I remember correctly, wearing the long white tunic and trousers of the typical rural Indian. He appeared to be extremely comfortable and relaxed as he addressed his waiting audience. Influenced, no doubt, by the value that Father Griffiths placed upon the infinite and invisible dimension, Sheldrake looked at two major unsolved problems of modern science: the nature of life and how the shapes and instincts of living organisms are determined.

The essential assumption behind Sheldrake's hypothesis of formative causation is that there is a level of reality beyond the one we know and beyond the material world in which we have our finite and time-bound existence. This level of reality corresponds to Plato's world of the ideal, Jung's collective unconscious, and the "prima materia" of the alchemists. From the standpoint of the ego, this other reality could be considered a "shadow universe." Enfolded within it is the potential for reality in *this* world. The other world contains the potentiality for patterning—that is, for creating the preforms for various types of structures or species. Sheldrake calls these preforms "morphogenetic fields" (from *morpho*, meaning form, and *genetic*, relating to or determined by the origin, development, or causal antecedents of something).

Morphogenetic Fields or "M Fields"

Sheldrake proposes that morphogenetic fields give rise to specific forms in nature, species by species, each with its own specific characteristics. His morphogenetic fields, or "M fields," give rise to the forms of total organisms. Sheldrake does not differentiate between physiological and psychological structures, but regards organisms as instances of undivided wholeness. An organism is complete within it- self and maintains its form amid changing circumstances. It may take in from its environment and put out into its environment, like a man or a cabbage or a frog, but it is a whole entity in and of itself. Nothing needs to be added or taken away to make it complete.

For Sheldrake, M fields are essential factors in the formation of pat- terns of organization. The particular character of an M field comes from the influence of the form and behavior of past organisms of the same species, through direct connections across space and time. He applies this principle to both archetypal patterning and instinctive behavior, since Sheldrake believes that these do not occur independently of one another.

Jung, among others, struggled with the problem of inheritance of behavioral patterns. At one time he suggested that this inheritance comes through germ plasm. As early as 1928, he wrote:

Although our inheritance consists of psychological paths, it was nevertheless mental processes in our ancestors that traced these paths. If they came to consciousness again in the individual, they can do so only in the form of other mental processes; and although these processes can become conscious only through individual experience and consequently appear as individual acqui- sitions, they are nevertheless pre-existent traces which are merely "filled out" by individual experience. Probably every "impressive" experience is just such a breakthrough into an old, previously unconscious river-bed. (1928/1969, par. 100)

Clearly, Sheldrake is not satisfied with this explanation. While the combined effect of DNA programming and the capacity of the organism to adapt to environmental conditions may account to some degree for the development of individual organisms, Sheldrake is not convinced that these explain all the variations over time in an entire species. Mor- phogenetic fields, through their own structure, affect or even give rise to the forms of developing cells, tissues, and organisms, says Sheld- rake. Although the existence of these fields has been considered by scientists for over fifty years, their nature and even their existence re- mains obscure. Sheldrake believes that they are as real as electromag- netic fields and that they have very remarkable properties. For example, they connect similar things across space with seemingly noth- ing in between, and, in addition, they connect things across time.

His theory that the M fields that shape the growing animal or plant are derived from the forms of previous organisms of the same species implies a kind of feedback loop in which the M field affects the development of the species. The species is subsequently modified by the environment, and, in turn, the modified species exerts an influence upon the M field. This would seem to suggest that the M field is dynamic, fluid, and evolving, rather than static, rigid, and fixed.

Morphic Resonance

Sheldrake is saying, essentially, that the inheritance of form depends upon both genetic inheritance and "morphic resonance" from similar past forms. Sheldrake defines *morphic resonance* as the process by which the forms of previous systems influence the morphogenesis of subsequent forms. Yet no visible connection exists between the forms of the past and the formation of the present organism. Since this cannot be explained in terms of existing concepts, Sheldrake uses an analogy with energetic resonance. The image of the radio is helpful, for a radio uses the principle of selectivity, an example of energetic resonance. Selectivity occurs when out of a mixture of vibrations called radio waves, the radio responds only to the particular frequency to which it has been tuned. The radio waves have neither mass nor weight, but they determine what is heard on the radio. Thus, radio depends on (1) the material structure of the set, (2) the energy that powers it, and (3) the transmission to which the set is tuned. Someone who knew nothing about radio would suppose that sounds arose from the interaction among the complex parts. He would dismiss the idea that something entered it from the outside when he found that the set weighed the same whether it was turned on or off. There would be no way to be aware that the music originated in a broadcasting studio hundreds of miles away. In fact, the transmission comes from previous similar systems, and reception depends upon the structure and organization of the receiving system. Changes in tuning lead to the reception of different transmissions.

Similarly, morphic resonance is a resonant effect of form upon form across space and time. The developing system of an organism can be tuned to different M fields. According to the hypothesis of formative causation, organisms of the same variety or race resemble each other not only because they are genetically similar and therefore subject to similar genetic influences, but also because their characteristic varietal patterns are reinforced and stabilized by morphic resonance from past organisms of the same variety. With its characteristic internal structure and vibrational frequencies, a past organism becomes present through morphic resonance to a subsequent system with a similar form, and the structural pattern of the former imposes itself on the latter.

While this theory has received some support, it is radical enough to have received substantial criticism as well as to have stimulated some promising research. Meanwhile, in his more recent book *The Presence of the Past* (1988), Sheldrake gives evidence that he is continuing to pursue the mysteries of the invisible world.

The Beginning and the End of the Universe

> In the beginning there was an explosion. Not an explosion like those familiar on earth, starting from a definite center and spreading out to engulf more and more of the circumambient air, but an explosion which occurred simultaneously everywhere, filling all space from the beginning, with every particle of matter rushing away from every other particle.
>
> WEINBERG, *The First Three Minutes*

Steven Weinberg, professor of physics at Harvard University and senior scientist at the Smithsonian Astrophysical Observatory, is another scientist in search of an answer to the question of what is fundamental reality. His particular area of research is how it all began. His book *The First Three Minutes* (1977) offers a contemporary view of the origin of the universe. In it, he reflects back to the fifties when he was a student and beginning his own research, a time when the study of the universe was widely regarded as not the sort of thing to which a respectable scientist would devote his time. "Nor was the judgment unreasonable," Weinberg writes. "Throughout most of the history of modern physics and astronomy, there has simply not existed an adequate observational and theoretical foundation on which to build a history of the early universe" (p. 4). Weinberg goes on to describe how all this has changed in just the past decade. A theory of the universe has been so widely accepted that astronomers often call it "the standard model." It is more commonly known as the "big bang" theory.

Weinberg discusses the cosmological principle that recently has come out of the speculations and mathematical formulations of physicists and astronomers. He states that much uncertainty remains surrounding the cosmological principle and that this becomes very important as people look back to the very beginning of the universe or forward to its end. He admits that the simple cosmological models of today may only describe a small part of the universe or a limited portion of its history.

Weinberg expresses the frustration of many scientists when he arrives at the edge of knowledge and must say that although—based on a good deal of highly speculative theory—scientists have been able to extrapolate the history of the universe back in time to a moment of infinite density, this leaves them unsatisfied. "We still want to know what there was before that moment, before the universe began to expand and cool. . . . That which we do now by mathematics was done in the very early universe by heat—physical phenomena directly exhibited the essential simplicity of nature. But no one was there to see it" (p. 149).

I am tempted to sigh at the futility of all this speculation. A new paradigm struggles for a hearing amidst disregard and rejection by the guardians of the past, and at last it is heard and given credence—only to be superceded eventually by a newer paradigm that also will endure only for a limited time. But the human spirit is indomitable, and I hear the voice of the scientist soften and begin to resemble the voice of the mystic.

However all these problems may be resolved, and whichever cosmological model may prove correct, Weinberg does not take much comfort in any of it. He finds it almost irresistible to believe that humans have some special relation to the universe, that human life is not just some more-or-less farcical outcome of a chain of accidents reaching back to the first three minutes, but that we were somehow built in from the beginning. He describes his feelings as he is flying in an airplane at 30,000 feet over Wyoming en route home from San Francisco to Boston. He sees the earth below, looking very soft and comfortable— "fluffy clouds here and there, snow turning pink as the sun sets, roads stretching straight across the country from one town to another." From this vantage point he finds it even harder to realize that all that appears so peaceful and serene is just a tiny part of an overwhelmingly hostile universe. It is even harder for him to realize that this present universe has evolved from an unspeakably unfamiliar earlier condition, and that it faces a future extinction of endless cold or intolerable heat.

He concludes:

The more the universe seems comprehensible, the more it seems pointless. But if there is no solace in the fruits of our research, there is at least some consolation in the research itself. Men and women are not content to comfort themselves with tales of gods and giants, or to confine their thoughts to daily affairs of life; they also build telescopes and satellites and accelerators, and sit at their desks for endless hours working out the meaning of the data they gather. The effort to understand the universe is one of the very few things that lifts human life a little above the level of farce, and gives it some of the grace of tragedy. (pp. 154–55)

Making Order Out of Chaos

James Gleick, in *Chaos* (1987), chronicles the history of the new science of chaotic systems and the physicists, biologists, astronomers, and economists who conceived it and brought it into being. The science of chaos cuts across traditional scientific disciplines in the same way that Thomas Kuhn's earlier *Structure of Scientific Revolutions* did. Gleick talks about how wildness and irregularity in nature thrust all preconceived notions about order into a seething caldron of chaos. It is something like what happens when a pan of water is slowly heating on the stove. It remains in a stable state for a while but soon there is perturbation on the surface of the water and then suddenly there is a roiling, boiling mass that begins to vaporize into steam, and no one can predict which molecule of water will end up where. The world is full of unrelated irregularities, but hidden somewhere in the chaos, scientists are coming to believe, is the possibility of a new sort of order.

One explanation for the existence of random or chaotic motion is that we are unable to predict the initial condition with sufficient clarity and precision. In addition, unknown factors always slip in, and this may reflect the fact that mere mortals are not possessed of infinite discrimination or unlimited attention. The errors in chaotic systems grow exponentially with time. More and more information must be processed to maintain the same level of accuracy. When calculations can no longer keep pace with the actual events, all power of prediction is lost. The good news is that although the word *chaos* implies something negative and destructive, there is a creative aspect to it as well. Random elements endow chaotic systems with the freedom to explore vast ranges of behavior patterns.

I can best point to what chaotic systems are about by telling about an analysand of mine, a computer programmer who had an academic background in physics and was still devoted to the mechanistic, deterministic viewpoint. We had endless discussions about whether, if you had all the relevant data, you could actually predict accurately what would happen next. Of course, in many instances that does hold true, but the point I was trying to make was that in some instances it does not hold true. I pointed to the chair in the corner of my consulting room.

"Do you see that chair?" I asked. "Has it been in that spot for the six months you have been coming to see me?"

"Yes," he answered.

"Based on your observations, would you care to predict where that chair will be one minute from now?"

He thought awhile and then ventured, "I would say it will be in the same place."

I went over to the chair and moved it. He got the point that one can seldom be certain that one has *all* the relevant data, especially when it comes to living creatures. For all our commitment to determinism, we cannot avoid the conclusion that while it may work very well in the abstract where we can view the world as a gigantic machine, when it comes to real conditions in the real world, or worlds, and especially with respect to living organisms, we cannot depend on it.

Before the science of chaos, as long as we understood the second law of thermodynamics we knew what we could expect in certain areas. The second law proved to be workable within the context for which it was formulated. But when entropy began to be generalized to disciplines where it did not fit, like economics, demographic studies, the social sciences, politics, it became an inaccurate and confusing metaphor. To think, for example, that civilizations must reach their zenith and then necessarily run down into degeneration and decay, is depotentiating. The process of degeneration is going on all the time, but creation is also taking place at the same time. Perhaps the Hindu has a better perspective than ours, when he projects onto the gods Brahma, Vishnu, and Shiva the attributes of Creator, Preserver, and Destroyer, each one always present, always active, and in the long run balancing each other out.

When scientists moved beyond Newtonian science and the second law of thermodynamics to chaos, they crossed into the invisible world. The science of chaos, says Gleick, raises the disturbing question as to how a purposeless flow of energy can wash life and consciousness into the world. The essence of chaos is a delicate balance between forces of stability and forces of instability. Chaos arises in the laboratory when normal science (in Kuhn's sense) goes astray. Where chaos begins, classical science stops. The time comes when the scientist can no longer avoid looking at anomalies. For any one scientist, the ideas of the new science of chaotic systems could not prevail until such a science became a necessity. It is well to bear in mind that when the theory of chaotic systems becomes accepted and common, it may become the new *classical* physics, and remain so for a time until some radical ideas emerge from the collective unconscious to threaten its existence.

Where Are We Going?

Paul Davies, professor of theoretical physics at the University of Newcastle upon Tyne, is another physicist who writes of his attempts to learn what there was before there was something. His research has ranged across much of fundamental physics and cosmology. His book *The Cosmic Blueprint: New Discoveries in Nature's Creative Ability to Order the Universe* (1988) uses the metaphor that I found useful also. It really poses the question, *Is* there a cosmic blueprint? Davies reviews the major historical theories in classical physics, specifically the Newtonian and the thermodynamic pictures of the universe. In both of those earlier views, he says, *creation* is an instantaneous affair. Atoms merely rearrange themselves in the Newtonian universe, while the thermodynamic view of the history of the universe is one of *loss* through entropy, leading toward "dreary featurelessness" (p. 200). But these deterministic views do not always prevail, and so the idea that everything can be predicted or retrodicted does not always fit our experience.

Davies then moves to discuss the newly burgeoning field of *chaotic systems.* He asserts that chaos can be employed as an efficient strategy for solving certain problems in mathematics and physics. He suggests that it is also used by nature itself, for example, in solving the problem of how the body's immune system reacts to pathogens. Here an interruption of normal bodily processes sets an unpredictable sequence of activities into motion. Furthermore, the occurrence of chaos is frequently accompanied by the spontaneous generation of spatial forms and structures. This is quite a different hypothesis of formative causation from that of Sheldrake, but perhaps equally intriguing. Davies concludes that nature can be *both* deterministic *in principle*, and random; but that *in practice*, strict determinism is a myth. In this he fulfills the prophecy of 1977 Nobel laureate Ilya Prigogine, who wrote:

The basis of the vision of classical physics was the conviction that the future is determined by the present, and therefore a careful study of the present permits an unveiling of the future. At no time, however, was this more than a theoretical possibility. Yet in some sense this unlimited predictability was an essential element of the scientific picture of the physical world. We may perhaps even call it the founding myth of classical science. The situation has greatly changed today. (1980, p. 214)

Time and Forever

Finally, we must take note of the man in the wheelchair who has been widely regarded as the most brilliant theoretical physicist since Einstein. Plagued by a serious neurological disorder, Stephen Hawking nevertheless has addressed himself to seeking the Grand Unification Theory (GUT), which attempts to link the two greatest achievements of the twentieth century, relativity and quantum mechanics. His most creative work has been an exploration of the possible existence and nature of "black holes." Although the existence of black holes was first posited in the eighteenth century, and black holes have been studied and written about ever since, Hawking says that there is still no conclusive evidence that they exist. His current work is on the subject of time. He asks such tantalizing questions as: Did time have a beginning? Will it have an end? Is the universe infinite? Or does it have boundaries?

Hawking admits that even if there is only one possible unified theory, it is just a set of rules and equations. "What is it," he asks in his book *A Brief History of Time* (1988), "that breathes fire into the equations and makes a universe for them to describe? The usual approach of science of constructing a mathematical model cannot answer the questions of why there should be a universe for the models to describe. Why does the universe go to all the bother of existing? Is the unified theory so compelling that it brings about its own existence? Or does it need a creator, and, if so, does he have any other effect on the universe? And who created him?" (p. 174).

He notes that up to now most scientists have been too occupied with the development of new theories that describe *what* the universe is, to ask the question *why*. One the other hand, the philosophers, whose business it is to ask *why*, have not been able to keep up with the advance of scientific theories. In the eighteenth century, philosophers considered the whole of human knowledge, including science, to be their field, and discussed such questions as, "Did the universe have a beginning?" However, in the nineteenth and twentieth centuries, science became too mathematical and technical for the philosophers, or anyone else except a few specialists. Philosophers reduced the scope of their inquiries so much that Wittgenstein, the most famous philosopher of this century, said, "The sole remaining task for philosophy is the analysis of language." "What a comedown," says Hawking, "from the great tradition of philosophy from Aristotle to Kant!"

Hawking concludes his book with the following statement: "However, if we do discover a complete theory, it should in time be understandable in broad principle by everyone, not just a few scientists. Then we shall all, philosophers and scientists, and just ordinary people, be able to take part in the discussion of the question of why it is that we and the universe exist. If we find the answer to that, it would be the ultimate triumph of human reason—for then we would know the mind of God" (pp. 174–75).

■

We can see a curious commonality in the statements of these new scientists. They are engaged in an endeavor to make the invisible, or at least some part of it, visible. Each one has moved beyond the old paradigm with its image of a *deus ex machina* who set the world in motion and determined its course. The image of a god who would create so perfect and fully complete a cosmic order was totally in keeping with the religious atmosphere at the time of Newton. It is not surprising that Newton spent his last years consumed by biblical prophecy. But today we can hardly escape the realization that there is not only order, but also chaos; and despite the magnitude of our knowledge about the visible world, our wisdom tells us that there is much more yet to be learned and that, even so, the unknowable exists in what is infinitely large and infinitely small.

Who knows but that the concept of chaos just recently washed up from a sea of ancient memory is like an earlier wave that touched the Kabbalists of the Middle Ages, prompting them to write in their sacred text the *Zohar* as their commentary on the first chapter of Genesis:

Now the earth had been void and without form. . . . Then a mighty fire beat upon it and produced in it a refuse. So it was transformed and became *Tohu* (chaos), the abode of slime, the nest of refuse, and also *Bohu* (formlessness), the finer part of which was sifted from the *Tohu* . . . namely the refuse, and was buoyed up by it. The "spirit of God" is a holy spirit (wind) that proceeded from *Elohim Hayyim* (living God), and this "was hovering over the face of the waters." When this wind blew, a certain film detached itself from the refuse, like the film which remains on top of boiling broth when the froth has been skimmed off two or three times. When *Tohu* had thus been sifted and purified, there issued from it "a great and strong wind rending the mountains and breaking in pieces the rocks." Similarly *Bohu* was sifted and purified and there issued from it earthquake. . . . Then what we call "darkness" was sifted and there was contained in it fire. . . . When what we call "spirit" was sifted, there was contained in it a still, small voice. (vol. 1, p. 66)

6

Gnosis—Another Kind of Knowledge

In the 1970s, when the women's movement was finding its genuine voice, I was writing my book *Androgyny* (1989). In it, I sought to show that women needed to find release from their traditional roles as defined by a male-dominated society, and to assume a specifically feminine identity that we ourselves would define in terms of our own capacities and our own special interests. I took the position that the behaviors and characteristics that were stereotypically associated with masculinity and femininity were in no sense the exclusive province of one or the other sex. However, as I saw quite often in my analytic practice, people resisted acknowledging in themselves those qualities typically associated with the opposite gender. It was well known, theoretically at least, that men have access to so-called feminine qualities within themselves, and that women possess attributes usually associated with the masculine gender. But since, in the socialization process, members of each sex learned to behave in ways that society deemed gender-appropriate, the contrasexual aspects in each person tended to be repressed.

In a time when women were entering the work force in unprecedented numbers and establishing their own identity as people, rather than as the wife of _____ or the mother of _____, the concept of androgyny offered a new model that incorporated the values and behaviors that had formerly been associated with only one or the other gender. If women could acknowledge those so-called masculine attributes that society had discouraged women from owning in the past, and if men could do the same with respect to their "feminine" attributes, people could become androgynous, and thereby more whole. This idea had been around for a long time, but had not been enunciated clearly in recent years. Difficult as it may be to believe from our vantage point in the present, when I told people in the early seventies that I was writing about androgyny, very few had any idea what I was talking about.

I decided to study various historical and mythological precursors of the contemporary idea of androgyny, to learn what androgyny had meant to people in the past and why it seemed to have vanished from the contemporary scene. My investigations led me to the pre-Hellenic mythology of ancient Greece, to Plato's myth on the origins of the sexes, to some anomalies in the biblical myth of Adam and Eve, to the yin/yang concept of Taoism, to astrology, alchemy, and the Kabbalah, and finally to the Gnosticism of the two centuries preceding and the two centuries following the time of Jesus. I found many gnostic myths that dealt with Creation and the world before human beings appeared on earth. I discovered gnostic mythology that pointed to an androgynous god-image, a primal deity who was neither male nor female, yet was both, containing all the attributes of each.

As a consequence of having written *Androgyny*, I was invited to give a seminar with Elaine Pagels, author of *The Gnostic Gospels* (1979). Pagels was working on a new book, *Adam, Eve, and the Serpent*, which has since been published (1988). The subject of our seminar was to be "Little-Known Stories about Adam and Eve." I hesitated about participating with this distinguished scholar whose knowledge about ancient Gnosticism so greatly exceeded my own, yet the challenge intrigued me. What could I possibly say about Gnosticism that Pagels could not say far better and with more authority? As I was puzzling over this question, I remembered having once heard that there was a gnostic church in Palo Alto, where I live. I had somehow dismissed it as probably being one more California New Age phenomenon using a historic name to conjure up a sense of mystery. I had no idea what sort of a church this might be, but it did occur to me that if I were to go there perhaps I would find out something about contemporary Gnosticism that Dr. Pagels might not be familiar with.

I set out to go to the Ecclesia Gnostica Mysteriorum one Sunday morning. Interestingly enough, it turned out to be only a mile or so from my home. I walked up the stairs of an office building that was part of a small shopping center. I entered the anteroom, where I was met by the faint fragrance of incense, and then went into the sanctuary itself. I was totally unprepared for what I found. The room was softly lit. Exterior light filtered through a rose and mauve stained glass window patterned with the forms of sun and moon and abstract shapes. What especially impressed me was the silence. As people entered there was hardly a sound, no handling of papers or shuffling of feet, but a sense of people perfectly composed, turning inward. I saw flowers delicately arranged behind the altar, not as a florist would arrange them but as someone who was creating a very personal work of art would do. The flowers surrounded a small statue of a Black Madonna seated with great dignity, her Child in her lap. I fell into my own reflections, and the image of the first Black Madonna I had ever seen came to me. She was the Lady of Einsiedeln, and I had made a pilgrimage to see her church when I was a student in Zurich.

I was startled out of my reverie to see a woman clothed in a black cassock and white surplice walking from the rear of the sanctuary toward the altar. She bowed before the statue, turned to the audience and began to preach. She told a simple teaching story about a little boy who was walking with his grandfather, asking the old man about whether he needed to do what his parents and teacher told him to do when he didn't understand why, or when something didn't make any sense to him. He had been told, "Do it just because I say so," and this had troubled him. The grandfather said that it was not necessary to follow blindly whoever was in charge. It was all right for the boy to sit quietly with his own thoughts and to listen to what came up in him. He was to understand that God did not only speak to parents or teachers or priests or rabbis, but that God spoke to everyone, to children and adults, and even to animals and plants. It is more important to discover the truth within ourselves than to look for it out in the world, Grandfather told the little boy. This was a very different message from what I had learned in Sunday School. I heard, too, that wisdom comes from the Self, in which our innate wisdom is lodged. This Self of the Gnostics sounded very much like Jung's description of the Self, the archetype of wholeness connecting the personal with the transpersonal dimensions of life.

After preaching, the priest[6] withdrew, and an acolyte lit the candles to signify the beginning of the rite. I found it interesting that the ser-

---

6. I have discussed with Bishop Rosamonde Miller the relative appropriateness of using the word "priest" or "priestess" when referring to the female who celebrates Mass in the Gnostic Church. We agreed that "priest" is preferable for two reasons. The first is that the woman who serves Mass performs exactly the same function that a man in that role does, and therefore, should not be differentiated—any more than one would call a female poet a "poetess." The other reason is that the term "priestess"

mon was not a part of the service itself. That had been the "teaching."
Now the priest returned, this time wearing a deep blue embroidered
cope and holding the aspergillum. Sprinkling holy water on the people
assembled, she said, "In thy strength, O Lord, do we command the
powers of chaos to wither into nothingness, that they shall not abide,
and that our temples within and our temples without may be so purified as to receive the blessing of those who come in thy name."

In the ritual that followed, there was no creed. No one was told
what to think, nor did anyone need to profess some collective belief.
There was no mention of "sin" or "guilt." I was to learn that in this
church's teachings, not sin, but ignorance is responsible for the unhappy condition of many human beings. Ignorance is an intoxication,
a drunkenness, a sleep. The soul's ignorance of itself, its origin, its
situation, is the cause of much human misery. The liturgy of this gnostic group was very different from any I had known in the past, not
something to be grasped with the intellect but to be entered into: another space, an archetypal space unbounded by ordinary time. This
experience, and others that flowed from it, inspired me to plunge into
the study of gnostic writings and literature about Gnosticism, in the
hope that these might shed some new light on the questions I had
been exploring. What follows now is the result of those studies.

Like the new scientists, who refuse to be limited by the textbooks
of the past but rely on their own direct observations, so the early Gnostics independently sought the answers to the eternal questions rather
than relying on Torah or Church dogma. They committed their own
experiences and thoughts to writing, and composed numerous texts
whose beauty and depth equaled that of many texts included in the
biblical canon. The questions to which they addressed themselves were
not so different from those addressed by the new scientists. Gnostics
asked in biblical times, and are still asking: Who are we? What have
we become? Where were we? Where are we going? What is birth? What
is rebirth?

A Spiritual Revolution

The structure of spiritual revolutions is not unlike the structure of
scientific revolutions. The old order changeth, yielding place to
new . . . but not without a great struggle in which the very foundations

---

today evokes an archaic goddess-worshipping cult, while the female priest of today
wishes to be regarded as the contemporary equivalent of a male priest.

of society are shaken to their depths. As Copernicus' declaration that the earth moved around the sun preceded and laid the groundwork for Galileo's observations and the resulting shift to modern astronomy, so Moses' leadership of the Children of Israel from slavery into existence as a free people prepared the Hebrew people spiritually for the message of individual freedom that Jesus was to bring.

Nearly two thousand years ago, Christianity appeared in the pagan Roman world as a movement that potentially could bring about a new paradigm. Of course, it was not recognized as such in the beginning, for incipient paradigms are rarely apparent to mainstream cultures. Rooted in the Judaism of its time, the new religion found its strength in the person of a messiah, an "anointed one," who seemed to his contemporaries to have been appointed to bring about a new world order. The appearance of Jesus in a Judea under the domination of Rome did indeed set on fire the spiritual aspirations of Jew and pagan alike, and radically changed the character and values of the entire Western world.

By the time of Jesus, Judea was a province of Rome ruled over by the puppet Jewish dynasty of Herod, and the punishment of crucifixion was regularly employed against those who spoke out against Rome. Jesus was born into a community of ancient peoples whose beliefs and practices were older than those of the Romans who then dominated them. The Hebrews had managed to keep their religion relatively pure despite the succession of foreign empires that ruled over them. They faced the temptation to accommodate to the pagan world and to participate in the economic and political advantages that such collaboration promised. Some Jews did ally themselves with their conquerors and were given in return an opportunity to serve as petty officials under Rome, to gain material wealth, and to assimilate to some degree, religiously and socially. Most Jews, however, resisted the pagan influence mightily, strengthening their own religious institutions and support systems as well as they could. They were tolerated under the Pax Romanum: as long as they paid their taxes—which sometimes reached the point of extortion—and refrained from creating any civil disturbances, they were as a general rule permitted to practice their faith in their own way. There were exceptions, of course, but on the whole Jews who did not rebel against Rome in word or deed were allowed to exist in peace.

Temple worship in Jerusalem was permitted as long as the priests and their wealthy supporters collaborated with Rome. The Pharisees resisted this practice by a firm insistence that their fellow Jews obey

strictly the laws put forth in Leviticus and Deuteronomy and so maintain their identity as holy people. Some Jews adopted customs borrowed from Greece and Rome, and became secularized and to some
degree assimilated. Other Jews, feeling that the Temple community had
been polluted by the influence of Rome and of the Jews who collaborated with Rome, withdrew from the Temple as an institution, and
indeed from Jerusalem itself. Among these latter were the Essenes,
who left the city and made their homes in the caves above the Dead
Sea. They took little in the way of worldly goods with them, but they
did carry away from Jerusalem the precious scrolls that contained the
teachings of their faith. These would be their guides and sustenance.
The Essenes pursued an ascetic life in the desert, living in caves, practicing monastic simplicity, and awaiting the Day of Judgment when
God would pass judgment upon the righteous and the unrighteous of
his people Israel. These were some of the mingled currents that existed
in Judea before, during, and immediately after the lifetime of Jesus.

The message of the Savior was radical and demanding, but it was
not altogether new. Almost all of what Jesus preached was founded in
the holy scriptures of the Jews. Even his interpretations were in the
Jewish tradition, which allows questioning and debating about the
meaning of the word of God and even permits putting a construction
different from the traditional one upon the holy writ. So one might say
that the historical Jesus, the Jewish teacher and religious reformer, was
the Jesus whose presence was seen in the visible world. Yet few would
deny that Jesus was a manifestation also of the invisible world, a mysterious presence who incarnated in his physical body a spiritual reality
that reached far beyond the consciousness of his contemporaries for
its source. His inspired message and his personal power drew people
around him to listen as he talked about the laws and customs of the
people, showing them which were antiquated and in need of being
discarded and which remained valid and needed to be upheld. But
most important, he was able to *see through* the texts of the law into
their true meaning. Under his creative interpretation, the words became symbols of an esoteric language that could not be spoken directly,
but which he transmitted through parables and allegories so that people not only understood but enshrined his words in their hearts and
their souls. Through Logos he brought a message of supernal wisdom,
and through Eros he brought a message of divine love.

In delivering his message, Jesus spared neither the pagan conquerors nor the Jews who collaborated with them. He assailed such
pagan practices as the subjugation of human beings, the accumulation

of great wealth, living purely for pleasure, homosexuality, prostitution, exploitation of the stranger, and many other "abominations" that were rejected by observant Jews as well. He went still further, to condemn the practices of some Jews whose literal observance of the law blinded them to the spirit in which it was conceived. Yet Jews were the first adherents of this fellow Jew, who was more than that and who promised them a Kingdom of the Spirit if they were willing to commit themselves fully to it and to him. The full impact of his message became apparent only after his death, when his disciples carried it out into the wider world and called the new faith Christianity, referring to the divine origin of the Christ, the anointed one, the Messiah, the expected one and the redeemer of the Jews.

Passion and Resistance

As Christianity spread beyond the confines of Judea and reached into far-flung parts of the Roman Empire, it became more and more of a threat to the status quo. Where the pagan world practiced all forms of licentiousness in the area of sexuality, Christianity offered chastity as a way to personal freedom for both sexes; while the pagan ethic allowed one to seek wealth for himself based on the exploitation of the labor of others, the Christian model offered communal sharing of the necessities of life; while racial separation was endorsed by the pagan, the Christian was proclaiming the equality of men and women of every race.

At first the Romans ruthlessly tried to suppress the new faith that was growing stronger day by day. The paradigm that was only being born aroused everything from rejection to derision, to the most severe forms of suppression possible. Yet through the influence of Christianity and despite the risk and hardship entailed, more and more people were awakening to the reality of a world beyond this world, and a Kingdom of the Spirit beyond the kingdom of the flesh. These Christians of the first century saw themselves as participants in a revolution of the spirit that would bring about a transformation of society in "the world to come." They had little interest in pursuing their usual daily activities or the lives they had led in the past; home and parents and children were nothing to them, for their hopes were fixed on eternal life. Temporal ties only interfered with their commitment to the world beyond. When they ceased to be docile servants of a foreign government they came into direct conflict with the Roman authorities. The literature of the period abounds with the stories of Christian martyrs who gladly gave their lives rather than capitulate to pagan Rome.

The effects of the teachings of Jesus and his followers and, even more, the strength of the new Christians' resistance to temporal power, could not fail to impress their rulers. The message of Christianity made itself heard in Rome, at first as the voice of an inconsequential ragtag group of people and later as a mighty, popular movement. Under the constant threat of persecution and extinction, Christians banded together in communities of the faithful. They found spiritual leaders and implored them to help develop institutionalized structures within which their radical movement might grow and endure. This entailed establishing a hierarchy of people who would formulate a community morality and provide education in the Christian doctrine. What this meant was to translate into the practical terms of everyday living what was and what was not acceptable behavior in the sight of God. The security of a common set of ethical principles that clearly set the Christian beliefs apart from those of the pagan world led the new Christians to accept willingly the increasing institutionalization of the Church. By the end of the second century, an organized church structure had developed, and with it a differentiation between true believers and dissidents.

Christianity Becomes an Institution

In any process of institutionalization, there is an inevitable reaction on the part of those "free spirits" who by their very nature resist a strong authoritarian presence. While Christianity was assuming the form of a "normal religion," at least among its adherents, some people within the Christian community resisted submitting to the requirement for conformity demanded by the new authority. These people wanted to discover for themselves the answers to certain questions. They would not accept unequivocally the so-called revealed knowledge handed down by the Church Fathers, but took upon themselves a personal search for truth through the direct experience of the divine presence.

These dissenters acquired the name Gnostic because they were seeking a special kind of knowledge concerning the nature of God and the relationship of the divine and human levels of consciousness. This special knowledge was called gnosis. It was not the knowledge that was transmitted through a sacred priesthood, nor by books filled with statements that were not to be questioned, nor through laws that were promulgated by officially recognized sectarian authorities. The kind of knowledge they sought would come from within themselves, for they understood God as being everywhere in the universe, including within the inner recesses of the individual. The Greek word *gnosis* most clearly expressed this kind of knowledge, for it means an inner knowing that is communicated directly from the divine origin to the human being, or—in another view—from the divine *in* the human being. Some critics assert that Gnostic was a term of derision applied to these people, meaning "know-it-all," since it appeared that they believed that anything worth knowing was already known to them on some level. From our viewpoint, there may indeed have been some validity to this allegation.

Gnostic Ideas Rediscovered

It is important to remember that Gnostics were setting down their gospels at the same time that the books that were to comprise the New Testament were being written. However, because there were no hierarchical controls over the Gnostics, these people felt free to give rein to their wildest fantasies, whether divinely inspired or strange visions of the night. Furthermore, because gnostic writings were the products of individual "revelations," a great variety of thought and expression abounds in them. Various gnostic seers drew about themselves groups of devotees and supporters, with the result that the gnostic movement was not one, but in fact a number of movements linked mainly by their unwillingness to accept a churchly authority that was unsupported by their own spiritual experience.

Until recently, we had to depend mainly upon the words of the Church Fathers as to what these books contained and what was their meaning and value, because we had access to very few of the original gnostic writings. French scholar Jean Doresse (1960) writes of the state of gnostic studies when he first learned of the Nag Hammadi finds, ". . . authentically Gnostic texts consisted hardly at all of original texts (only the smallest fragments of which survived) but almost entirely of works written against these sects by their contemporary opponents. . . . Essentially all that we knew about Gnosticism was what we had learned from texts—most of them Christian—denouncing these sects as heretical" (p. 4). Since gnostic writings often took positions at variance with the developing Christian tradition, as well as the earlier Judaic tradition, they were treated as gross heresies.

Rather than risk having their books burned or, still worse, having their authors burned, the Gnostics learned to keep themselves out of view, and their books remained for the most part secret doctrines, imparted only to those who had been initiated into this special company. Until recently, very little of the original gnostic writing was available for study, and so it was impossible for scholars to determine for themselves what the true nature and import of this material was.

In 1945, the discovery of a number of ancient gnostic books hidden in jars in a cave near Nag Hammadi, Egypt, brought to light a large and substantial body of gnostic literature. This astounded religious historians from many nations, and a race would have been on among these scholars, archaeologists, and biblical exegetes to piece together and translate the works had the Egyptian government not stepped in with its insistence on keeping control of the materials found on its soil, and made it difficult, if not impossible, for research to be done without the use of considerable ingenuity and political intrigue.

James M. Robinson, an American theologian and general editor of *The Nag Hammadi Library* (third edition, 1988), was unsatisfied with the hazy descriptions of the site of the discovery, and determined to go there and see for himself. He also wanted to make sure that all the documents in question had actually been found. It took many years of wrangling with the Egyptian government and countless personal contacts before Robinson could gain permission to look for the precise location where the books had been found. It was not until thirty years after the original discovery that Robinson managed to locate one of the brothers who had inadvertently come upon the manuscripts, and to persuade this camel driver, Muhammed Ali, to accompany him to the area of ancient Chenoboskia. Muhammed agreed only upon the payment of some money and the provision that he would be dressed in American clothes and ride with Robinson on the back of a Russian-made jeep owned by the director of the Nag Hammadi Sugar Factory. (The camel driver was still wanted for a murder to avenge a family blood feud of which he was accused, and did not wish to draw attention to himself.) After several abortive attempts, Muhammed Ali managed to bring Robinson to the place. As Robinson describes it in *The Nag Hammadi Library* (1988):

On each side of the Nile Valley cliffs rise abruptly to the desert above. The section of the cliff on the right bank marking the limit of the Nile Valley and the arable land between Chenoboskia and Pabau is called Jabal al-Tārif. A protruding boulder shaped somewhat like a stalagmite had broken off in prehistoric time from the face of the cliff and fallen down onto the talus (the inclined plane of fallen rock that over the ages naturally collects like a buttress at the foot of a cliff). Under the northern flank of one of the huge barrel-shaped pieces of this shattered boulder the jar containing the Nag Hammadi Library was secreted. (p. 22)

This discovery made it possible for the first time to examine this original textual material, instead of relying on what the detractors of Gnosticism asserted the doctrines contained. It has taken several teams of scholars some forty-five years to piece together the fragments of these Coptic writings and to translate them and study them, but the major work has been completed at last and it is possible to read this material in English today. The books provide insight into a group of people and a concept of the world that is so stunning in its originality that it compels us to try to understand what may have been going on in the minds of this small group of dissidents in the formative years of the Judeo-Christian culture.

One can read the gnostic texts in a number of different ways: for their literal meaning alone, in their historical context, as the foundation of a perennial philosophy that served in those days and continues to serve in ours, or as a countercultural element compensating the current culture. Any of these ways is useful and provides much insight into both the historical and the spiritual phenomenon of Gnosticism. I find myself fascinated by any and all of these approaches. My inquiry here, however, is into the nature of the visible and invisible worlds and how they have been understood and portrayed in Western culture. Gnosticism takes a radical view of this question in that, unlike most Western religions, it places a highly negative valuation on the visible world and a great investment in the sphere of the unknowable. The mythology of the Gnostics comes out of their lack of trust in the created world and in the intentions of its creator-god.

Creation According to the Gnostics

One of the most interesting and well known of the gnostic writers was Valentinus, a brilliant religious thinker of the mid-second century, Egyptian born and Latin educated. At one time Valentinus was the loser in the election of a new bishop of Rome. Historical evidence does not show whether Valentinus turned more gnostic after losing the election, or whether he lost the election because of his gnostic view of Christianity. Nevertheless, some early Church Fathers had a grudging admiration for Valentinus and one of them, Jerome, has been quoted as saying, "No one can bring heresy into being unless he is possessed, by nature, of an outstanding intellect and has gifts provided by God. Such a person was Valentinus" (Dart 1988, p. 102).

A gnostic tractate titled "On the Origin of the World" is ascribed in part to Valentinus and in part to other sources, including Jewish, Hellenic, and Manichaean. It is a compendium of gnostic ideas, especially on cosmogony, anthropogony, and eschatology. According to one of its translators, Hans-Gebhard Bethge, this text "can help us understand how the gnostic world view, in debate with other intellectual currents, but also making use of them, could maintain itself or perhaps at times even win the field" (Robinson 1988, p. 171). "On the Origin of the World" relates that the highest God was passive, resting in majesty, and disinterested in creation. The Sophia, as active principle, thought about creating a work alone, without her consort. Her thought *became* a work, an image of heaven, a curtain between heaven and the lower regions that were called aeons. Then a shadow was cast forth and the shadow took note that there was something stronger than itself. It became filled with envy and immediately gave birth to envy. From that day on the beginning (*arche*) of envy made its appearance in all the regions (*aeons*) and their worlds. But that envy was found to be an abortion in which there was no divine spirit (Rudolph 1983, p. 73).

Some versions of this myth relate that this spiritless being was such because Sophia's consort had not concurred with her. The hatred or envy that originated from the shadow was cast into a part of chaos. In this way, matter originated from a negative action on the part of the shadow, and as a consequence it was discounted from the beginning. Following the origin of matter, the demi-urge, the subordinate deity who created the material world, came into being. As the text recounts: "And when Sophia desired to cause the thing that had no spirit to be formed into a likeness and to rule over matter and all her forces, there appeared for the first time a ruler, out of the waters, lionlike in appearance, androgynous, having great authority within him, and ignorant of whence he had come into being. Now when Sophia saw him moving about in the depths of the waters she said to him, 'Child, pass through to here,' whose equivalent is '*yalda baoth*' " (Robinson 1988, p. 173). He is called Yaldabaoth, "the accursed god," in most of the gnostic writings, because he created the visible world and withheld knowledge from humanity, beginning with his warning to Adam and Eve not to eat of the fruit of the tree of knowledge (Rudolph 1983, p. 73).

When the Sophia saw what had happened through her error—that envy, the matter of chaos, was like an abortion because there was no spirit in it—she was sorely troubled. Out of compassion, she descended into the world of matter to breathe life into the face of the abyss. There she encountered out of the depths of matter the ruler or chief archon,[7] Yaldabaoth, who was full of power in himself. Yaldabaoth had embarked upon his creative activity, and through his word the lower heavens and the earth and all the hierarchies of heaven (*archons*) were created, each having its own heavens and thrones, glories, temples, and chariots.

After the heavens and earth had been established and all the gods and angels praised Yaldabaoth, he exalted himself and boasted continually, saying to them, "I have need of no one. I am God, and there is no other apart from me." In one version, Sophia cries out to him, "You are mistaken, Samael."[8] Again he exalts himself, saying, "I am a jealous God and there is no other God beside me." The text continues: "[Thereby] he indicated to the angels who attended him that there exists another God. For if there were no other one, of whom whould he be jealous?" (Robinson 1988, p. 112). This passage indicates a crucial point with respect to gnostic values: why they regarded blindness, or ignorance—not sin—to be the cause of evil. For blindness and ignorance give rise to pride and vainglory, lack of respect for others, arrogance, ambition, self-importance, conceit, greed, licentiousness, and those other powers of the world that separate person from person and country from country. From our perspective of psychological hindsight, we can see that the Gnostics projected the evil in the human heart onto the powers of the world, the archons. The archons, in turn, could exert their negative influences upon men and women.

The narrative now returns to Sophia. In the world of matter to which she has descended, she is overcome and defiled by the archons, and made blind. In her suffering, she repents and recognizes her deficiency and the loss of her perfection. She understands that Yaldabaoth, the abortion of darkness, envy, and chaos, is imperfect because she separated from her consort and he did not concur with her. She repents of her arrogance and weeps bitterly, and calls upon the "Father" to hear her prayer. It is also the prayer of all those who have fallen away from their knowledge of their true selves from antiquity until the present.

The echo of the prayer of Sophia finds its way into a contemporary gnostic Holy Eucharist service (Miller 1988):

---

7. *Archon* originally meant the high magistrate in Athens, and later referred to magistrates in the Jewish communities of the Diaspora in the Graeco-Roman period.
8. Samael means "the blind god."

I have been apart and I have lost my way. The archons have taken my vision. At times I am filled with Thee, but often I am blind to Thy presence when all I see is this world of form. My ignorance and blindness are all I have to offer but these I give to Thee holding back nothing. And in my hours of darkness when I am not even sure there is a Thou hearing my call, I still call to Thee with all my heart. Hear the cry of my voice, clamoring from this desert, for my soul is parched and my heart can barely stand this longing.

The Highest God hears the prayer of the suffering feminine and sends redemption in the form of the Logos to Sophia, who clearly manifests Eros separated from an essential part of her being. The Logos takes the earthly form of Jesus, descends to this world, and with a touch restores the sight of the suppliant. Sophia, thus redeemed, begins the archetypal process that in the dimension of time will offer redemption to all of humankind.

In commemoration of this, the following is read in the contemporary gnostic service (Miller 1984):

And Jesus answered: They say I came for all, but in truth I came for Her Who came for all. For it came to pass that there were those who had lost their way and, lacking in spark, could not return to the Father, and seeing this, She came unto them, giving her life to the depths of matter. And in truth She did suffer and become blind. But our Father, sensing Her anguish, sent Me forth, being of Him, so that She might see and We be as One again. Though they see it not it is She, the tender Mother of Mercy, Who is the great redeemer.

The separation of the feminine principle from the masculine principle, or Eros from Logos, results in the incomplete or one-sided being. With the assumption into heaven of the holy Sophia, the invisible world can be healed—that is, made whole again. But the visible world, presided over by the creator-god Yaldabaoth, remains imperfect and fragmented, and its imperfection results in the many warring factions of the visible world that have yet to find a way to peace.

The gnostic narrative moves from creation to the Garden of Eden. In the primal history of Adam and Eve, emanations of the Ineffable Light in the highest heaven move through successive stages, with the light becoming more dense with each transformation. The Tree of Knowledge in the garden is the Tree of Gnosis. A heavenly god-man, a primal man, emanates from, or has a close relationship with, the Highest God. This "Anthropos," or first Adam, is earlier and superior to the demi-urge or creator-god. The first Eve or Heavenly Eve is an emanation of the Sophia. She is mother, wife, and virgin in one being and thus represents the female trinity of the kingdom of light. A drop

of light passes from the Sophia to the Heavenly Eve, and from this the
"Instructor of Life" is born. He later appears as the serpent in Paradise,
the wise one who instructs Adam.

The creator-god then creates a man, the second Adam, modeled on
the image of the first Adam, the archetypal Man of Light. But the
second Adam has no real life in him until he can be imbued with the
Divine Spirit, the pneumatic substance. This comes about either
through the intervention of the Highest God or of the Heavenly Eve,
who is the prototype of the earthly Eve. In the gnostic hierarchy, this
then places the second Adam above the creator-god, who does not
breathe the pneumatic substance. Furthermore, the inspiration of the
Heavenly Eve bestows the capacity for redemption upon the first man.

The archons, the powers of darkness, see that the second Adam is
alive. They see Eve (the Heavenly Eve) speaking to him and are confused.[9] They do not wish Adam to have power over them, so they fall
upon this Eve in order to cast their seed into her so that they, and not
Adam, shall have control over her children. But the Heavenly Eve turns
herself into the Tree of Gnosis, and only her likeness (the second Eve
or earthly Eve of the Garden) remains with Adam. The archons make
the sleep of forgetfulness fall upon Adam and they say to him in his
sleep that she (Eve) originated from his rib, so that the woman might
be subject to him and he be lord over her. The archons defile the likeness, and then they become confused and take counsel together and
go in fear to Adam and Eve and say to him [sic], "The fruit of all the
trees created for you in Paradise shall be eaten; but as for the tree of
acquaintance, control yourselves and do not eat from it. If you eat you
will die" (Robinson 1988, p. 184).

The serpent plays a thoroughly positive role in this myth. He appears at this point and says to her, "What did God say to you (pl.).
Was it, 'do not eat from the tree of acquaintance (*gnosis*)'?" She says,

9. It should be added here that the confusion of the archons is paralleled only by the
confusion of the reader of the gnostic gospels. Those texts contain multiple stories of
the core myths, not all of which agree in details. Furthermore, there are different
levels of understanding of the major mythic characters, and it is not always clear which
one is meant in a given portion of text. For example, some texts suggest the existence
of a first or Higher Adam; a second or psychic Adam; and a third or earthly Adam.
It is not altogether clear whether these are different entities, or whether they are all
the same Adam as he appears to people of three different levels of consciousness.
Likewise, references made to Jesus are suggestive both of a fleshly Jesus, who is not
the true one, and the nonfleshly, the Christ of Glory, the Logos. And further, the
first Adam is sometimes understood as the nonfleshly Jesus. My inclination is not to
try to determine too precisely which layer of the mythos is being referred to in the
text, but rather to recognize that the text is meant to be understood on more than
one level.

"He said, 'Not only do not eat from it, but do not touch it lest you (sg.) die.' " The beast says to her, "Do not be afraid. In death you (pl.) shall not die. For he knows that when you eat from it, your intellect will become sober and you will come to be like gods, recognizing the difference that obtains between evil men and good ones. Indeed, it was in jealousy that he said this to you, so that you would not eat from it" (Robinson 1988, p. 184). Eve eats the fruit and gives it to her husband, who also eats. Then their understanding (*nous*) is opened, for when they have eaten, the light of knowledge (*gnosis*) is opened to them.

The archons see what has happened, and in their dismay they curse Adam and Eve and all their children, and cast them out of Paradise and into the world. As if what they have done is not sufficient, they go to the Tree of Life and surround it with great terror, fiery creatures called cherubim, and they set a fiery sword into her midst, which turns about so that no one can ever return to that place. The Sophia, seeing that the archons have cursed her likeness, is enraged. She drives the archons out of their heavens and casts them down into the sinful cosmos, so that they become like wicked demons upon the earth.

We have here the open recognition that evil exists in this world, the visible world, and we have an explanation for its existence. This is not to say that the invisible world is all good; quite the contrary. The invisible world contains the All, visible and invisible. If evil manifests in the visible world of mortal existence, then it must be a manifestation of the Fullness beyond. The Fullness of the Gnostics is without qualities in and of itself, yet it contains the potentials for all that is, has been, and will be. We cannot fail to notice the parallel between this visible world and David Bohm's implicate order, and this invisible world and his explicate order.

The Gnostic Heresy

Just as the early Christians had a difficult time setting themselves free from the culture in which they were embedded so that they could clarify their own vision, so the Gnostics struggled with the necessity they felt to differentiate themselves from the new Church. They saw the Church becoming an institution with a set of rules and regulations, and they found this intolerable. Not that they disagreed in principle with the tenets of Christianity as they were being written into law and taught to the followers of the faith. The teachings of Jesus and the principles espoused by the members of the Christian community served to establish the religion in the minds and hearts of the people. The discipline provided the spiritual sustenance and the common belief that would make it possible for the faith to survive and become firmly established in a milieu that was hostile to it. The Gnostics felt that for most people, an elementary understanding of the rules, moral guidance, and submission to authority was necessary and sufficient. But they felt that they were in a special category. For them, the Christian teaching as formalized into a doctrine was only a beginning—a step along the pathway to spiritual freedom. Total freedom as seen by the Gnostics meant the right of a person to find a direct relationship to God, without interpreters or intermediaries, if that seemed authentic to the individual. This is why Gnosticism arose as a protest movement for individual freedom against the growing constraints of orthodoxy.

The Gnostics saw how the new religion of Christianity, which promised so much to those who would follow it, had to struggle for its existence in a society that negated its ideals. They saw, too, how the Church had to exert its own powerful authority over its adherents, destroying (in the gnostic view) the very freedoms for which the early Christians had been ready and willing to die. The Gnostics could understand why the Christians had to disown those people who deviated from the orthodox path; and they realized that as a consequence they would have to conceal their writings lest an ignorant people destroy them.

These early dissidents could not easily reconcile the image of a limiting and punishing god as portrayed in the authoritative doctrines of the Church, with their own concept of the Highest God, who filled all space and time. They could only acknowledge their despair over the ignorance (*agnosis*) of those who took literally the Judeo-Christian god-image, and still retain their own faith by ascribing the evils of this world to a creator-god who was separate from the unknown God whom they called Father. The unknown God was for them also unknowable, partaking of a level of reality or consciousness beyond the capacities of mortal human beings to comprehend. They used the term *Father* symbolically, to mean that which stands above all the gods who are called Father by others, and they likewise transposed additional literal terms from church teachings to symbolic expressions of the unknown.[10] For

---

10. In *Psychological Types* (1921/1971), Jung defined the symbol as follows: "A symbol always presupposes that the chosen expression is the best possible description or formulation of a relatively unknown fact, which is nevertheless known to exist or postulated as existing" (par. 814).

example, Father, Son, and Holy Spirit become "Father of All Father-hoods," "Logos who bridges the worlds," and "celestial Bride and Charming Heart to the heavens and earth alike."

The Gnostics asserted that they wished to become spiritually mature. This meant that they desired—indeed, felt a strong need—to go beyond being told how to think, what to believe, and how to behave (Pagels 1988, p. 59). They believed they were subject to being called by the Highest God, and that if they listened to the voice of this God within their own souls they would be shown how to live in concord with the order of the universe. They insisted that women were certainly as capable as men of receiving God's word and preaching from their own base in gnosis. From earliest times, gnostic women have served all spiritual functions, including those of the priesthood, in complete equality with men. The Gnostics have always maintained that God called to those to whom he wished to speak, and no institution should stand between the individual and the voice of God.

The Gnostics of the first two or three centuries of the Common Era had a different concept of the nature of the world from that of orthodox Christians, one that would necessarily cause them to reject the authority of the Church over them, and indeed, any authority that might be imposed upon them from without. For Gnostics, the world of form was of lesser importance than the eternal world. They could endure hardship and privation, because they made it a point not to be possessive of the things of this world. They did not wish to be trapped in materialistic values or materialistic goals. Some groups practiced an ascetic discipline; others lived actively *in* the world, but did not consider themselves *of* it. Their authority stemmed from a divine spark that imbued each human being with life, and that emanated from an Unknown Source beyond this world. Their God was all-encompassing and beyond description. Their God did everything in a mystery, and the invisible world was the place where their God dwelt:

Not one of the names which are conceived, or spoken, seen or grasped, not one of them applies to him, even though they are exceedingly glorious, magnifying and honored . . . it is impossible for mind to conceive him, nor can any speech convey him, nor can any eye see him, nor can any body grasp him, because of his inscrutable greatness, and his incomprehensible depth, and his immeasurable height, and his illimitable will. This is the nature of the unbegotten one, which does not touch anything else; nor is it joined (to anything) in the manner of something which is limited. Rather, he possesses this constitution, without having a face or form, things which are understood through perception. (Robinson 1988, p. 62)

Such a God would be no more accessible to the bishops of the Church than to individuals. Remote and unknowable, he was yet present in every living being and in every part of the universe, wherefore it is said, "No place is empty of me." Therefore, to the Gnostics there seemed little cause for seeking this unknown God anywhere but within the self, for they viewed the self as a manifestation of the illimitable divine presence, containing the divine and being also contained in it.

Inasmuch as the Gnostics did not submit to any overall discipline, and inasmuch as no one apparently ever censored their writings or "normalized" them, great disparity exists among the various gospels. There was little agreement, even among the Gnostics, as to what Gnosticism really was. Because of its very openness to interpretation, many versions of their curious doctrines and many different kinds of rituals and practices developed out of their beliefs. Yet the spirit in which all Gnostics shared these rituals and practices affords us insight into the fairly coherent infrastructure of attitudes they held in common. Their mythology is more than an attempt to understand why the worlds are as they are; it provides cryptic images of the psyches of the people who wrote the various texts. When I read the gnostic gospels I address myself to the meanings that their authors apparently intended to convey, and at the same time to unconscious meanings present on a deeper level. The objective is twofold: to read what the Gnostics have had to say about the visible and the invisible worlds, and to differentiate between the manifest and the hidden content in what they have written.

Dualism and Wholeness

One element in Gnosticism that distinguishes it from some other religious views is what many see as its characteristic dualism. On the one hand, its evaluation of the visible world together with its creator is unequivocally negative. The visible world is regarded as a kingdom of evil and darkness. On the other hand, it sees a totally different order of existence where the otherworldly and Unknown God who is the real Lord of the Universe dwells. This God is neither begotten, nor does he create worlds, and in this respect stands in contrast to all other tribal gods and world gods of the historic religions. Gnostic literature even makes reference to the folly of those who do not know the true God and therefore behave as though he did not exist (Rudolph 1983, pp. 61–62, 69).

It is hard for me to understand how a people who conceived their Highest God to be all-encompassing, otherworldly, and yet present in every aspect of existence, could consider dualism more fundamental than their view of the universe as an undivided and indivisible whole. In their Alien God they found also an Eternal Presence who comes out of the Fullness, the "Pleroma," to be with all who are open to receive him. The otherworldliness of this God does not refer to a *literal* other space, but to a level of comprehension beyond the range of the ego. We cannot understand the limitless any more than an ant can understand the workings of a doorknob. But we can recognize that it is surely different from the dimensions of the world that we can see.

So dualism for the Gnostic must refer to division within the Fullness whereby the Unmanifest can take form and thereby creation can occur. The Unmanifest refers to the invisible world, or the implicate order. The Unmanifest is, by definition, formless. As it enters the world of form, it begins to manifest. When this happens, the separation of the visible world from the invisible one is possible. So the One becomes two, yet it is still One in the higher sense. The negative valuation the Gnostics placed on the visible world was explained in their myth of how this world came into being, a radical departure in spirit from the canonized creation narrative.

Gnosis and Depth Psychology

It would be arrogant and condescending to suppose that the Gnostics of antiquity had no sense of the power of unconscious forces in the human psyche. These were people who thought for themselves and who penetrated by means of introspection the many veils of illusion that obscured inner knowledge from their contemporaries. One can imagine Jung poring over the gnostic legends late into the night and reflecting that here are the myths that deal with the troubling questions of the sick psyche. Here are the demons who inhabit people's dreams and fantasies, who give rise to unwelcome suspicions, justifiable and irrational fears, compulsions and complexes of all kinds. Here is the mischief out of which psychosis is fashioned. But in a more subtle way, here is the basis for ignorant and thoughtless behavior that sets people apart from each other and nation against nation. For all these archons still exist as powers in the psyche, able to give rise to all manner of human suffering.

Clearly, it was no mere happenstance that Jung studied Gnosticism with great interest and care, and that gnostic myths and symbols informed his thinking about the greater Self—the archetype of wholeness that underlies ego-consciousness. The Self, as Jung understood it, is comparable to the gnostic concept of the alien and unknown God. Indeed, I find it easier to agree with Jung that the Gnostics were wise beyond their contemporaries, than to dismiss them as a heretical sect who preached the wildest fantasies. Jung says unequivocally, "It is clear beyond a doubt that many of the Gnostics were nothing other than psychologists" (1951/1968, par. 347). To support his statement he cites Clement of Alexandria as saying in the *Paedagogus,* "Therefore, as it seems, it is the greatest of all disciplines to know oneself; for when a man knows himself, he knows God" (par. 347); and the Gnostic Monoimus "the Arab," who writes in a letter to Theophrastus:

Seek him from out thyself, and learn who it is that taketh possession of everything in thee, saying *my* god, *my* spirit, *my* understanding, *my* soul, *my* body; and learn whence is sorrow and joy, and love and hate, and waking though one would not, and sleeping though one would not, and getting angry though one would not, and falling in love though one would not. And if thou shouldst closely investigate these things, thou wilt find Him within thyself, the One and the Many . . . for in thyself thou wilt find the starting point of thy transition and of thy deliverance. (par. 347)

Nor is this profoundly psychological concept the province of the Gnostics alone, though it went strongly against the current of Western thought at the time it was enunciated. Jung compares it to the Indian idea of the Self as Brahman and Atman, citing a passage from the Brihadaranyaka Upanishad: "He who dwells in all beings, yet is apart from all beings, whom no beings know, whose body is in all beings, who controls all beings from within, he is your Self, the inner controller, the immortal" (par. 349). So we may properly suppose that the gnostic myths were part of a spiritual tradition and more; they were also a self-conscious rendering of psychological truth in spiritual terms on that mysterious ground where psyche and spirit meet.

Jung's contemporary depth psychology was strongly influenced by his explorations into gnostic literature. His archetypal world with the unfathomable Self as its central archetype also goes beyond the mundane world in which the ego is the prime moving force. Gnostic writing is surely ahistorical: it has nothing to do with people who ever lived in this world or with events that have any historical reality. But it has a psychological validity, in that it comes from the soul or psyche of the human being, and is expressed in the language of the collective soul, or the collective unconscious as Jung would say—a language that finds its way to us through myth and metaphor.

What the Gnostics sought was an understanding of their place in the visible world and their role in bringing to consciousness the invisible world. They realized, to their eternal credit, that the invisible world existed within themselves, and that therefore within themselves lay the promise and the potential for wholeness. One way in which they lived this out was in their recognition that the feminine principle and the masculine principle—in visible world terms, men and women—were equal before God and equally necessary to achieve the balanced state of wholeness that they sought to attain. Women, therefore, from the beginning of the gnostic consciousness, held an equal role with men in every aspect of their spiritual life. Women, as well as men, were priests; they administered sacraments, they could be bishops, they could teach; in fact, no facet of spiritual practice was denied to them.

Another important aspect of early Gnosticism was its unending search for inner truth through intense introspective observation. As Jung put it, Gnosticism "reached its insights by concentrating on the 'subjective factor,' which consists empirically in the demonstrable influence that the collective unconscious exerts on the conscious mind. This would explain the astonishing parallelism between Gnostic symbolism and the findings of the psychology of the unconscious" (1951/ 1968, par. 350).

The gnostic world view was not altogether buried in the caves at Nag Hammadi. Threads of Gnosticism are interwoven throughout the fabric of traditional religions. If they are not evident, they lend a richness of texture to what might otherwise be flat repetitions of traditional patterns. Gnostic views have always been present, usually in those more personal encounters with the divine presence that are referred to as mystical experiences. They have also lent inspiration to the more inward movements related to the traditional Western religions, such as monasticism in Christianity, Sufism in Islam, and Kabbalah in Judaism. And recently, since so much more of the literature of the Gnostics has come to light, we find again small groups of people coming together to study the old texts and finding in them inspiration for a religious expression that, strangely enough, meets the needs of some few people who have not found themselves at home in the more traditional churches and synagogues.

Contemporary Gnosticism and the Judeo-Christian Tradition

To compare as diverse and complex a body of ideas as the gnostic texts reveal, with the equally complex and diverse expressions of the Judeo-Christian tradition, is an impossible task. It is complicated by the fact that since Gnosticism has no credo and each person seeks the truth from inner wisdom, Gnostics do not always agree on what Gnosticism is. So if I dare to make some comparisons of a few features of each, it is to be understood that these necessarily consist of the broadest generalities and are not to be too concretely taken. My intention is to indicate something of the spirit of Gnosticism, as compared with that of the more traditional religious forms.

Jewish and Christian authorities closed the canons of the Old and the New Testaments, implying by this that revelation happened at a certain time in history, for all time. Gnosticism recognizes many sacred texts that were written during the same period as the New Testament and later, and it sees revelation as an ongoing process.

Orthodox Christianity places authority within the church establishment, with the head of the Church as the final authority on certain important issues. Gnosticism stresses the authority of the inner voice, sometimes referred to as the Voice of God, within each person. Authority, in Gnosticism, becomes a function of each person's inner perception of Divine Will, as discerned through self-knowledge and contemplation.

The Judeo-Christian God is referred to as a jealous God who says "Thou shalt have no other gods before me," thereby recognizing that there are other gods, but that they are inferior. Gnosticism sees the creator-god, Jesus, and Yahweh, as well as the gods of all other cultures, as manifestations in this world of manifestations, of something pointing toward, but not equivalent to, the God who is unknown and whose nature is unknowable. All other gods, who can be described, to the Gnostic are but imperfect approximations of the True God.

The Mass, for the orthodox Christian, is celebrated in commemoration of a past event, with vicarious benefits to those who partake of it. In the Gnostic celebration of the Eucharist, the participant enters into the immediate experience of the death of the personal ego, symbolized by the crucified Christ; and the resurrection that follows is that of an integrated ego-Self union, symbolized by a sense of oneness with the risen Christ.

In traditional Christianity, the Trinity consists of Father, Son, and Holy Spirit. Notable for its absence is a fourth element, which could be matter, the feminine principle, or the demonic element. Gnosticism takes all four into account. It restores matter to a vitally important place in the visible world; redeems the feminine principle, in the image of Sophia; and recognizes the presence of the demonic, in the form of the archons. The archons represent the noncreative powers in this world, who must be recognized for what they are and confronted directly.

Both Judaism and Christianity see God as a father figure, creating a world through the agency of the word or Logos. In the Old Testament, creation proceeds with the word issuing from God: "And God said, 'Let there be light, and there was light' " (Gen. 1:3), and the New Testament Gospel of John opens with, "In the beginning was the Word." Gnosticism sees the ongoing creative power in the universe as the Father-Mother principle, emanating light or energy; and in the human spirit as the principle of individuation.

In traditional Christianity, the feminine power is subdued. Where woman is recognized as an element in spirituality, it is either in her biological function as Mother and bearer of the Divine Child, or as a compulsory virgin in religious orders. But as a fully independent woman who may choose to be sexual or not, she has little status. In Gnosticism, the feminine is redeemed from the depths of matter and returned in her totality to coequal status with the masculine.

Christianity regards as a high virtue the *Imitatio Dei*, the imitation of God, with the words, "Be ye perfect." Not so in Gnosticism, where what is sought is not perfection, but wholeness. Wholeness or completion comes about symbolically in the mystical marriage between the Christ or Logos figure and the Sophia or Eros figure. The meaning of this for the Gnostic is that the union is to be realized not only upon the altar in the Mass, but also in the individual person. This involves the recognition of the dark side within oneself and in the world, and a willingness to face up to it.

The traditional religions, with their litanies of thou-shalt-nots, encourage the repression of the shadow, the part of the self that is unacceptable in terms of collective mores. Gnosticism urges the integration of the shadow by progressively dealing with the ignorant and destructive parts of one's own nature. To approach wholeness, the gnostic ritual seeks the "bringing together of the fragments." The prayer that concludes a contemporary gnostic Eucharist expresses this major intention of the gnostic way: "I have recognized myself and gathered myself together from all sides. I have sown no children to the ruler of this world, but have torn up his roots. I have gathered together my limbs that were scattered abroad, and I know Thee Who Thou art" (Miller 1988).

7

The Apocalypse and the Messiah

How is it we have walk'd thro fires
& yet are not consum'd?
How is it that all things are chang'd,
even as in ancient times?
                                        BLAKE, *The Four Zoas*

Signs and Wonders

I am often struck by the number of catastrophes we bring upon ourselves day by day out of our own meanness or heedlessness. Slowly and barely noticed, they add up. They receive attention in the press, on television, from the pulpit, and on the lecture-seminar circuit, but in a strange way all this seems almost like entertainment. We watch, we listen absently to reports of vials of AIDS-tainted blood being washed up on the ocean beaches of our country, of fish dying in polluted waters, of the pesticides being used on fruit that may poison human beings as well as fruit flies, and we may even go so far as to stop buying grapes to support a protest. We buy peaches instead. We read about the controversy over whether we should use the research on hypothermia that comes out of the Nazi experiments in murder at Dachau and feel some moments of agony until the press stops publicizing the issue. We grieve when we see a quilt larger than two football fields commemorating the loss of thousands of people from an epidemic, nearly a plague, but if we are not homosexual or intravenous drug users we don't feel personally threatened. Acid rain, we hear, despoils our crops, but that problem doesn't touch us much either. Beautiful fresh fruits and vegetables are always available in the grocery store. Wages are up and most people are managing. True, some are not; there are the homeless in every large city, and sometimes we are moved to give charity. To make it even easier, grocery stores accept our small change and put it into a special fund for food for the homeless, and give us a receipt so that we can claim a tax exemption. Political prisoners languish in jails in many "civilized" countries. Terrorism is still tolerated as a legitimate weapon of those who cannot afford a huge investment in armaments.

We can avoid being preoccupied with the evidence that the world is in deep distress as we approach the ending of another millennium. But something in us does notice. Under the surface of a bountiful economy lies a sense of despair and frustration. We cannot totally avoid the recognition that the results of all our excesses are about to come tumbling down upon our heads. Other civilizations have come and gone. Could it be that ours is not here forever? When will it end, and how? We have noted that astrophysicists have been asking these questions lately. Most often, they place the death of our planet from natural causes in the distant future. But will we human beings bring about the ultimate catastrophe in the next millennium, the next century, the next generation? These are the secret questions we dare not ask aloud. But we respond to these questions indirectly by drinking too much, by using drugs to help us escape our sense of impending doom, or by going to the movies where we can have all our violence and destruction in fantasy without really being touched by it. We tend to associate with people who think and feel as we do, so that our attitudes and behavior do not get challenged.

It is only when something that happens in the world causes pain or dislocation to us personally that we begin to recognize for whom the bell tolls. Earthquake, drought, other "acts of God" remind us that when all the potential disasters finally add up, it is possible that none of us will escape. We feel foreboding under the surface of our cultivated minds when we read the newspaper accounts of disaster that corroborate our own disquietude.

In the summer of 1988, suffocating heat made life miserable for most of the country. It pushed temperatures to record levels in a dozen states, causing power failures in Boston and simmering Lake Erie waters at a record 80 degrees. This has been ascribed to a "greenhouse effect" supposedly caused by pollution of the atmosphere. What if the countries of the world cannot cooperate to resolve this problem? What if each succeeding summer is just two or three degrees hotter than the last?

Politicians are talking about the end of the world in flood, pestilence, and famine. Looking ahead to the next few years, a former secretary of state says, "We will see a new international agenda, different from the outdated issues of the 1900s. Climate, population, and acid rain are creating security problems of a different order." Harvard professor Joseph Nye says, "The world will be more economically and ecologically interdependent. We will be required to live together in different ways than in the past." The *San Francisco Chronicle* carried a column by Richard Reeves, "People who may have been inclined to dismiss such thoughts as '60s talk aren't so sure as they look up, down and around at a world that seems at odds with nature. . . . I, for one, writing on the 46th straight 90-degree day in Washington, am willing to listen to the scientists being paraded before Congress now. A few days ago I was standing on a beach in Long Island in the late afternoon. The sun was hotter and brighter than I ever could remember it in the many summers I have stood in that same place."

We begin hearing what can only be called apocalyptic visions. *Apocalypse* comes from a Greek word meaning revelation, and it is surely appropriate in these times when nature and the newspapers are beginning to reveal to us what can no longer be wished away. The apocalyptists of our time take care not to attribute what they predict to the actions of a wrathful god. They assign the responsibility to "nature" and "human folly." But if there were a creator-god who had covenanted with humankind that he would protect them in all their ways provided they strictly observed his law and his commandments, then surely he would issue warnings such as those we read today in the daily press.

We are in the early days of the new paradigm in science, and in some ways it looks as though we are not surviving it very well. While many people read about the scientists' theories on how the world began and their predictions of how it may possibly end, there seems to be a selective blindness when it comes to recognizing any personal responsibility we may have for our eventual fate. The speculations and discoveries of the scientific theorists of our day have brought us an ever-increasing knowledge about the way things are, how the world works, and what the system is that holds it together and makes it function in a generally orderly way. Laws and principles are applied to create new technologies that serve us in every aspect of physical life. The human mind penetrates farther than ever before into the infinite spaces of the unknown. Scientists probe the limits of knowledge and stand on the edge of the abyss.

This is not the first time anyone has been there. In those dark centuries around the time of Jesus, when the visible and invisible worlds were totally at odds with each other, it is not surprising that many

Christians and Jews and pagan Gnostics withdrew into their separate communities and commiserated with each other about the discrepancies between what they saw as the ideal or archetypal world, and the world in which they lived. In each other's company and often out of sight of the establishment culture, they told their own stories to rationalize the presence of evil in the world, and came to understand in their own way how to insulate themselves from contamination by worldly powers—what Gnostics referred to as the archons, and what the others called temptation, corruption, and sin. These groups shared a common belief in a better life after their temporary sojourn in this imperfect world. Each community developed its own practices and wrote its own sacred literature. They instituted rituals to initiate new members and to bond together the companies of the faithful, who would wait patiently for the end of days and the world to come.

The Visionaries

In every age there have been those few—madmen or geniuses, prophets or shamans, visionaries or fools—who have seen through the surface of ordinary consciousness and looked directly into the interior. These individuals have almost unanimously reported that they did not make a conscious decision to do so. It has seemed to them that they were "chosen" in some inexplicable way. They were called, they heard their names, and they responded. To them have been given visions of another world, a world without boundaries, out of space and out of time. Such people are around today, but they do not ordinarily proclaim themselves. One has to be prepared to recognize them when they appear, or else they pass unnoticed like a breeze in the morning. They are the latest of a long line carried on by the likes of Ezekiel, St. John of the Cross, Hildegarde of Bingen, Dante, Milton, Blake, and many others. They serve as teachers for those who know that it is possible to transcend the ego world and look in upon another. For me, William Blake has been such a mentor. In his early work *The Marriage of Heaven and Hell*, he describes his own particular method of printing, an allegory for how a creative person uncovers and gives expression to true knowledge. William did not have enough money to get his works published by a proper printer, and he reflected long upon what he might do. Then his dead brother Robert came to him in a dream and described the method that, in fact, William did employ thereafter. He laboriously traced on a copper plate his text with all its embellishments. Then he printed by "the infernal method, by corrosives, which in Hell are salutary, melting apparent surfaces away, and displaying the infinite which was hid."

In *Milton,* one of Blake's later "prophetic works," he made clear how limited he felt the senses were when it came to perceiving truth. For him, there was a great difference between ordinary perception and perception that was "seeing through":

> Ah weak & wide astray! Ah shut in narrow doleful form,
> Creeping in reptile flesh upon the bosom of the ground!
> The Eye of Man a narrow orb, clos'd up and dark,
> Scarcely beholding the great light, conversing with the Void;
> The Ear a little shell, in small volutions shutting out
> All melodies & comprehending only Discord and Harmony;
> The Tongue a little moisture fills, a little food it cloys,
> A little sound it utters & its cries are faintly heard,
> Then brings forth Moral Virtue the cruel Virgin Babylon.
>
> Can such an Eye judge the stars? & looking thro' its tubes
> Measure the sunny rays that point their spears on Udanadan?
> Can such an Ear, fill'd with the vapours of the yawning pit,
> Judge of the pure melodious harp struck by a hand divine?
> Can such closed Nostrils feel a joy? or tell of autumn fruits
>
> When grapes & figs burst their covering to the joyful air?
> Can such a Tongue boast of the living waters? or take in
> Ought but the Vegetable Ratio & loathe the faint delight?
> Can such gross Lips percieve? alas, folded within themselves
> They touch not ought, but pallid turn & tremble at every wind.
>
> (1957, pp. 484–85)

Voices of the Apocalypse

The centuries just before and after the time of Jesus were times of tremendous emotional ferment. Those times, like these, were millenarian times and people were looking backward as if to take stock of where they were and where the world was, before pressing forward into the next millennium. At such crucial points it seems that the stars are brighter, and on earth, passions are heightened. When the Roman Empire had passed its zenith and its once heroic leadership had become effete and the glories of Greece were scarcely remembered, people of every class and station struggled to find their way into a new sort of existence. The poor and the homeless came together in little groups to listen to anyone who would bring them a message of promise in a world that offered them little hope for the future. For some, the new Christian communities brought meaning and a sense that this corrupt and difficult world was not all that existed.

The apocalyptic seers couched their dire warnings in strange symbolic language. Their imagery called forth the visionary capacities of every person to imagine the fantastic beasts that represented every vice and sin imaginable, and the wrath of God smashing the earth with lightning and fire, and with storm, disease, and pestilence. It seems clear to me that their visions derived from extraordinary states of consciousness, as when the ego is either shattered or transcended. Anyone who has experienced extreme sensory deprivation, who has used hallucinogenic substances, or who has had fantastic and powerfully moving dreams, knows how real a vision can be. The reality is not necessarily the consensual reality, but it is an individual reality that is completely valid in terms of the person's own experience.

The images and symbols in which the apocalyptic visions presented themselves evoked through analogy many different levels of meaning. For example, when the apocalyptists speak of "the fire next time," that fire may evoke the devouring passion of the human heart, the threat of world destruction by violence, the hell fire of divine retribution, or the secret guilts that eat away at the image one has of oneself. Everything depends upon the receptivity of the person who hears the prophecy. The process that entails "seeing," communicating what is seen, receiving it, and being moved to action, is not a rational process at all.

Yet ever and always there are those who insist on a logical explanation for what I would call nonrational behavior and events. One of the "explanations" of the apocalyptic visions—both those foreseeing total destruction and those offering a slim shred of hope for life after it is all over—is that they have a polemic aspect. Perhaps these visionaries spoke as they did, the skeptics claim, to frighten naive people into conforming to certain patterns of behavior out of mortal fear of what would happen to them if they did not. Surely every age has its false prophets, who use real or fabricated "visions" to manipulate people for their own purposes. But there are also those gifted individuals who are able to see through the visible world.

What is the source of the warnings of the coming destruction and the horrific symbols that describe it? I suggest that the images are archetypal, and that they originate in the collective psyche. As has been repeatedly shown in mythology, every culture produces images of its own destruction. These are often accompanied by hints of a potential reconstitution at a higher level. Those individual tellers of tales at the time of Christ may have felt impelled from within to warn of the coming catastrophe; and the polemics, if they can properly be called that, represented an honest attempt to waken the people to what lay in store for them. Conversely, it may be that the prophets of doom looked about them, and seeing a world of moral dissolution, became afraid. Their fears took the form of wrathful gods and vast destructive powers. In either case, those who presaged the end were gazing into a darker reality than the one that is familiar to all of us. They looked into the depths of evil and saw what had not yet come to pass.

The apocalyptic predictions had to do with the end of an era and the beginning of a new age. The changeover (what we might see in retrospect as a paradigm shift) was to be marked by the appearance of a bright star in the east as the sign of the zodiacal shift from the Age of Aries to the Age of Pisces. Aries, with its symbol the ram, corresponds to the historical period from about 2000 B.C. to the time of Jesus. It was the age of the Old Testament patriarchy, beginning with Abraham's coming out of Ur of the Chaldees, a land in which astrologers were the most respected scientists of their time. It ended when Jesus, the last lamb of Aries, took on the symbol of the fish, the image of Pisces and of the new astrological era. With the appearance of Jesus, new hope was offered. If sin and death came into the world through one man, Adam (Rom. 5:12), then the abundance of grace and the gift of righteousness might also be possible through one man, Jesus Christ (Rom. 5:17). So redemption was held out as the ultimate hope.

Messianic Expectations

Converts to Christianity proclaimed Jesus the Messiah, the Christ. They expected a messianic age to come about forthwith, with the promise speedily fulfilled of peace on earth and good will toward men. They expected that when all had "received the wrath of great God to their bosoms," God would again make a great sign, a radiant star brightly beaming from heaven, and he would show a victor's crown for those who contended in the contest. And then would every people in immortal contests

Contend for glorious victory; for there shall none
Be able shamelessly to purchase a crown for silver.
For Christ the holy shall adjudge to them just rewards
and crown the excellent, and a prize immortal he will give
to martyrs who endure the contest even unto death.
And to virgins who run their course well a prize incorruptible

He will give, and to all among men who deal justly
And to nations from far-distant lands
Who live holy lives and recognize one God.

(Barnstone 1984, p. 557)

Isaiah had said, "There shall come forth a shoot from the stump of Jesse, and a branch shall grow out of his roots, and the spirit of the Lord shall rest upon him. . . . The wolf shall dwell with the lamb, and the leopard shall lie down with the kid . . . and a little child shall lead them" (Isa. 11:1–2, 6, RSV). The Jews who did not convert to Christianity maintained their reservations. If Jesus were indeed the Messiah as proclaimed, then the world would be a better place, at least for the followers of Jesus. Observing the persecution of the new Christians and the continuing hard lot of the Jewish people, the Jews saw that the promise of a new age had not yet been realized. At least two conclusions could be drawn from this. One was that Jesus was the Messiah but that his kingdom would not be accomplished on earth in the near future, but in heaven at some unspecified time after humankind had been judged and those found worthy had been elevated to the kingdom. This became a matter of faith to the many people who found it acceptable. Another conclusion was that Jesus was a great spiritual teacher and religious reformer, but that he was not the promised Messiah. The evidence given for this was the observation that the visible world was not necessarily better after the crucifixion of Jesus than before his birth. The day of the Messiah was not yet. The glorious promise of a new Jerusalem was yet to be fulfilled. So, while the growing community of Christians believed that Christ had come, Christ had risen, and Christ would come again, there were others, especially the Jews, who awaited not the second coming, but the first.

According to some teachers of Judaism, the Messiah would not necessarily arrive as a person, but more likely as a state of mind, an awakening of a people, an enlightenment. That an individual might have some role in the coming of the Messiah was accepted as a possibility. Such a person, or persons, would serve the function of a midwife bringing a child into the world: she or he might be the agent of the event, but not its cause. In the Judaism of the biblical and intertestamentary periods, the messianic age was not expected to come about as a historic outgrowth of previous events. It was not to occur as a developmental stage of a people but, as Gershom Scholem (1971) puts it, messianism "is transcendence breaking in upon history, an intrusion in which history itself perishes, transformed in its ruin because it is struck by a beam of light shining into it from an outside source" (p. 10). The messianic hope is conceived in apocalyptic despair.

The seers of the apocalypse foresaw the consummation of history. They sought to have revealed to them the time when God's mighty acts would bring an end to history and recreate a new world for the elect, the chosen ones. There were prophecies of the signs that would precede the end; for example, Ezra's vision of the fall of Jerusalem that would come about as a consequence of the evil acts of human beings, beginning with Adam's first transgression and continuing with Israel's sins:

Days come when the inhabitants of the earth are seized with great panic
and the way of truth hidden
and the land will be barren of faith.

Then the sun will suddenly shine by night
and the moon by day.
Blood will trickle forth from wood
and stone speak its voice.
People will be confounded
and stars change course. . . .

Sown fields will dry up, full storehouses be empty,
salt waters turn sweet,
friends attack each other fiercely.
Then intelligence will hide
and wisdom withdraw to its chamber
where none can find it.
Unrighteousness and lust will cloud the earth
and lands will ask each other:
"Has righteousness come your way?"
And the answer will be No.
In that time all hope will fail,
all labor fail.
These signs I tell you, but if you pray, weep, and fast seven days,
you will hear wondrous things.

(Barnstone 1984, p. 514)

The question was asked of a talmudic teacher of the third century, "When will the Messiah come?" The people were told, "Three things come unawares: the Messiah, a found article, and a scorpion" (Sanhedrin 97a, cited in Scholem 1971, p. 11). The importance of repentance was stressed and it was said that if Israel would repent even for a single day, it would be instantly redeemed and the Son of David would instantly come—as it says in Psalm 95:7, "Today, if you will listen to his voice!" (*Exodus Rabba*, xxv, 16, cited in Scholem 1971, p. 11). The redemption could not be realized without terror and destruction, but in its hopeful aspect this prophecy suggested the possibility of a utopian age.

■

"They shall not hurt or destroy in all my holy mountain; for the earth shall be full of the knowledge of the Lord as the waters cover the sea" (Isa. 11:9, RSV). These prophetic words refer to the reestablishment of the Davidic kingdom as a spiritual kingdom on earth, but they were seen in many old midrashim as referring to the reestablishment of the condition of Paradise. For the mystics, the correspondence of the First Days in Paradise and the Last Days, when the messianic prophecy would be fulfilled, was a living reality. In Lurianic Kabbalism, the utopian dream went even farther. In the First Days when the cosmos came into being, God sent his light—those generative sparks— into the universe, but they met with "the breaking of the vessels." The interpretation of this is that the divine inspiration could not be contained in an imperfect world or by the imperfect beings who resided in it. Yet the world was not wholly without the divine inspiration, either. Perhaps there were some vessels that did hold, and in these the messianic hopes were born. The Kabbalah suggested that the Last Days would even surpass the First Days, going beyond the condition of a renewed humanity and a renewed Kingdom of David to the unrestrained utopianianism of a renewed condition of nature and a new harmony in the cosmos as a whole.

The Interior Messiah

The mystics interpreted this hope less in an activist way and more in terms of the interiorization of the messianic ideal. For them, the promised reality of a messianic age would appear as an outward symbol of an inner condition of the world and of its people. While some interpretations of Christianity suggested that a pure inwardness might burst forth and bring about redemption, in Judaism, even among the mystics, there could be no redemption of the spirit without a corresponding manifestation in the outer world as well. The Jewish mystics saw this movement to the interior, to the soul, to be the requisite balance to the outward movement. As a matter of fact, in Judaism the redemption of the practical world was clearly understood as the meaning of messianism until the Middle Ages, at which time inwardness and introspection became a crucial part of the process.

The *Zohar*, a masterpiece of Spanish Kabbalism that came into being during the late years of the thirteenth century and the beginning of the fourteenth, gathered together medieval works that possessed all the urgency of the foreseen End and the passionate messianic expectations. Here an unnamed Kabbalist in the book *Ra'ya Mehmemna* expresses his visions by means of the old biblical symbols of the Tree of Knowledge and the Tree of Life. The Tree of Knowledge is the tree of the apocalypse, because its fruit brings about death for Adam and Eve and all the generations of their progeny. Death is related to the visible world, in which good and evil coexist, and in which human beings by their willfulness turn knowledge to self-serving and destructive ends. The Tree of Life represents the pure, undiluted power of the Holy Spirit, diffused throughout the world but mostly unseen. To taste the fruit of the Tree of Life requires an act of faith in the ability of all living things to communicate with each other and with their source in the invisible world.

There is an analogy between the development of the messianic hope in Kabbalistic Judaism and the process of individuation as envisaged by Jung in our own time. In Judaism, the Tree of Knowledge is characterized as the "Torah of the Exile" and the Tree of Life as the "Torah of the Redemption." In Jungian terms, the Torah of the Exile would correspond to the state of the individual who is dominated by purely ego concerns (such as survival, security, ambition, prestige, wealth, sexual gratification, status, and the approval of others). "Exile" refers to the separation of the ego from its source in the unconscious and from its connection with life's meaning and purpose. Whence did we come? What are we here for? Whence comes our end? Where are we going? These questions are rarely asked when we are dominated by the ego state, in which knowledge is valued for its own sake and without regard to the meaning and implications of what it uncovers. Without wisdom, knowledge is reduced to science, which, for all the ways in which it has been able to enhance our life-styles, has nevertheless brought us to a condition where for the first time in history we hold in our hands the means of total and final annihilation of the planet we call home and all its people. Nuclear disaster stands at our left hand as a means of bringing on the apocalypse—and it will not be God who has done it but we who will bring it upon ourselves. But at our right hand stands the possibility of personal freedom.

Beyond the ego state lies the state of wholeness in which the ego serves a larger reality than itself. This is the reality of wholeness, and its central dominating factor is the Self, in Jung's terminology. The Torah of Redemption represents the state of the Self, the archetype of Wholeness, which is experienced when conscious intent and purpose are in harmony with the direction and flow of the unconscious. For Jung, the Self is the central focus of the totality of an individual, in which consciousness and the unconscious communicate with each other in an open, undefended manner. This state, then, corresponds to the Tree of Life, while the purely ego state is controlled by the Tree of Knowledge, which also is the Tree of Death. The ego is oriented toward knowledge (in its limited sense), while the Self is oriented toward wisdom.

Redemption Here and Now

Although I have been writing in theoretical and abstract terms for some time now, I want to make clear that I am dealing not in idle speculation, but with human experience. Whatever I have to say comes out of my living, breathing contact with real people. The process in which we engage in analysis is what Jung called "the way of individuation." It is a process that seeks to establish a harmonious relationship between the ego as the historical aspect of the person, and the Self as the timeless aspect.

Once in a great while I have the rare privilege of accompanying a person who is traveling this path and discovering for herself some of the ancient truths that have always been known to a special few. My analysand Laurel, for instance, knew very little about Judaism in general, about the messianic tradition in Judaism or about the Kabbalah. But she did understand that the unconscious often breaks in upon consciousness, and when this happened to her she was alert and receptive.

One day during a session, she said to me, "My unconscious is telling me that there is something more important than any task I perform. It is *a way of being*, a form of *redemption*. I don't know exactly what I mean by 'redemption,' or even by 'a way of being.' We have talked in here about goals. *That* is my goal. It is not an easy path, and I don't get any rewards for it in this world. I pick up things, realizations. I realize that there are particular persons who give off an extraordinary kind of message—they are like a lighthouse in the dark night. There aren't very many of these people. They were singled out before they were born. I have a special term for these people. 'Carriers of consciousness,' I call them."

I reminded her that the literature of Gnosticism refers to these special people, whom God calls by name as "the elect." He knows their names before they are born. She was familiar with the concept and said, "In my lifetime I have known only about five. They are the redeemed." I asked her what sort of redemption she was talking about.

"I am not talking about the redemption of people, or about the redemption of God," Laurel answered. "It has a much more profound meaning for me. It's tied up with evil in some way. As a young person it seemed to me that evil was very active in the world. I used to try to grapple with evil, but it appeared to me that no one else did. Maybe that was why I had such a strong sense that I was different. I have always seen myself as being involved in the process of redeeming evil. I am one among others who are on the same course. It is not so much by my actions, but by my way of being that I am redemptive."

I asked her how she knew this. She replied that this knowing came from within herself, from an inner source that she trusted. "I simply know certain things," she insisted. "I know that evil for most people is something outside themselves; it is in the world or in other people. To me evil is right here, at my side. That knowing doesn't come from books. I recognize that evil exists in myself, and I don't try to avoid searching it out and confronting it in a very personal way. But there is more to evil than just the personal aspect. There is a collective evil, a sickness in society. Evil is like the toxic substance that was loaded onto a barge and sent off to sea. No country wanted to accept it. It's your evil, not ours, they all said. So the barge went from port to port in search of a place to dump its cargo."

She went on to explain her notion of evil on a grand scale: "Jesus was supposed to bring this [redemption] about, but he didn't. He was one light. This way of being I'm talking about allows one light to appear in the great sea of blackness, then one here and another there. These lights matter incredibly—these lights, this way of being, transcends my individual light. While I am here on this earth I can help in some way I cannot comprehend. I add my light (which is not really mine in the sense of possession) to the redemptive process. It requires my willingness and the willingness of others to look in the face of this absolute evil and to acknowledge it, not to gloss it over—to live in it and with it as if one were a voluntary exile. I don't have this way of being yet, but the structure is there—the beginning."

I saw this as evidence that Laurel was far along on the path to individuation. In the process she was gaining more understanding, and this was leading to more consciousness. Consciousness was the constant factor in what she had called a "way of being." "As you move in the direction of wholeness," I told her, "you gain in strength. People who do not have the strength cannot hold the light. It is the strengthening that makes it possible to hold the light."

Laurel said that she was not surprised that there are so few on this path. So much is asked.

"There must be some reward, then," I suggested.

"The reward?" Laurel reflected back to me. "The reward must be finding the meaning of my existence."

Reconciliation of the Opposites

It is difficult to reconcile the dire predictions of the apocalyptists, ancient and modern, with the notion of a just and merciful god. The god of Abraham and of Jonah might visit punishment upon his people for their heedlessness and wrongdoing, but he could be cajoled or persuaded to forgive his people and give them yet another chance to make amends and again find favor with him. But the god of the apocalyptists finds the world utterly base and corrupt, its people perverted and dissolute. There will be no reprieve this time, but utter destruction, including the annihilation of the human race. We saw in the gnostic mythology the seeds of this state of affairs: the world was brought into being through error, and is consequently imperfect. It contains the seeds of its own destruction. Yet, because the Sophia was of divine origin, and because she brought sparks of divinity with her when she descended into the world of matter, the sparks came down also and entered into the human condition. Therefore, from the beginning the possibility has existed that some people might be found who could contain the sparks; some people who could serve as vessels for the imperishable aspect of humanity. Scattered throughout the apocalyptic writings one can find the possibility, even the promise, that a new order will spring forth after the old order has been destroyed. It will be like a forest that has suffered the rages of wildfire and has been totally denuded of underbrush and leaves and branches. But the fire releases the spark in the seed. In the weeks that follow, the thunder and lightning come, the spring rains flood the blackened earth, and slowly the forest comes to life again and dares to put forth green shoots.

Apocalypse and redemption occur in the inner lives of human beings also. It can happen that in times of utter personal ruin, when an individual has fallen into the abyss of depression or anxiety and all hope is gone and nothing is left to cling to, a new path will suddenly open up in the tangled wood and a ray of sunlight will shatter the darkness. Again, it may happen when a person has left a comfortable and secure life behind and is floundering around trying to find another way. The light appears unexpectedly and without any seeming prior cause, but it is greeted by a gasp of recognition, as though what now is seen was always known but had been forgotten and is now instantly remembered.

8

The Kingdom of
the Spirit

A Stranger here
Strange things doth meet, strange Glory see.
Strange treasures lodg'd in this fair world appear.
Strange all and New to me:
But that they mine should be who Nothing was,
That Strangest is of all; yet brought to pass.
THOMAS TRAHERNE, "Lines from the Salutation,"
read at Henry Moore's posthumous service at his request

Seeking the Kingdom

The Kingdom of the Spirit means different things to different people. For some it is a way to escape the dreaded apocalypse and to achieve the longed-for messianic age. For others it may be like a fairytale world that one must enter through some mysterious aperture, leaving the ordinary world behind. Today a number of flourishing groups propose to give their members some kind of spiritually oriented experience. These range all the way from fundamentalist Christian retreat camps to Western recreations of Hindu ashrams. Some people go off on vacation to secluded areas where nudism is accepted, as a means of doing away with the falseness with which people clothe themselves in everyday lives. There, bathing together in hot mineral springs, they seek to recapture the living waters of the baptismal fount by literalizing the spirit. Perhaps, we can conjecture, there may be other motives. Meditation weekends at some Zen monasteries in California are booked a year in advance. International guided tours are arranged to the great power spots of the earth: Glastonbury, Stonehenge, the pyramids, the rock temple at Elephanta, the Dome of the Rock. In addition, there are many groups that can only be called cults. By this I mean a small or narrow circle of people united by some system of beliefs and practices usually regarded by the mainstream as unorthodox or spurious, and including special devotion to a leader whose word is law within the context of the group. What is the meaning of this plethora of vigorous contemporary interest in an otherworldly consciousness, a Kingdom of the Spirit?

The Glass Bead Game

Once upon a time I made a journey to explore this very question. I left the city where I lived and the country of my birth and set out for the mythical land of Castalia. I rode through the sky in the belly of a gigantic silver bird for many hours across the land and the ocean and again over the land. Below, snowy mountains thrust their tops through a sea of billowing clouds. We descended slowly and came to rest in the city made famous by a wise old man who had lived there, and whose disciples had taught me in years gone by. Though they were filled with his spirit, the disciples had never failed to acknowledge the source of their inspiration by beginning an inordinate number of sentences with the words, "Jung says . . ."

From the landing field in Zurich I made my way to the city, and there, in an old railway station in its center, multitudes of people scurried about speaking their strange language. I inquired of a prim-looking woman who sat on a high stool behind a counter, where I would find the next train to Vezia. I could not speak the language of the people in the station, nor could this woman speak mine, but we were able to communicate in German, the language most Swiss reluctantly use when they have to speak to foreigners.

The train left at the very moment the woman had said it would. It wound a circuitous path around mountains, along the edges of lakes, and through river valleys, until all of a sudden the rush of noise in my ears told me that we were entering the interior of a mountain. In the darkness of the tunnel, illuminated only by the train's dim headlight, it appeared that we were traveling toward the center of the earth with absolutely no chance of escape. After several long minutes, however, a ray of light shone into the tunnel from the far end. In another instant we were out in the bright daylight, in a strange and beautiful country called the Tessin. "Veeeeyzia!" called the conductor. I gathered up my belongings and got off. A car was waiting for me and took me up and up and up the laborious way to the very top, to my destination at "Castalia." It was to be the scene of a six-week seminar designed to explore spiritual issues in much the same way as the gathering that took place at its earlier namesake in one of the great novels of all time.

Castalia is a place that does not exist on this earth, yet it does exist as a Kingdom of the Spirit. Or at least it was created by Hermann Hesse, whose last and most profound novel, *The Glass Bead Game*, also published as *Magister Ludi, (Das Glasperlenspiel)* (1969), was set at some unspecified time in the future in a secret mountain fastness named Castalia, for the sacred spring at Delphi under Mount Parnassus, held in ancient times to be the center of the world. Parnassus is also the mountain of the muses, the daughters of Zeus and Mnemosyne (Memory), who said, "We know how to speak false things that seem true, but we know, when we will, to utter true things."

According to Hesiod and Aeschylus, men had grown so wicked upon the earth that Zeus determined to destroy them. He sent the Great Deluge; but the visionary Prometheus, knowing what was going to happen, advised his son Deucalion and his niece Pyrrha to build a chest and stock it with provisions and to embark in it and wait out the storm and tempest that Zeus's brother Poseidon, the god of the sea, would send to annihilate mortal man. When the flood receded, the first dry land to appear was Mount Parnassus. Pyrrha and Deucalion, now the only living creatures in a dead world, came down from Parnassus and prayed for help. They heard a voice saying, "Veil your heads and throw behind you the bones of your mother." They did not understand these cryptic words at first, for oracles are rarely comprehensible when they are given. At last Deucalion saw their meaning and said to Pyrrha, "Earth is the mother of all. Her bones are the stones. These we may cast behind us without doing wrong." This they did, and from the stones arose a new race, hard and enduring as it needed to be. From that time forth at Castalia, seekers for Truth were answered by a priestess of Apollo, who went into a trance before she spoke. We may understand the trance as her way of entering into the invisible world.

I had come to Switzerland to participate in a summer's retreat that was supposed to recreate something like Hermann Hesse's fabled Castalia. The place was chosen because it was close to Montagnola, where Hermann Hesse had lived while he was writing the masterpiece that brought him the Nobel Prize in literature. Here scholars and students were brought together in the spirit of the Glass Bead Game, to contribute their expertise on various subjects in the realm of art and intellect so that the spirit of those assembled might be nourished. As soon as I arrived I became aware of the rarified atmosphere. It resembled Hesse's Castalia in that it was above all the socioeconomic and political tensions of the lower world. In our Swiss mountain fortress we could bar the doors against poverty of body and soul. We were not people who had to struggle for our sustenance and that of our families. We were free to pursue our intellectual pleasures, to set our sights on the movement of the spirit, and to study the myths and symbols that pointed to the ultimate mysteries of life. We were free also to tone our bodies by hiking across alpine meadows or, following the ancient discipline of the East, to strengthen our muscles in the practice of hatha yoga. We were free to listen to those who had come to impart wisdom; we were free in the daytime and long summer evenings to indulge in conversation about esoteric matters or, if weary of that, to enjoy the pleasures of the senses away from any rules and conventions that might have limited us at home. We were here in "Castalia." I wondered if it was to be the summer of the Glass Bead Game.

This Game of Games, as Hesse alluded to it (he never really described it), could be played only by those who had been admitted to the Order after a long period of study and apprenticeship. The preparation demanded achievement of superb knowledge in a particular field of specialization, and the task was the transformation of that knowledge into the secret systematics of the Game. Scholars from many disciplines in the arts and sciences sought to codify, translate, or syncretize the essence of what they knew into a common body of rules and procedures. From a contemporary perspective, one might see that they were trying to formulate a unified field theory of the intellect—so enormous an undertaking as to be hardly imaginable! I wondered, would each person retire into an area of expertise and perfect it and then bring it forth in its pristine purity like a crystal bauble, to join a hundred other crystal baubles of all sizes and colors, a gem of glass to be put into play? Would each one maneuver it through the intricate labyrinth of the intellect, contending with others for precedence in pushing his own bead through the narrow straits of the Game?

What better metaphor for isolation, for separateness, for a single idea, an area of specialization, a parochial point of view than Hesse's glass bead! If each isolated person identifies with that single bead, playing the great Game with other isolated human beings joined only by the common striving of the mind, they play with pretty but essentially worthless marbles. They remain separate from their fellows and also alone within themselves, fragmented, because they exercise only one part of their being—the intellect—and not the totality of themselves.

In a poem that Hesse composed while he was working on the novel, he wrote of "a game of thoughts called the Glass Bead Game" that he practiced while he worked in his garden. As he watched the ashes of his burning leaves filter down through a grate, he said, "I hear music and see men of the past and future. I see wise men and poets and scholars harmoniously building the hundred-gated cathedral of the Mind." Hesse's Glass Bead Game is a parable of the microcosm. All thought and skill, all philosophy, art, and science, are reduced into one complicated and intricate Game. This cosmic Game becomes a vortex into which young boys of unusual intellectual prowess are drawn, in some mysterious way, to a rigorous training that will bring them to twirl their lives away in a spiral of ever-decreasing size and ever-increasing intensity.

When he began to write *The Glass Bead Game*, Hesse had not even thought of the central character Joseph Knecht,[11] who eventually bears the title Magister Ludi[12] (which is also the title of one version of his book). His major purpose was to design a sort of spiritual kingdom, a utopia where peace and harmony might reign under the aegis of the intellect and the aesthetic sensibilities. But Hesse realized that music and art, mathematics and history, do not exist apart from those who make them, and do not survive apart from those who cultivate them. This point is frequently overlooked by contemporary critics of literature and writers of scientific papers, which is why their works are so often dull and lifeless. Hesse wrote in a letter, "In the beginning I was concerned, above all—almost exclusively—with making Castalia visible" (Ziolkowski 1965, p. 294).

Castalia is viewed from the position of a fictitious narrator, in reality Hesse himself. He is actually doing what he charges the young, developing students at Castalia to do. They are to immerse themselves in the life history and the cultural surroundings of some particular individual who lived and worked in another time and place, to the degree that they can actually think that person's thoughts and feel his emotions. The task, then, will be to write an "autobiography" or "memoir" of this fictitious character as he would see himself, and through his eyes to delineate the part of the world in which he had his existence. This is precisely what Hesse has done through the fictitious narrator with the "person" of Joseph Knecht. In the beginning, Hesse, and therefore Knecht, is convinced of the value of the spiritual realm represented by Castalia.

Life in Castalia is very different from that simple, more primitive, more dangerous, more disorderly, and less sheltered existence of most

---

11. *Knecht* means servant, aide-de-camp, or foot soldier.
12. *Magister Ludi* means, literally, schoolmaster; but *Ludi* can also be understood as play, game, pastime, or to imitate, ridicule, deceive, fool around, or make love.

human beings. This primitive world is a part of everyone, but in coming to Castalia the young students have left that world behind. Each person can feel it, has some curiosity about it, some nostalgia for it, some sympathy with it. It is, after all, the visible world. Hesse sets out as the "true task" to be fair to it, to keep a place for it in one's own heart, yet not to relapse into it. The other world, the World of the Mind, exists alongside it and is superior to it. It is highly cultivated, more orderly, and aspiring to it requires ongoing supervision and study. Students are charged to serve the brilliant hierarchy, but without doing an injustice to the lesser world from which they have come, and also without eyeing that world with desire or nostalgia. The purpose of the small monastic world of Castalia is to serve the larger but lesser world, to provide it with teachers and books, and to guard the purity of its intellectual functions and its morality. Castalia exists as a training ground and refuge for that small group of men who have consecrated their lives to the Mind and to Truth.

Knecht's early existence in this lofty kingdom goes through three stages. At first, Knecht is convinced of the utopian character of Castalia. The study and severe discipline of the monastic life bring him a sense of destiny, of mission. Through unusual devotion and not inconsiderable talent, he rises quite rapidly through the levels of training to full membership in the Order, and from there upward through the hierarchy. Eventually, his inner discipline and his subtle competence in dealing with his colleagues win for him the respect and honor that result in his being chosen to fill the highest position in all of Castalia, that of Magister Ludi, Master of the Game.

Within a short period after Joseph Knecht's investiture, the second stage begins. He takes up his task as Magister Ludi and in due course has so thoroughly converted himself into the wearer of robes and the keeper of an office that such personal matters as friendship vanish into the realm of the impossible. No longer does he see his former friends as personalities, but as members of an elite, as students or candidates, as soldiers in the regiment he has to train. When a member is guilty of some mild discourtesy, Knecht reproves him wordlessly, by a gesture of the finger, and later sends a meditation master to calm the guilty member's troubled soul. And so, bit by bit, Magister Ludi attains his goal, which Hesse describes as "a great labor to subdue this elite, to drill them until they were weary, to tame the ambitious, win over the undecided, impress the arrogant." But now the work is done; the candidates at the Game Village have acknowledged him their master and submitted to him. Suddenly everything goes smoothly, "as if only a drop of oil had been needed." How sharply Hesse's metaphor lets us know that the Kingdom of the Spirit has turned into a machine.

The third stage occurs when Knecht feels a vague dissatisfaction set in, despite the honor accorded him, despite the serenity with which he lives through his days, and despite the courtesy and efficiency with which he carries out his duties. He becomes aware of this when one of his friends, Designori, who had been with him as a student from the beginning but had left the Order, returns for a visit. Designori is explaining to Joseph the reasons for his defection from Castalia: "The protection that Castalia had given me proved dangerous and dubious, for I did not want to live as a hermit, cultivating my soul and preserving a calm, meditative state of mind. I wanted to conquer the world, you see, to understand it, to force it to understand me. In my own person I wanted to bring Castalia and the world together, to reconcile them."

The Master of the Glass Bead Game responds to his friend in a way that seems as much to shore up his own uncertain faith as to convince his former colleague who stands before him of the value of the serenity of the stars and of the mind, and of the Castalian kind of serenity as well. He says to Designori, "You are averse to serenity, presumably because you have had to walk the ways of sadness. Now all brightness and good cheer, especially our Castalian kind, strikes you as shallow and childish, and cowardly to boot, a flight from the terrors and abysses of reality into a clear, well-ordered world of mere forms and formulas. Even if the majority of us were, in fact, of this sort—it would not lesson the value and splendor of genuine serenity."

The two points of view represented by the rules of the Order and Designori's challenge come into conflict in Joseph Knecht. At last they destroy that very serenity that is Castalia's whole raison d'être. Knecht finally makes the fateful decision to resign his exalted post and return to the world as a humble schoolteacher. He says in his letter of resignation that he considers the Glass Bead Game itself to be in a state of crisis. He uses the parable of a man sitting in his attic room, engaged in a work of scholarship. Suddenly he becomes aware that fire has broken out in the house below. He does not stop to reason whether it is his function to see to it or whether he had better continue his tabulations. He runs downstairs and attempts to save the house. Knecht sees himself as sitting in the top story of the Castalian edifice occupied with the Glass Bead Game, while his nose tells him that something down below is burning and the whole structure is imperiled.

In leaving and reentering the world, Joseph Knecht reflects that before entering Castalia he loved this world that is forever growing and seeking nourishment. But in Castalia there is nothing to nourish it. Castalia—which aspires to be a Kingdom of the Spirit—is outside of the world, a small perfect world in itself, but it is no longer changing or growing. Knecht serves Castalia best when he leaves it by warning it to forsake its elitist stance and its self-indulgent autonomy, which must ultimately lead to its destruction.

My summer in "Castalia" was my first visit to Switzerland of any length beyond a few days since I had left after completing my analytic training at the Jung Institute in Zurich eight years earlier. I could not help thinking how much my nearly four years of living in Zurich had resembled Joseph Knecht's time in the fictional land of Castalia. Going to Zurich had required me to give up a home, sell all the furniture, and put every material asset into the adventure across the sea, without having any knowledge of the final destination. There in a land of strangers it had become necessary for me to learn a new language, new customs, and above all, to learn to look for the truth both within myself and all about me, insofar as this was possible. It had meant shucking off all the accoutrements of background and social position, and becoming just like everyone else, a lowly student treading ever so tentatively on the ground that was possessed by others so much wiser and more accomplished than myself.

Although individual freedom was preached, there were strict rules that had to be obeyed. The first was absolute secrecy about what went on in the analytic process. The analyst was the mentor, and she worked with what she observed and what you told her, and she never ventured outside of her consulting room to gather information that might reveal whether what you told her was or was not accurate. The second had to do with the transference. Nothing that you said in the analytic hour was to be taken at face value. The analyst could safely assume that you were not able to perceive her directly, but always through the distorting lens of your history, which you would transfer into the hour like invisible baggage. On the other hand, she could see *you* quite clearly and understand your deepest motivations. If you did not agree with her statements it was likely that the problem was in you, and unlikely that it was in her. Another rule was that you could not be friends with your analyst. Another rule was precise punctuality. Another was that you did not discuss your dreams with anyone except your analyst. Another was that you did not engage in any other kind of therapy outside of the analysis without express permission from your analyst. Also, you were not to ask to enter the training program, or even to be motivated to become an analyst. You were supposed to await some message, some call, from the unconscious. If it came, you were practically assured of being considered for entrance into the training program.

At the time, I did not understand the reasons for all these restrictions, but I was not encouraged to ask questions. I understand these regulations better now. But in those days, like Joseph Knecht, I was to learn all I could about the mysterious game, hoping to acquire the skills to become a player. I was virtually cut off from the rest of the world, living in a place where the inner life was regarded as important and the outer life as a necessary structure with which one should make peace but not involve oneself too much. Training, for me, became a possibility only after becoming deeply involved in the Institute and in my personal analysis.

I noticed that some people who came to Zurich to attend the Institute stayed around for many years, so that training became a way of life in and of itself. I became restive after about three years. I was temperamentally more like Designori than I was like Magister Ludi. I became bored with continually gazing at my own reflection and an eagerness came upon me to be back in the world where I could deal with earthy people and their practical problems. Moreover, I found myself wanting to participate in the changes that were going on in the United States in the turbulent sixties. During the last months in Zurich I began to wonder if it were really necessary to retreat from the world for lengthy periods to find the domicile of spirit. I still cannot give an unequivocal answer to this question. It seems to me that retreat is necessary, but I am not sure that the retreat needs always to be so disconnected from the everyday world of nuts and bolts. Surely, for some people it may be necessary at some times, but I do not feel that one has to make a rule about it.

The Separate Kingdoms

Today I see all around me a greatly renewed interest in the spiritual aspects of life. The search for the Kingdom is a preoccupation, especially with people who have managed to be sufficiently successful in the visible world so that they do not need to concern themselves with matters of survival, providing for their families, or establishing a sense of their own worth. I have been wondering if this search could be, in part, a reaction against the excessive materialism of our times. Despite the phenomenal rise in wealth and fame on the part of some privileged members of the younger generation, many more people suffer painfully as a result of the maldistribution of the world's goods. I ask myself, is the hope for the realization of the Kingdom of the Spirit a defense against millenarian forecasts of the disintegration of our civilization or the destruction of our planet?

A dream brought into analysis by Laurel suggests an unconscious fear of impending doom, and a glimmer of hope. She dreamed that she had awakened one morning to discover that most of humankind had disappeared. A woman informed her that she knew who was responsible—Wug the trickster. He evidently had hidden most of humankind, and the feeling was that he would redeem them eventually. In the meantime, Laurel moved to a basement of some kind. She noticed that there were lots of people around—evidently Wug only fooled people. The woman and Laurel went off on their bicycles in an effort to find a material, perhaps silver, that would somehow help the "stolen" people to return.

Talking about the dream, Laurel said that as she moved to different levels of awareness, she "lost" most other people. She saw them as being "asleep," going about their daily activities as if in a dream, never knowing why they were brought to do what they did, not knowing how their actions affected others nor to what degree they were acting out a script not of their own making. Wug was the trickster who tricked the sleepy ones into believing they could have what they wanted—be it a new car or a new house or a cream for removing wrinkles—and that it would make them happy. So they wandered after Wug and his promises, while the dreamer sought a way to help the "stolen" people return.

Do the many attempts on the part of people within traditional mainstream churches, to find a Kingdom of the Spirit and a spiritual teacher who will lead them there, arise out of a feeling of disillusion? Are these people turning away from institutions that insist on being maintained as they are, in their solid edifices?

Another of my analysands told me, "My minister laughed at my mysticism. He said that the Holy Spirit works through community and not through the individual." I asked her why she thought he said that. She reflected on this for a moment, and then answered, "Maybe he was afraid that we would come to believe something that was at odds with the Church. I asked him once, 'Don't *you* have any *personal* experience with God?' He said, 'I keep my personal experiences to myself. My congregation isn't interested in them. I replied, 'Not even in your sermons do you speak of your own personal experience of God.' He ended the discussion with, 'My sermons have nothing to do with my own personal beliefs or my relationship with God. That's nobody's business.' I sat in church, looking at the colored light streaming through the rose window in the rear, touching the altar with beauty. I took the Holy Eucharist. A voice said to me, 'You don't have to do it alone.' "

I believe that the urge to search for the Kingdom of the Spirit arises from within the individual. This is not to exclude any of the other possible motivating factors I have mentioned, for this inner direction can occur alone or in the presence of any or all of them. Given that the natural, elemental human drive toward matters of the spirit, toward the *Mysterium Tremendum,* is inborn in all of us but veiled over as we become "civilized" by the continuing necessity to adapt to the "real world," it is not surprising that the repressed yearning for the divine emerges into consciousness at times. The forgotten Self is layered over by veil after veil of conditioning. Then come the winds of change or the hurricanes of traumatic experiences, and the veils are either temporarily parted or torn away and we see beyond the narrow limits of our conscious minds. Perfect redemption, according to Valentinus, is the cognition itself of the ineffable Greatness. But the cognition, like redemption, tends to be elusive. Again the veils return, and what remains is a vague longing for something precious, the special substance that could possibly make us whole. And so we are open to the hope and the promise that someone can show us the way, the certain path to the Kingdom.

Spiritual Teachers—Spurious and Genuine

Plenty of people are certainly ready and willing these days to assist the seeker. Once you get on the "New Age" mailing list, scarcely a day passes without your mailbox being stuffed with advertisements of workshops, seminars, meditation weekends, lectures, tours, books, records, audio tapes, videotapes, and special pants to wear while doing yoga. I do not intend to comment here on the relative merits of any of the royal roads to spiritual fulfillment. They have always existed, as have teachers who offer guidance on the way. The spiritual path is not for everyone, nor is it an easy path, despite all claims to the contrary. Nor is it a superhighway upon which masses of people can travel. Not that it is reserved for an elite, for people of particular gifts, as Castalia was. But it is somewhere hidden, and the people who truly may be able to help us find it are not wearing placards announcing their availability. The Taoists who lived around the time of Jesus maintained their sacred traditions in their monasteries in China and Tibet, far from Western influence, yet they perceived also the distinction between genuine and spurious spiritual teachers; as noted in the *Tao Te Ching:*

> The ancient masters were subtle, mysterious, profound, responsive.
> The depth of their knowledge is unfathomable.
> Because it is unfathomable,
> All we can do is describe their appearance.
> Watchful, like men crossing a winter stream.
> Alert, like men aware of danger.
> Courteous, like visiting guests.
> Yielding, like ice about to melt.
> Simple, like uncarved blocks of wood.
> Hollow, like caves.
> Opaque, like muddy pools.
>
> (Lao Tsu, 1972 translation, chap. 15)

When we seek to find out what spiritual teachers in esoteric traditions have been like over the centuries, we discover a theme common to many parts of the world. It has to do with the wise old man or woman who does not go about proclaiming wisdom but who, on the contrary, is engaged in some ordinary profession behind which an extraordinary wisdom is hidden. You may have heard of Gurdjieff, who sometimes appeared as an odd sort of con man selling painted canaries, or of a kosher butcher in a Jewish neighborhood who was also a Zaddik, or of an elderly nun who picked dying people off the streets of Calcutta and restored their spirits. You would not recognize an exceedingly wise spiritual teacher behind the person's relatively ordinary appearance—surely not before you looked directly into the depths of the eyes and caught a glimpse of the soul's fire behind them.

The real mission of the spiritual teacher is to transmit esoteric knowledge. By esoteric I do not mean necessarily secret, but rather, subtle, obscure, ambiguous, cryptic, or veiled. Nor is esoteric knowledge factual knowledge. It is inner knowledge intuitively arrived at, what we have referred to earlier as gnosis. For gnosis is not limited to that group of people who called themselves Gnostics in the two or three centuries after the time of the historical Jesus. In its broader sense, gnosis has spoken to all those who have depended for their spiritual sustenance upon a particular and uncommon way of knowing. Still today, the inner path is chosen by people—there is no way of knowing how few or how many—or perhaps it is the path that chooses *them*.

The teacher can only point out the path and perhaps accompany the initiate a little way. The seeker must take the first step and every step thereafter until the end. The way is often solitary, yet it is not too difficult to find. Notwithstanding, many individuals look for mentors or gurus or psychics or mediums or channels to tell them what they "need to know." Often they find people who claim to speak the absolute truth and who demand loyalty and strict adherence to their doctrine from those who sit at their feet. When anyone promises peace, bliss, freedom from pain or stress, love, improved health, increased earnings, nirvana—be careful. No one can transmit any of this to another person, no matter what the claim. What we need to know, we already know on some level; but we have to rediscover it. We, ourselves. No one can do it for us.

True spiritual teachers do not hide this reality, even though it may be difficult to accept. They themselves are open to the possibilities inherent in the unimaginable, the enigmatic, the roiling, boiling fullness of the universe. They serve as conduits for the invisible to all those with ears to hear and eyes to see and a willing heart. Swami Muktananda referred to the capacity to function in this way as the "guru principle." He said that the guru is absolutely necessary, since the guru principle is the natural force that enables us to know the Self. He told his disciples: "A person can say, 'Who needs gravity? I'll stay on this earth through my own efforts,' but he has no power of his own to cling to earth. He is dependent on the natural force of gravity. In the same way, it is through the natural force of the guru that we break free from the limiting *samskaras* and perceive the Truth of our nature. This is the right understanding of the guru. If we think of the guru as a person, as an individual human being, then we have the wrong understanding of the guru. Of course when that cosmic principle works through a human being to uplift and free others, then we have a physical guru. Still, the guru is the Shakti [the empowering energy], and not the person. If a person understands this, he can relate to a physical guru in the right way."

The Spiritual Teacher Within

Transmitting the capacity to know in this way is not simply a matter of educating the mind. The sacred mysteries are everywhere accessible, but not everyone will discover them. It is necessary to be attentive, to search within oneself for that which is present. Not everyone is willing to enter into the search, for it may reveal much that is uncomfortable, even painful. Even if the teacher is willing to teach, the people are not always willing to learn. One of the books discovered in the cave at Nag Hammadi yielded an extensive collection of *logia*, sayings of Jesus. They belong to the Gospel of Thomas, a document containing Jesus' response to his disciples when they asked him how they might attain the Kingdom of the Spirit.

The book begins with the statement, "These are the secret words which the Living Jesus spoke and *Didymos* Judas Thomas wrote."[13] The Living Jesus is not to be understood as the historical Jesus who was born, lived, and died on the cross, but as the Eternal Jesus who is alive now in spirit, and who was and is beyond birth and death. When this Jesus speaks, his concern is not with the visible world, but with the necessity for looking beyond it, beyond the boundaries of time. The writer of the Gospel of Thomas relates that the disciples said, "Lord, there are many around the cistern, but nobody in the cistern." Jesus said, "Many are standing at the door, but it is the solitary who will enter the bridal chamber" (Robinson 1988, p. 134). And again, "He who is near to me is near the fire, and he who is far from me is far from the kingdom" (p. 135). One cannot expect to learn before one is prepared to know. Yet it is necessary to continue attending to the inner discipline or one will not be prepared when it is time to learn. This idea is expressed in words attributed to Jesus: "Seek and you will find. Yet what you asked me about in former times and which I did not tell you then, now I desire to tell, but you do not inquire after it" (p. 136).

What then, are we to seek? Are we to look for the Kingdom of the Spirit in some pristine place unsullied by the commerce of the everyday world, as the hucksters who feed off the popularity of the "New Age" would have us believe? Again the Gospel of Thomas offers guidance. "Jesus said: If those who lead you say to you: 'See, the Kingdom is in the sky,' then the birds of the sky will precede you. If they say to you, 'It is in the sea,' then the fish will precede you. *Rather, the Kingdom is inside of you and it is outside of you. When you come to know yourselves* [emphasis mine] then you will become known. But if you do not know yourselves, you dwell in poverty and it is you who are that poverty" (p. 126).

---

13. *Didymos* means double or twin. It suggests that the scribe, Thomas, is aware that he has also an eternal aspect, like that of Jesus. This may be meant to convey the proposition that this likeness, this eternal twinship, is a property of those who have gnosis—that is, of those who understand the meaning of the Eternal Jesus.

If failing to know ourselves is equivalent to living in spiritual poverty, then there are many of us whose lives are impoverished, despite any material goods we may possess. Perhaps it is some vague awareness of this that is leading so many people in our time to seek nourishment for the soul or psyche. There is a place where the spiritual and the psychological meet, and there are some spiritual teachers and some psychologists who are attempting to meet on that bridge. Their aim is to restore the psyche to psychology; for psychology is, or is intended to be, the study of the psyche—and *psyche* comes from the Greek word that means soul.

9

Psychology Encounters the New Paradigm

> The really decisive moments in psychotherapy, as every patient or therapist who has ever experienced them knows, are unpredictable, unique, unforgettable, always unrepeatable and often indescribable.
>
> LAING, *The Politics of Experience*

Psychology Reflects the New Paradigm

In the past, psychology paid lip service to the world view that had prevailed so long in classical physics and the other hard sciences. If the universe were a giant machine obeying fixed laws, and deterministic in the sense that if we had sufficient data we could predict the outcome of events, then it should follow that some of these same laws ought to be applicable to the life sciences. For many purposes, it is true that objects and events can be broken down into their simplest components and that these can be analyzed, manipulated, and controlled. When it comes to the life sciences, however, the clockwork metaphor ceases to be useful, because life is extremely complex and is subject to the continuing interplay of random variables. One may know a great deal about the psychology of cats, for instance, but it is hardly possible to predict which way the cat on the fence will jump. Because organisms have the capacity to adapt to unforeseen circumstances in unpredictable ways, much that happens in the life sciences is better described in terms of randomness and chaotic systems.

If life itself, even in its simpler forms, cannot be adequately treated through a mechanistic world view, how much less able can such a view be to inform so tenuous a concept as mind or psyche, or even the vagaries of human behavior? Nevertheless, in the short history of psychology—as a science distinct from such disciplines as neurology or philosophy or theology—the metaphors of the old paradigm have been and continue to be used in an effort to penetrate its ever-elusive subject matter, the psyche. Three of the most common approaches being used in psychology today—the objectivist approach, the positivist approach, and the reductionist approach—are remnants of the old paradigms in the physical sciences.

The Objectivist Approach:
Experimental Psychology

The objectivist approach in psychology has been most evident in experimental psychology, where behavior is brought into the laboratory and observed and manipulated. The earliest examples of this approach were experiments designed to train rats to run mazes and perform other simple actions by rewarding the desired behavior with a pellet of food and/or punishing the undesirable behavior by administering an electric shock. With human beings, the experimenter might arrange to test two groups, a control group in which no treatment has been given and an experimental group that matches the control group as closely as possible and that has been treated in a special way, verbally or otherwise. Then the difference between the two groups is precisely measured, under the assumption that the treatment will account for the difference between the groups. Objectivist psychology rejects introspective data and introspective interpretations of data.

Experimenters have believed they can be neutral, remaining outside of and unrelated to the effects of the experiment. They have chosen to overlook, or at least to try to minimize, the ever-present factor of human interaction. Such "objectivity" fails to allow sufficiently for the influence of the experimenter's presence on the outcome of the experiment; or, when the role of the experimenter is considered, the illusion is maintained that this role can be accounted for precisely. One of the criteria as to whether a psychological experiment is "reliable" is whether it can be repeated and the same results obtained in repeated tests as in the first administration of the stimuli or the test. This is extremely difficult to establish in working with living creatures, and especially with human beings, because organisms are constantly growing and changing over time, so that exact replication of an experiment in the life sciences is well-nigh impossible. Consequently, when "scientific objectivity" is applied to human beings, it tends to fall short of its aims. Psyche and behavior are far too complex, and there are far too many variables that cannot be kept under the control of the experimenter.

The Positivist Approach: Social Psychology

Positivism has also been borrowed from classical physics. It postulates, in essence, that what is physically observable is what is real. This poses a problem, since the psyche is not directly observable. The effects or manifestations of the psyche as they occur in behavior can be treated, but just what property of the human organism causes this behavior to occur, and what factors in the psyche generate one sort of behavior and not another, remain mysterious. It is true that behavior can be observed and even measured when it is broken down into discrete parts, but the very process of breaking it down necessitates leaving out such factors as motivation, emotions, values, and goals—those very aspects of behavior that are crucial to its form and character but are not directly observable.

Much of contemporary social psychology exemplifies the positivist approach. This approach tends to find the causation of psychological problems primarily in the environment. Concerned as it is with readily observable facts, the positivist approach collects detailed data on the external influences that cause certain types of behavior, with the goal in mind of modifying the environment and thereby affecting the behavior of the persons who live in it. Little attention is paid to the genetic potentials of individuals or to the particular characterological qualities that determine how an individual may react to situations.

The Reductionist Approach: Psychoanalysis

Reductionism is the general point of view that holds that complex phenomena can be understood and explained by analyzing them into ever-simpler, and ultimately into elementary, components. Psychoanalysis, an example of a reductionistic approach, differs from social psychology in that the psychoanalytic approach seeks the cause of the disturbance within the individual, while social psychology finds the sources of human problems mostly outside of the individual (in the visible world). Positivism, which holds that the analyzed parts are real and that the whole can be completely explained as made up *only* of the analyzed parts, has had a profound effect on the psychoanalytic method. Its assumption leads the psychoanalyst to delve more and more deeply into the mysteries of the psyche in order to uncover and analyze what was formerly unknown or not understood. An objective of the psychoanalytic method is to bring as much unconscious material as posssible into consciousness. Like the classical attitude of the physical sciences, psychoanalysis holds that every effect can be attributed to a prior cause. In psychoanalysis, these causes are often extremely subtle and difficult to discern.

The psychoanalytic approach allows for the many imponderables that must be considered when dealing with the intricacies of human nature. The possibility of mysterious unknown or unconscious elements is admitted in this approach, but these are considered likely to be accessible to treatment. The following assumptions are made: There is a problem. Something is wrong with the individual. The problem is that the organism is not working properly. Something must be causing this problem. So if one works back from the problem itself through the causal chain, one will, theoretically at least, arrive at the initial cause. This will require working through the blocks or defenses between effect and cause. Once the cause or source of the disturbed functioning is known and is brought into ego-consciousness, it should be possible to repair the damage by going over the material from every aspect until it is integrated into awareness. So by reducing the pattern of disturbing behavior or ideation to its secondary and then to its primary causal elements, including all the emotions associated with the precipitating events and their sequelae, the repair of the psyche should be achieved. It is clear enough why this process takes so long, but it is surely unclear whether the more successful cures are due to the basic underlying theories of psychoanalysis or to the relational connection, support, and attention the therapist supplies to the client.

The Developmental Approach: Supplanting Theory with Direct Observation

It has been as difficult for psychotherapists trained under the old paradigm to consider a totally different approach to the psyche as it has been for classical physicists to accept a radically different view of the planet and its place in the universe from that in which they were schooled. The resistance is especially strong in psychology because the relevance of the new physics has not yet been generally felt in this field. We saw how difficult it was for the new physicists to relinquish attitudes that had been fostered and trained over a period of many years and that had become a part of their identity as well as the source of their livelihood. It has been no easier in psychology. In the transitional period around the middle of the twentieth century, when the old paradigm was beginning to show cracks and the new paradigm was still amorphous and tentative, attempts were made to reconcile the then-current psychological theories with a systems view that sees the human organism as a whole that cannot be reduced, either to its component parts or to clearly defined prior causes.

Into this breach came the developmental approach to the psyche and to human behavior. To Piaget, the great Swiss psychologist, belongs the credit of being one of the first psychologists to observe the behavior of children directly and with great care, instead of inferring what had happened in infancy and childhood on the basis of selective memory traces in the adult, or on the basis of anterior theories. Piaget (1951) mapped early childhood development and established norms of conceptualization and behavior in children of various ages. His studies were the first of many subsequent efforts to show that certain kinds of behaviors and the attitudes leading to them could be expected to appear typically at certain ages or stages of development. Heir to this approach were the Gesell studies at Yale University, and the work of Erik Erikson, Jane Loevinger, Lawrence Kohlberg, Daniel Levinson, and others. The studies themselves became more sophisticated as time went on, passing from observation of relatively simple behavior patterns to Kohlberg's (1964) consideration of complex stages of moral development.

Loevinger (1966) follows the individual through a succession of stages from infancy's "pre-social symbiotic stage," through adulthood, toward the highest or "integrated" stage, which, she clearly states, is not attained by everyone. Describing this last stage, Loevinger says, "the person proceeds beyond coping with conflict to reconciliation of conflicting demands, and, where necessary, to renunciation of the unattainable, beyond toleration to the cherishing of individual differences, beyond role differentiation to the achievement of a sense of integrated identity" (p. 20).

A Time of Transition

Loevinger's work was the product of the developmental research that had been done during the two or three decades leading up to the precedent-shattering sixties. If ever a culture has run into turbulence that has produced chaos, at least in some sectors, ours surely experienced it with "the dawning of the Age of Aquarius." When I returned to the United States from Zurich in 1964 after completing my analytic training at the Jung Institute, I found a very different country from the one I had left four years earlier. It was the time of the hippies and flower children, of idealism and pacifism, of breaking out of the constraints and disciplines of the nuclear family, and of experimentation with new sexual freedoms and with mind-expanding drugs. I saw a generation of people in their late teens and twenties who had discovered that not all learning comes under the rubric of formal education. There was communal sharing, in some ways a retreat from individualism with its power games, a disdain for authority, an openness to seeing the world in new ways, and an appetite for gurus who would lead the young people on the path of the heart.

Today, more than two decades later, these people have reached an age of discretion. Most of them have exchanged their beads for neckties and silk scarves and have taken their places in society as teachers, scientists, entrepreneurs, businessmen and women, and yes, even psychologists. The flower children have grown up to attain positions of importance and power in the world. Furthermore, many of them have grown beyond, one might even claim outgrown, Loevinger's "integrated stage." They have gone beyond reconciling conflicting demands and beyond renouncing the "unattainable." They have even recognized that to cherish individual differences overmuch can lead to an exaggerated sense of self-importance. The attitudes so prevalent in the sixties were indeed followed in the seventies, by what Christopher Lasch so aptly called "the culture of narcissism."

Today more and more people are beginning to loosen their hold on their sense of integrated individual identity and to replace it with a sense of participation in an organic planetary society. Perhaps this is a reaction to the culture in which the domination of the ego, the "I," the individual in charge of his or her own destiny, has been central. These people, now mostly in their forties, may appear to some to be following in their parents' footsteps, but they are not. For one thing, a sizeable proportion of the positions they hold in the workaday world were not even in existence twenty years ago. For another, we have changed from an industrial society to an information society. We equate information with computers, but it is important to remember that computers don't generate new information, they just organize the available information and manipulate it. They also enable people to retrieve information and use it more rapidly and more effectively than could have been imagined a couple of decades ago. Where this information has its strongest impact is on the human psyche. We *know* more of our world than ever before, and we know from our own experience that it is a living system.

The Beginnings of a New Psychology

It is clear that the paradigm of the old physics is no longer applicable to the exploration of the human psyche, if indeed it ever was. The question naturally arises, when we move beyond the objectivistic approach, as to whether we should abandon our standards of testing and replication and controlled experiments in the field of psychology. The answer surely is no. These belong to the ego-world, the visible world, where they provide useful and needed information. As we move into a wider concept of the psyche and its potential, we need also to be willing to subject experience to scrutiny, even to measurement, when there is good and sufficient reason for doing so. No more than we can abandon the classical physics that explains how things work in everyday life, can we abandon in psychology the necessity to deal with personal problems on a personal level. But we do not need to stop at the personal level.

The new psychologists will take a different view from the positivistic approach to the psyche and the world. They will not find it necessary to abandon the viewpoint that what is real is physical. We do not know, exactly, what reality is. The physical world is surely one reality, if we can know any dimension of reality at all. The physical world is, in fact, identical with the visible world. This is where we live most of the time. We depend upon our sensory apparatus to perceive it, and we would not get very far in this world if we did not trust our senses. Yet we need to be fully aware of how limited our senses are. If we do not hear as well as our dog or see at night as well as our cat, how little do we really know of the world that lies beyond the reach of our senses?

The reductionist approach, as it found its way into psychoanalysis, has also seen some modification. While Jung was a member of the psychoanalytic circle in Vienna, he had certain reservations about Freud's methods—not so much as to their correctness in principle, as to their limitations in practice. Nevertheless, he resisted the temptation to criticize Freud's pioneering work until he had used the psychoanalytic method in his own therapeutic practice and tested Freud's assumptions and techniques thoroughly. Jung carefully noted and studied the results of this work, and came to the conclusion, stated in *Freud and Psychoanalysis* (1906–30/1961) that the efforts made in psychoanalysis to bring the contents of the unconscious to consciousness were workable only to the degree that the unconscious was construed primarily as the repository of personal material that had been repressed. Jung called this finite portion of the unconscious the "personal unconscious." He saw it as a liminal area between consciousness and the deep unfathomable collective unconscious. Freud's "unconscious" might approach the threshold between the visible world and the invisible world, but in itself it could never provide entry into the mysteries beyond. This is because the principal focus of psychoanalysis, and of all the theoretical and practical approaches that have grown out of psychoanalysis, has been the so-called ego. These psychologies see the ego—understood as the repository and organizer of consciousness and the sense of personal identity and continuity—as needing to be supported, repaired, strengthened, healed, expanded, freed from neurotic constraints, and, often, given a new facade. In other words, the objective of ego-psychology is to enable the individual to function better and with more joy in the visible world.

Jung saw that this objective, worthy as it was, did not deal with the deeper levels of the unconscious. He acknowledged that these deeper levels did not necessarily have to come into play in every psychotherapeutic encounter. But he felt strongly that if one were to be able to view the psyche in its larger context, it was incumbent upon the psychotherapist to gain some familiarity with the ground upon which the psyche rests, namely the collective unconscious. Having plumbed these depths through one's own personal search, one would then be ready to lead others upon the path as far or as deep as they were prepared to go.

Now that the new physicists have expanded their purview beyond its earlier frame, some of their contemporaries in the field of psychology are seeing that for them, too, a new way of looking at the psyche and human behavior is not only necessary but long overdue. The new approaches begin with a different set of assumptions. The first is that we may not exclude from consideration any classes of experience or phenomena that have been observed in human societies over centuries, simply because they do not fit into preconceived notions of the province of a particular field of inquiry. Just a few of the phenomena that have been included in the new psychology are the study of dreams and their meanings, behavior and ideation in altered states of consciousness, initiatory experiences, the effect on the psyche of various rituals and spiritual practices, near-death experiences, and preparation for dying.

The new psychologists bring to the field some approaches that add vitally important dimensions not previously dealt with by most traditional clinical and academic psychologists. The humanistic psychology movement has contributed to this new openness, led by such individuals as Carl Rogers, Abraham Maslow, and Virginia Satir. Their emphasis has been largely on developing the human potential, self-actualization, and the management of human relationships. Other forms of psychology and psychotherapy have been taking into account the whole person in his or her life situation. These include family therapies, body therapies, psychodrama, Gestalt therapy, and many others.

The earlier focus on objectivity in psychology is being shifted toward mutuality, and the former subject-object dichotomy is being dissolved. The new psychologists tend to be participant-observers, with stress on the "participant" aspect. The "observer at a distance" is being replaced by the observer close at hand. The new psychotherapists do not take the position when working with clients that they have the wisdom and training to understand the client better than the client does. Working *with* an individual means a partnership in which each one brings something of value to the encounter. The psychotherapist has a broad understanding of how people relate to their inner process, to other people, and to their own vision of the world. The client possesses a profound knowledge concerning his or her own history and experience. Since each is an expert on one part of the process, they complement each other by bringing new and challenging information and insights that the other does not have.

In addition, these psychotherapists will usually have explored their own unconscious material in the course of their training, and so they will know—better than most people—who they themselves are. This kind of psychological training by experiencing the process oneself is absolutely necessary so that the issues that belong to the psychotherapist do not get confused with those of the client. It is this "inner training," more than anything else, that enables the psychotherapist to "see through" the presenting problems and into the real issues that the "problems" conceal.

A Transpersonal Perspective

When we speak of "unfathomable depths," we quickly recognize that there is no question of assimilating the contents of the unconscious (personal *and* collective) into the ego, any more than the infant can take itself back into the mother's womb. This is far more obvious today than it was twenty or thirty years ago, because the time between has been marked by a burgeoning interest on the part of a broad segment of the population of the United States and Europe in mythology, anthropology, archeology, and comparative religions. We are deeply interested in what people believed to be truth in ages past, in far-flung places of the world, in societies that no longer exist, and in societies whose values and practices are diverse and dissimilar to our own. These places, these peoples, these societies, these worlds are not part of our everyday experience, yet we have gained a certain familiarity with them.

We even project ourselves with delight and amazement into worlds of the future as created by the imagination of filmmakers and science fiction writers. This material intrigues and excites us for two reasons. The first is that it is so utterly alien to our own experience that we stand in awe before the mysteries it conveys. The second is that it is so utterly familiar. People out of the ancient past, people of faraway lands, and people who have been created wholly out of the imagination all experience the same fears and dreads, curiosities and affections, that we do. On my bookshelf is Joseph Campbell's *The Hero with a Thousand Faces*, the first printing, dated 1949. I read it when it first came out. It was required reading at the Jung Institute in Zurich. But it took forty years, until Joseph Campbell appeared on nationwide television with Bill Moyers, for the book to rise to the top of the best-seller lists.

Something similar has happened with respect to the psychology of Jung, as well, during those years. When I returned from Zurich in 1964, Jung's work was not taken seriously by the psychological community. Today there is a ready audience for seminars on subjects relating to analytical psychology (the term Jung used to differentiate his approach from psychoanalysis), and books by Jungian authors are in wide demand. The parallel concepts of the collective unconscious and the invisible world have been around for a long time, but the time was not ripe for them. Today it is.

Jung was the chief pioneer of transpersonal thought, and he remains a leading figure in the field. He first used the word *transpersonal* in connection with psychology when he spoke of the collective or "transpersonal" unconscious in 1917. The transpersonal perspective is a view of people and their relations to the larger world that is compatible with the new world view that sees the universe and everything in it, including human beings, as a series of interconnected, interacting, and mutually influencing systems. Transpersonal psychology approaches human beings in the context of the wider world, including the invisible world of spirit. It insists on recognition by individuals of the breadth of the context in which they live. But transpersonal psychology does not exclude the practical world of everyday living, for it is through our daily lives that we make our imprint upon the wider world; while we, in turn, are in the process of being transformed by the practical world every moment of every day. In the transpersonal view, the only way the spiritual world can manifest is through ordinary people in the visible world.

Jung's Contribution to Transpersonal Psychology

Jung, as pioneer in transpersonal thought, helped people to recognize the many dangers that beset the path toward awareness of oneself and the Other. These dangers are so universal and so pervasive that Jung accords them an archetypal dimension. First comes the *persona*, the mask we adopt to ease our way into the external world, in order to be "appropriate" to whatever is our task or our role. We may even believe we are that person, that image we have tried so hard to present. More often than not, the persona conceals the true person. This may happen out of fear that the true person may not be acceptable to others or in a particular situation, or simply because the individual has not recognized who he or she really is. An important task in the individuation process is seeing through the personae, our own and those of others.

Because the mask, or persona, is a kind of unconscious theater, we can learn something about this from Japanese Noh theater, as Sirkku Hiltunen (1988) explains: "The powerful metamorphosis caused by putting on a mask, then slowing down and stylizing the movement in pantomime to improvise expressions appropriate to the particular mask, created a state of mind which, for the first time, made me understand why some tribal societies give magical attributes to masked rituals. I could see a visible transformation take place in the person who put on the mask. He or she not only assumed another character through movement and pace, but also seemed to become one with the mask in the process" (p. 71).

The formation of the persona, the image we present to the world for the sake of creating a certain impression, gives rise to the archetype of the *shadow*. The shadow comprises those aspects of ourselves that are obscured by our desire to present ourselves in a way that is acceptable to ourselves and to others. These darker aspects are inadmissible to consciousness—at least to our own consciousness, while they may be perfectly apparent to others. It is just those shadow qualities that we do not accept in ourselves that we tend to project onto others, where we can feel free to dislike them with great intensity. Jung's concept of the shadow archetype is not limited to individuals. Groups and nations frequently project the collective shadow onto each other. The enemy nation sends spies to stealthily infiltrate our land, while *we* use intelligence procedures to legitimately protect ourselves. But if we would see the world as a unified system, with interrelated and interacting parts, we would not be so quick to assign blame to "the other," whoever that might be, and the nobler motives exclusively to ourselves. Someday we may even say in our schools, "I pledge allegiance to the flag of the United Nations, and to all the countries for which it stands, one planet, indivisible, with liberty and justice for all."

But in the meantime we have other archetypes to confront. Among them are *anima* and *animus*, which have to do with the balance of masculine and feminine principles in ourselves and in our world; the *divine child*, who comes out of the spiritual union of opposing elements both in ourselves and beyond anything personal; the *trickster*, who mediates the unexpected and thrives on chaos, both in our personal lives and in the mysteries of the physical world; and several other lesser powers of this world—until we confront at last the *Self*. Jung describes the Self as the archetype of wholeness, containing everything in consciousness and everything outside of consciousness, from the smallest elementary particle to the farthest star, from the Author of it all to his devilish antagonist, and from all the gods we know to the unknown One who stands above it and yet is present in all of it. The archetypes range about the psyche producing varying degrees of consciousness and unconsciousness, as the archons once roamed the many aeons of the gnostic universe.

Jung's Gnosticism

Some people see in transpersonal psychology a tendency to pass over the arduous work of discovering who we are and what our purpose is in this world, and also that of establishing fruitful relationships with others, and to proceed directly to attempting to transcend the limitations of the visible world. It is often seen as easier to avoid dealing with personal issues and to retreat into "the spiritual life" than it is to struggle through the practical difficulties that beset us. Jung learned the lesson well, as he pored over the ancient gnostic manuscripts in the dark days following his break with Freud and his retreat into his own confrontation with the unconscious, that the archons, or powers of the world, are very real aspects of the psyche, encountered daily. These dangers inevitably lurk on the path of the individual who seeks release from inner conflict and a sense of harmony with the whole of existence.

By stressing the depth and dynamic dimensions of psychology and the mythology and rituals that give rise to spiritual symbols, Jung opened the way to a blending of the psychological and spiritual aspects of the person in a larger context. His Gnosticism led him to view the individual as divided in two. One part is associated with the visible world and functions through day-by-day activities by means of a practical consciousness that mediates thoughts and feelings and environmental conditions. This aspect is commonly referred to as ego. The other part is the Self, that aspect of the individual that yearns toward the timeless dimensions of the universe that can transcend the everyday concerns and view life "under the aspect of eternity," as Jung was fond of saying. The fundamental gnostic questions, Who am I? Where did I come from? For what purpose am I here? What is my destiny? are basically about Self-knowledge, the sine qua non for understanding the outer world and for affirming the connection with the unknown God. Jung called this quest, this journey, "the way of individuation." Individuation is not individuality. It does not mean separating ourselves from others, but rather, it means recognizing ourselves for the unique beings that we are, and discovering our place in the pattern of the fabric of the universe.

The Roar of Awakening

Moving toward the Self is a quest for self-understanding—the revelation to ourselves of who we really are. This is not something that happens once and for all time, but is a gradual process, punctuated by sudden startling recognitions that move us toward a deeper sense of our true identity. In my own analysis it often seemed to me that I was searching for a lost self, someone or something that needed to express itself but did not know how. Then one day when I was not really searching, but reading in the totally unrelated area of East Indian mythology, I came upon what I had sought. In Heinrich Zimmer's *Philosophies of India* (1953), I found a story that set my teeth on edge. It is called "The Roar of Awakening."

A tigress, pregnant and nearly ready to deliver, walked stealthily along the edge of a high cliff foraging for food. She looked over into the grassland below and spied a flock of goats grazing in the sunshine. Hungry as she was, she hesitated, because the drop was precipitous.

Then she took the great leap, and in the fall she lost her balance. The noise sent the goats scurrying into the forest for shelter. The neck of the tigress was broken as she hit the ground, but in her death throes she managed to give birth to her cub. Then all was silent.

Little by little the curious goats reemerged from the woods and came close to the dead beast. They found the small creature, took him, and reared him as their own. The little tiger learned to subsist on grass, to adapt his voice to the gentle language of the goats. The vegetarian diet kept him very slim and imparted to his temperament a remarkable meekness. One night when this young tiger among the goats lay awake while the others were sleeping, a great roar suddenly put the flock to flight, and he alone remained in the meadow, without a trace of fear. A fierce old male tiger walked slowly toward him and he gazed in utter amazement at the apparition facing him.

"What are you doing here among these goats?" the mighty intruder demanded, in a voice he could understand. The young tiger only bleated in response. The jungle tiger picked up the young one by the scruff of his neck and carried him off to a nearby pond and forced him to look at his image in its mirrorlike surface that shone in the moonlight. "Look at these two faces. Can you see that your face is just like mine? We both have these fine stripes. Then why do you imagine yourself to be a goat, bleating in that funny tone and chewing on grass?"

The little one looked and shivered in wonder. Before he could respond, the older tiger carried him off to his den and offered him a piece of bleeding meat left over from a kill that same night. "Take it, eat it!" When the young one shrank back, the old tiger forced his mouth open and put some meat into it. To the little one's surprise, it tasted strangely good. Amazed, he reached for more, enjoying every mouthful as the new food filled him with a glowing strength and feeling of pleasure. He stretched out his paws, lashed his tail, and opened his mouth with a mighty yawn, as though he were awakening from a long, long sleep. Then he threw back his head and gave forth a powerful roar. The older tiger had been watching him intently as the transformation had taken place. "Now do you know who you are?" he asked, and completed the initiation of his young disciple into the knowledge of his own true nature by saying, "Now we shall go off together into the jungle."

This myth spoke of another time, another place, but it opened for me the doors of perception. I remembered what I had long ago forgotten, that I was, and still might be, an imaginative child filled with wonder and able to live in two worlds, the sunny world of every day and the forests of the night. This is how mythology can transport us into the place where the prepersonal and transpersonal meet. In the confrontation of the archaic world with the potential world, a person may be able to discover his or her own identity and meaning.

One of Jung's important contributions to transpersonal thought was his willingness to see both the darkest aspects of human nature that propel us toward apocalypse and the possibility of redemption through self-knowledge. Drawing from the Judeo-Christian background of the culture in which we live, he shows both the main currents and the coexisting streams of dissent. It is a spiritual way with which we are familiar, speaking to us from our own backgrounds and giving us a sense of continuity.

Transpersonal Psychology as Formulated by Ken Wilber

One of the most prolific contemporary interpreters of the transpersonal perspective has been Ken Wilber. Unlike Jung, who drew mainly upon the Judeo-Christian culture-myths as his sources, Wilber has looked often to the East, most particularly to Buddhism, for his inspiration. He focuses on an evolutionary perspective, tracing the rise of consciousness from archaic times to the present day. Among his many writings, perhaps his book *The Atman Project* (1980) sets forth most cogently his view of the structure and process of transpersonal development. Wilber has, in a very broad sense, extended the concepts of developmental psychology into the realm of the new world view. He has incorporated what has been learned about human development from observation and study in the sciences, in philosophy, and in comparative religion. Not only has he brought together and synthesized many fields of knowledge, but he has also gone beyond these and beyond the recent advances in developmental psychology, to envision still-higher states to which human beings may be able to rise. He suggests that through the insights of philosophers and scientists, and by rising above the goals and temptations of the ego, we may eventually be able to transcend our personal desires and ambitions and come to that selfless state that the Buddhists seek in Nirvana. In the broadest terms, Wilber's hierarchy portrays human evolution as going through three major stages (divided into many substages, which we need not explore here): the prepersonal (or pre-egoic) stage, the personal (or egoic) stage, and the transpersonal (or trans-egoic) stage. Individuals go through these developmental stages as well, up to the level of their psychospiritual maturity.

The prepersonal stage is a rudimentary consciousness, a consciousness prompted by survival needs. It is archaic, childish, grasping, self-centered. It is unconscious of itself except with regard to basic needs and desires, and has little regard for the world and its inhabitants except as they serve these needs and desires.

The personal or egoic stage is an advanced stage in which the individual develops a social awareness and is able to function in the world with varying degrees of success and varying degrees of awareness. He or she is a person with a clear identity, some sense of purpose, and the capacity to relate to others in increasingly meaningful and fruitful ways.

The transpersonal or trans-egoic stage is one in which persons are able to subordinate their sense of self-importance to the sense of membership in a larger society, a planetary society, with all that this implies. At the higher transpersonal stages one might transcend even the social order, and seek to become a part of the "Wisdom Culture" in a "bonding consciousness that shows everyone to be an ultimately equal member of the body of Christ/Krishna/Buddha" (Wilber 1981, p. 326).

Wilber is not so naive as to expect that transpersonal consciousness will evolve naturally, without having to face powerful opposition from the culture as well as from inner resistance to radical change in thought and behavior. But he seems to believe that the millennium (if not *this* millennium, then perhaps the next one) could bring about the capacity to transcend ego. He sees transpersonalists as people striving for higher and higher levels of consciousness. Ordinary people, in the egoic or personal stage, also evolve, but because of their foci of interest in the visible world they cannot participate in the higher transformations of consciousness until and unless they can break through to higher levels. It is the responsibility of the transpersonal psychologist to facilitate, for people who do not see beyond the egoic stage, their becoming more Self-aware and more aware of their condition.

One of Wilber's important concerns is that the pre-egoic or prepersonal stage may be confused with the trans-egoic or transpersonal. For example, mystical states that, in Wilber's view, belong to the transpersonal, could be confused with the pre-egoic myth and ritual of tribal practices that arouse an archaic feeling of community and bondedness. For Wilber, evolution occurs in a hierarchical line, running from immersion in the archaic collective unconscious to the experience of unity with a spiritual reality. He criticizes Jung for not sufficiently differentiating the primitive collective unconscious from the highly evolved collective unconscious that contains the sacred sources of spirituality.

Wilber is quite right—Jung did not divide the unconscious conceptually into the primordial unconscious and the superior unconscious world of spirit. The unconscious *is unconscious*, and for Jung that meant that everything that is beyond or outside of or anterior to consciousness reposes in it. Jung did not believe in hierarchies of value with respect to the unconscious. Whether something is higher or lower, good or bad, depends on the value or meaning human beings assign to it. In making assessments, people bring to bear all their own subjectivity as well as the conditioning to which they have been subjected by their environment and which they can never totally escape. The persona, the shadow, and all the other archetypes, like the poor, are always with us. We may learn to recognize them and deal kindly with them, but the likelihood of our totally eradicating them is slim. One lifetime is too short for most of us to achieve perfection; the most we can hope for is completion. By completion, Jung meant an acceptance of oneself with all the parts, the prepersonal as well as the personal and the transpersonal. As we gain in consciousness, we would expect to spend more time in transpersonal consciousness and less frequently to regress to prepersonal petulance or intolerance. But Jung rightly feared that just when we come to feel that we have transcended earthly concerns and can dwell in a loftier psychological atmosphere, we are most likely to stumble over a curbstone and break an ankle. Hence he insisted upon eternal watchfulness for the emergence of shadow aspects that might seduce people into the darkness of unconsciousness—the psychological correlates of the old and ever-present archons, or, if you will, our personal and collective demons. Unlike Wilber, Jung was not so ready to make a clean separation between the pre-egoic unconscious and the trans-egoic or transpersonal "superconscious." He knew that just when we believe that we have transcended the darkness and ascended into the light, we are most vulnerable to the incomprehensibility of the mystery.

Transpersonal Psychology, a New Gnosis

The transpersonal view has brought us full circle. In the old paradigm of physics and the psychologies that stemmed from it, people believed that the world was a machine and that human beings functioned like a machine and would eventually run out of energy and fall to pieces. In the Judeo-Christian tradition, this position tended toward apocalyptic thinking. For a short while, the wonders of technology held out the hope that we might avert the tragedy. Then came the new paradigm in physics that gradually reached out to embrace other sciences, even eventually the life sciences. Concepts such as Ilya Prigogine's theory of dissipative structures suggested that the world and its people would not necessarily fall apart, because the process of *regeneration* works in tandem with the process of *degeneration*. Translated into practical terms, this could mean that though we now have the tools to bring about total destruction of the world we know, we can also use these same tools to redistribute the world's goods, provide plenty for all, conquer disease and famine, end war, provide security from birth to old age for every person, and possibly even improve the general moral tone of the world. This point of view reflects faintly the messianic hopes that arose in bygone days in the face of threatened annihilation.

This position is consistent with Jung's, that psychologically we still exist, all of us, simultaneously in the prepersonal, personal, *and* transpersonal stages, although one or another may dominate our lives at any particular time. They *are* often confused, because to sort them out would require acts of careful reason and thoughtful logic, and these principles do not yet operate consistently in our world or in our minds. We need to learn how to recognize when we are functioning out of a prepersonal consciousness, when we are functioning out of an ego-consciousness, and when we are in touch with the transpersonal aspect of our lives. To do this requires self-knowledge. It raises again the necessity to seek the answers to the old questions:

Where did I come from? What is the source of my being? How am I related to it, and it to me?

Who am I? What is the nature of my being? How can I come into knowledge of myself? What are the highest potentials to which I may rise? What are my limitations?

For what purpose am I here? What is my path in this life? How am I called upon to live? What am I called upon to do?

What is my destiny? Is there more to life than birth, existence, and annihilation? How is my fate bound up with that of every other creature, with the earth itself?

I look at these questions not as boulders that block the way to understanding the mysteries beyond the visible world, but as doors through which we may go—if we dare—to face the unknown within and without.

PART III

Dancing in Both Worlds

Transformation does not occur only in the mind. Knowledge without behavioral change is sterile. Consciousness without corresponding action brings nothing to birth. People of every age have always known this, and have created rituals and practices to enact in the body and in the world what the psyche knows. Every religion prescribes certain rules and practices to bring the meaning of its symbols and structures into the procedures of everyday life. So does scientific work require certain procedures in order to be effective, and rituals find their way into many other aspects of living. In part I, we reminded ourselves of our sometimes forgotten notion that we have experiences in two worlds, one visible, one invisible. In part II, we were concerned with understanding how people from various disciplines—spiritual, scientific, and psychological—have come to a recognition of and familiarity with the invisible world. Part III will deal with the means of bringing our knowledge of the invisible world back to the world of everyday problems and issues, without ever again forgetting that the limits of the visible world are not the limits of the human being.

Practices and rituals actualize the ephemeral. They are the word made flesh. Without them, insights tend to fade; with them, insights may be deepened. It is important, therefore, to bring our knowledge, our gnosis, into what we do each day, each hour, each moment. We need not despair of fulfillment in this life, nor wait for another life in which to realize completion. In the words of the Buddhist teacher Soygal Rinpoche, "The next minute is a reincarnation of this minute." With this in mind, we will now turn to consider what we can do in *this minute* to effect a reconciliation between the opposite worlds—both within ourselves and where we touch the rest of the universe.

I must warn you that the practices I will describe in part III are not what they may seem to be. They are not—though they appear to be—things one does for a specific purpose. They are not, and yet they are. They become like the ground under the feet, the place of reference to which one returns and returns. There is an element of mystery in every spiritual practice. It brings us closer to being able to perceive the essence of things, even while attending to their appearances. For this reason, I have not been any more specific in indicating just how the practices are to be carried out and what will be the effects of performing the rituals. If one could say what these were, there would be no need of performing them, but the word is not enough: it only points the way to the mystery. The practice is essentially carried on in silence. The action itself reveals its own meaning.

The total human personality that surpasses and includes ordinary man and that transcends consciousness is represented by the figure of Original Man, the Anthropos, or Christ, according to Jung. This aspect of Christ was said to have gathered all his disciples together after the Last Supper and before he was taken over by those who would crucify him. He said to his disciples, "Before I give myself over to them, let us praise the Father in a hymn of praise, and so let us go to meet what is to come." Then he bade them form a circle and he was in the middle. He led them in a sacred dance of praise, singing to them such praises as drew together the opposites of this world and that world, and they responded, "Amen."

> We praise thee, Father.
> We give thanks to thee, Light, where there is no darkness. Amen.
> And wherefore we give thanks, that I will utter:
> I will be saved and I will save. Amen.
> I will be freed and I will free. Amen.
> I will be wounded and I will wound. Amen.
> I will be begotten and I will beget. Amen.
> I will consume and I will be consumed. Amen. . . .
> Grace paces the round. I will blow the pipe.
> Dance the round all. Amen.
>
> (Pulver 1955, p. 179)

The sacred dance is many things to many people. For us, it offers itself as a symbolic expression of living out fully and bodily what we understand to be the essence of our own nature and the purpose for which we are here.

10

Acquiring Tools for Contacting the Invisible World

The Practice

There is no single way to come into touch with the invisible world, nor is there a practice that suits everyone. Among the many paths that seekers have discovered over the centuries, each person can find a way to the inner kingdom and a key that will open the "doors of perception." There is no particular way to begin; the beginning will come where an opening is found. Everyone would like to have a sure technique that would succeed unfailingly when put to use. The word *technique* comes from the Greek, and does not mean a specific way of doing something; rather, it refers to the art or skill of getting ready. *Text* comes from the same root, and suggests speaking or writing or in some way committing the practice to a clearly defined form. I understand *technique* to mean a certain way of approaching a task that perfects itself in the doing. So the practice is a learning process that can be carried on throughout life. *Technique* implies that through carrying on a practice with diligence, it may be possible to develop a certain skill in finding one's way across the thresholds of the worlds and back.

Many books have been written describing in detail methods and practices that people have used for centuries, or have recently discovered or designed, for entering into the secret invisible worlds. While such books can often serve as helpful guides, the value of them is measurable only in terms of what an individual actually does, not what he or she reads or studies or observes. I have not wanted, therefore, to offer in a prescriptive way the "how to" of the many disciplines that people find useful. Instead, I have chosen to draw upon a few practices

that I have personally experienced and through which I have guided
others, to serve as illustrations of what practices are and what they
may mean in terms of opening gateways to a wider consciousness.
Finally, however, each person must discover the ways that are consonant with her or his inner purpose, and find harmony between that
pathway and the way the person lives.

The Practice of Sweeping the Temple

Our ancestors saw the sacred in everything around them. Not so
today. We have our sacred places: Saint Peter's in Rome, the Temple
in Jerusalem, and the churches or synagogues we may attend. In one
gnostic church, the priest sprinkles holy water on the altar as she says,
"In thy strength, O Lord, do we command all the powers of chaos to
wither into nothingness, that they shall not abide, and that our temples
within and our temples without may be so purified as to receive the
blessings of those who come in thy name." I take this to mean that it
is not necessary to go on a pilgrimage to find a sacred place, for one
can create a sacred place wherever one is, the sacred space within.
This involves clearing away the overwhelming trash and debris of self-
imposed concerns, petty resentments and angers, the need to prove
oneself right, mean competitiveness, little lies, taking advantage of people who are weaker and more defenseless, piling up money for its own
sake, and all the other aids devised to puff up the ego. Practicing dying
would be a method that leads to recognizing the futility of such efforts.
The first step, however, is to clean house, inside and out.

To the apprentice in the medieval guild house and to the novice in
the monastery the most menial tasks were regularly assigned. We can
call these tasks "sweeping the temple." They require people to take up
the responsibility of preparing the space in which they will carry on
their life work. "Life work" means that to which one will devote one's
energies. It is the work of the soul, as well as the material work done
in the visible world. These categories of tasks are not separate; they
are not inimical to one another any more than sweeping the temple,
washing the vestments, or cleaning and arranging the altar are inimical
to the act of prayer. On the contrary, these tasks *are* prayer. They are
the work of the soul in that they provide a suitable atmosphere for the
cultivation of a contemplative and receptive attitude.

Sweeping the temple—what does this mean in terms of our everyday lives? It means dealing with our environment in a way that shows
that we regard it as having potential for initiating creative change.

When considering the environment, we can begin looking at it from the outside and move gradually inward to the inner recesses of the heart, or we can begin with our inner condition and move outward.

This thought can be extended to our hearth and home, our country and our planet, and all spaces in between. To begin with, for most people hearth and home have ceased to be a center and a refuge, much less a sacred place. It is particularly difficult for many today who work outside of their homes to regard the home as anything but a stopping place, a resting place to eat and sleep and perform the necessary chores to make the machinery of life run as smoothly as possible. Efficiency is highly desirable. So many people who have been liberated from what they consider the drudgery of housework resent the amount they actually do. It seems especially burdensome when it is required in addition to the demanding activities outside the home, and often much anger is attached to it. Our society has forgotten what those disciplinarians of the atelier and the cloister knew: that all of life can be a work of art, even the most mundane-seeming tasks. These tasks need to be seen in the context of preparing and providing an environment that fosters mutual caring and mutual concern. There is great beauty in cleanliness and order and in bringing it into being. Watering the plants is as necessary as cleaning the stove, and vice versa. All these tasks bespeak care for oneself and others, and appreciation of the opportunity to create a *temenos*—a sanctuary, a safe and sacred space.

The *temenos* in ancient Greece was not limited to the temple, but included the enclosed court that surrounded it. Likewise, one cannot limit the temple sweeping to one's own home. No walled-off castle is this, but a part of a community with shared needs and shared concerns. I live near a major university that received a great deal of publicity a couple of years ago when students demanded sanctions against South Africa to exert pressure to end apartheid. Now we learn that racism has increased considerably on this same campus and in the surrounding community. It would seem desirable and necessary to sweep the temple that is close at hand before telling people in distant lands how to sweep theirs.

And yet we cannot overlook the wider environment in which we live. We are so busy building up a strong defense to save our nation from the threat of nuclear war that we are in danger of forgetting that unless we attend to the worldwide environment we may find ourselves on a planet not worth saving. Exploiting our natural resources without adequately replenishing them is but another example of mortgaging our future for the baubles of today. The environment is surely at risk, and yet it contains the resources needed to heal itself. The earth can be redeemed, but it will take sacrifice, intelligence, and skill, and the concerted efforts of many people.

To view the environment without prejudice and to observe what is happening, some people may find it useful to withdraw from it for a while. Reflection occurs best in quiet, away from the turbulence of too much stimuli. For this reason I find that it is important to stake out a sacred place. It may be the corner of a room, a hearth, or a spot in front of a small table upon which have been laid objects that serve as reminders of another world or another aspect of consciousness. It may be a section of a garden, or a special tree, a bench in the park, a chair by the window. One need not go far. Again, the Gospel of Thomas: "Split a piece of wood and I am there. Lift up the stone, and you will find me there" (Robinson 1988, p. 135). That sacred place, then, has the possibility of becoming the matrix, the womb wherein may form the thoughts and images that later can be put into action.

Because the sacred place is envisaged as something like an atelier or a cloister, the possibility exists that a work of art may come from it. It will not be an easy or simple process at all. In that quiet reflective space, there will be times of uncertainty and confusion. It is important to experience our self-doubt as fully as possible. This is what moves us forward, away from our complexes and fears and preconceived no-tions—although at the same time a panic may ensue that throws us right back into them. But the self-doubt pushes us on and through. This process and the way it happens presents us with an opportunity to discover how the barriers were breached, and to share this discovery with others. The work of art that emerges when we leave the place of interiority and reenter the visible world may be something tangible or it may take the form of a special kind of life, a life that is in itself an art. The sharing or the communication, in whatever form that may take, is the essence of the creative act. But the seed begins to germinate in aloneness and in silence.

The Practice of Dying

I have chosen the practice of dying as an exercise that surely marks a crossing over from the visible to the invisible world. When we die, consciousness as we know it ceases to exist. Before us lies the mystery. It is a passage we all must make, and who has not pushed it out of mind at one time or another? We know that we entered this life at some point, and what has become ourselves was once somewhere or something else. In what form it existed we do not know or do not remember, or even if we have some inkling we cannot be certain. In the same way, we do not know where we are going, although we may have some ideas about it. But certitude here, even if it seems to exist, may turn out to be an illusion, and rare is the person who has not at some time been afraid that there is nothing, absolutely nothing, ahead.

What we fear or what we would prefer not to think about often surfaces in our dreams. If we can allow the full impact of such uninvited dreams to stay with us, they may bring us unexpected gifts. I have dreamed of death at least twice, and the dreams were so numinous that thinking about them today fills me with as much awe as when they originally came upon me. The first dream occurred when I was in Zurich in analytic training and living with my husband and teenage daughter:

> *I open a door to a bedroom just slightly, enough to see into the room. The room is bare of furniture except for one bed that is in the far corner. Around the bed is a strange glow, as if a bright radiance were emanating from it. Although the light is nearly blinding, I cannot help looking at it and trying to make out what is there. I realize that my husband and my daughter are in that bed. Apparently my husband sees me at the door, and he throws a heavy object at me, perhaps a shoe, which I take to be a sign that I do not belong there, the sight is not for me. I quickly close the door. I am shocked and trembling.*

For years I did not understand the dream, yet it was always with me. I knew from the emotion I felt that it was very important. It was trying to tell me something, but I did not know what. All I knew was that the two of them were in a place that I was not permitted to enter. I felt cheated, cut off from the mystery of it, isolated and alone. Five years later, my husband died. Still I did not understand the dream. Another five years passed and then my daughter died. So I was left outside the luminous place of death to which they had gone. I knew that I now understood the dream. There was no doubt in my mind.

The other time I dreamed of death was of my own death. The dream came perhaps ten years ago. I was feeling perfectly well at the time, and had no anxiety or foreboding. Still, I had this dream:

> *I am lying on a narrow hospital bed, perhaps a gurney such as they use to wheel a patient into an operating room. I am very comfortable. I notice that I am hooked up to all sorts of wires and tubes. It strikes me as strange that I should be in this place and in this condition and*

feeling very well, unusually well. I am relaxed and peaceful. But I feel weak, not in an unpleasant way, simply weak. I do not feel that I can get up, but then I have no inclination to do so. It is as if my strength were slowly ebbing away, and the realization comes to me that I must be dying. Oh well, I think, if this is the way it is, just let it happen and observe it carefully. You may not have another opportunity. I pay close attention to the sense of everything slowing down, my body, my thoughts. Yet I keep a keen awareness of a growing calm and a very quiet pleasure, as it is to sleep in the arms of the Beloved. I feel my life slipping away from me and I feel myself slipping like a drop of water sliding into the sea. And then I am no more myself alone, but merged into the fullness.

Since having this dream I have not experienced any fear of death. Sometimes when I am fretful or worried or anxious about something, I am able to regain a sense of proportion and value and the peace that comes with it by practicing the art of dying, as I learned it from my dream. I have come to believe that most people have not actively prepared themselves for death, and for that reason are not adequately prepared for life. For unless we are truly in touch with our entire beings—body, mind, and soul—and with our death, we cannot appreciate the value and the brevity of this little bit of life in which we can actively participate. Our lives in this body and on this planet are short. As we get older we become more and more conscious of this simple fact. It will soon be over anyway. There may not be much left of it, perhaps only twenty years, perhaps only ten, perhaps there is only tomorrow. We do not know exactly, only that it is limited. Will we then spend these days getting and spending, wishing we had something we have not or we were better at something than we are? It would be better to prepare for the last act of the earthly drama, and decide what is important and what is not, what to hold onto and what to relinquish. When you have become sufficiently skilled in the practice of dying, all the other practices will seem relatively easy.

It goes something like this: You close your eyes and imagine that you are on your deathbed. You feel yourself drifting. You don't have any more energy to do anything. Your desk is piled high with unanswered letters, bills to be paid, unfinished projects. Either someone else will pick them up for you or they will remain undone. It doesn't matter much. No one will know that the idea you meant to work out never came to expression. No one will feel the poorer for it. Then there are the people in your life. If you loved them well, they will miss you and grieve for you. Over time the poignancy of your absence will fade and only a warm remembrance will be left. There will be those for whom you did not care enough, those you rejected, those with whom there is still some unfinished business. It doesn't matter now. There is nothing you can do about it.

There is only one thing you can do, and that is to let go. Let the tasks of the world slip away. Let your very identity slip away. Let your loved ones mourn a little while for you and then go on their way. Let go of everything, your home, your possessions, your feelings, and your thoughts.

Allow yourself to float. You begin to feel lighter. You have shed the heavy load you have been carrying. What was the heavy load? It was your sense of self-importance. It was your belief that everything you did had intrinsic importance, therefore you had to do it fully and perfectly no matter what it cost. Or, conversely, it was your belief that your work was so important that you couldn't possibly do it well enough, so the burden you carried was the unfulfilled responsibility. But either way, don't you see how temporal it is, when you are facing your own death? This practice can help you learn to do a little less, do it a bit more slowly, do it with care, and do it with love.

Life Provides the Practice: Utterance

> I was angry with my friend:
> I told my wrath, my wrath did end.
> I was angry with my foe:
> I told it not, my wrath did grow.
>   BLAKE, "The Poison Tree"

Bringing forth what is within you requires the act of utterance. This is more than the willingness to know or to understand. It is to communicate to another being the truth of who you are; it is putting yourself in jeopardy, baring your jugular vein. To fail in this is to depreciate yourself, to count yourself of little value, to bottle yourself up so that you become stagnant and lifeless. Without this communication, you are self-enclosed; you become moody, sick, or depressed. To open yourself up for the sake of another person is life-giving, as it was in the beginning when you first emerged from the womb.

Whether or not we practice dying as a form of meditation, sooner or later we are likely to have to face the imminent possibility of dying. For Ruby this came about unexpectedly. I had not seen her for a week, and when she came in it was clear to me that something very important had happened or was happening to her. She told me that in the course of a routine medical examination, the doctor had found something that looked suspicious, so he had ordered some laboratory tests and further examination. While she was telling me this, she was also reassuring herself by saying that nine chances out of ten were that they would find nothing. I knew that a time of testing her inner strength was at hand.

In past weeks and months, Ruby's insights into her true nature had been deepening. Although her relationships with people were more relaxed and genuine than they had ever been, she was far less compulsive than in the past about responding to everyone else's needs before her own. Now a new challenge had suddenly thrust itself into her life, and insight alone would not be sufficient to meet it. She would need to call upon her inner resources for the strength to deal with the dread possibility that was being presented to her. Ruby was in the position that each of us may be in at one time or another. Something changes in our lives, or threatens to change, and we have to draw upon our own inner resources for the tools with which to deal effectively with a new situation. Let us see how Ruby experienced this process.

First of all, it was necessary for her to get in touch with her most elemental feelings. After assuring me that everything was probably going to be all right, Ruby's eyes began to water. I waited. She bit her lip. Then, in a timid voice that belied the bravado of the moment before, she spoke haltingly. "I recognize . . . I have a lot of fear . . . walking down the street, I have a vague fear. Not a fear of being attacked. A vague fear of not being equal to whatever may arise. It's pervasive . . . it has to do with my view of other people. If you're not concerned with other people, what they'll think, then you don't care so much what happens to you. But I can't help being concerned . . . that's the way I am. It's one of the reasons I like being alone."

I observed that when Ruby was alone she did not have to worry about what other people thought of her. Solitude could be one way an Eros person could choose to get away from the pressures of real or fancied demands from others. But it was not that simple for Ruby. There were the friends who wanted to spend time with her, even when she did not want to be with them. She had learned that if she refused to recognize that sometimes she must reject her friends, then her body would intervene so that she could not take care of these people. This was what she was now experiencing.

When I asked her what she was feeling now, she replied in a hesitant way as if she were searching for words in some unfamiliar place: "I feel . . . the words that come to me are 'like embedding myself in a matrix.' I want aloneness, to be unsheltered, to be unconnected. It's like wanting myself to be slowly unveiled so I can see . . . this is on a feeling level . . . what matrix I am embedded in. I feel like Hesse's monk, Brother Narcissus—who could not help being seduced by the pleasures of this world—when Brother Goldmund tells him, 'I don't know what you will do when you come to die.' I feel like I want my mother. But not my real mother."

The archetypal matrix in which we are all embedded is often symbolized on an individual level by the personal mother. The word *matrix* has its source in the Greek word of two meanings: archaic and uterus. But it has come to mean more than these. The dictionary defines matrix as "the intercellular substance of a tissue. Something (as a surrounding or pervading substance or element) within which something else originates or takes form or develops (an atmosphere of understanding and friendliness that is the *matrix* of peace), the natural material in which a fossil, metal, gem, or crystal is embedded." For Ruby it was all of these. She was feeling a need to return bodily to the matrix. She said, "I need to find *my*self in *my* place. It's not that the body is the matrix for the conscious part of me. It's more like the physical and spiritual parts are together in a matrix. Finding the real matrix is like getting out of the narrow world of my immediate surroundings. The whole world doesn't respond to things the way people in the West do. In the East they don't fear death as we do."

She was able to see the possibility of imminent death from a very different point of view from the one she had been conditioned into accepting. We spoke of the kamikaze pilots of World War II; how they would dive down into a ship to blow it up and commit suicide at the same time. For them it was not fearsome, but the fulfillment of a duty. They were returning their lives to the matrix, the mother country that gave them birth. It was, for them, the natural thing to do.

Ruby questioned whether, no matter how it came about, death had to be accepted as the natural end of life. I looked around my consulting room: "In the quiet space we create in this room, we experience a world as still as a landscape painting. Outside, birds sing. Sunlight falls through the trees and makes dancing patterns on the ground. Leaves wither and fall from the trees. Birds peck at the persimmons on the tree outside the window; the ripe persimmons drop off and rot on the ground. Why are we not allowed to feel that this is right, that it is true? It's what we have. Do you see that, Ruby?"

"I see that other people are afraid of the ending of life. They were afraid before I was taught to be afraid. They got their messages from someone else, their parents perhaps. They taught me to be afraid— they did it on my behalf—on the basis of what they were told as to how things were supposed to be. When I was little I learned that there are feelings you just don't show to people. Then the next level is that you manufacture other things to put in their place, in the place of the real things. But I think there must be some people who wake up in the morning and think that everything is open. I have something in me that's closed—like an iron box. But I also know of a chink in the wall. You can see how blue the sky is through it. That chink, that's the real given."

I told her that she was expressing a feeling that reminded me of Blake's poem "London," where he writes of "the mind-forged manacles":

In every cry of every Man,
In every Infant's cry of fear,
In every voice, in every ban
The mind-forg'd manacles I hear.
(1957, p. 216)

"We forge them," I said. "We construct the iron boxes in which we live. We bind our own hands." That image helped Ruby to see what she needed to do. She saw that she had to discriminate the real givens from the responsibilities she placed upon herself or that others placed on her. Then she would be free to take responsibility for her own life and, when the time came, for her own death. This realization gave Ruby a sense of great relief. I watched the anxiety leave her face, to be replaced by a quiet sense of joy.

Ruby spoke. "I can see a new morning stepping out from behind the sun bearing the gift of another day. I feel it's all ahead of me. I feel like crying, 'Wait for me!' "

"What do you have to do to get there?" I asked.

"I have to be lighthearted and daring! Not grim about setting out on the spiritual path. You ask me what I am going to do. I think I'm going to speak my mind!"

"That sounds wonderful!"

She thought a moment, and then asked, half of me and half of herself, "It does, but can I live up to my wild expectations?"

Now I needed to support her newly born willingness to accept her life on its own terms. "Ruby, are you willing to be a fool?" I asked her. "To be surprised? Not to do everything according to your plan or according to what other people expect? Can you let the window be open? Let the rain or the sunshine or the butterfly come in?"

Ruby responded with playful determination, "I didn't say I was just going to think. I'm going to speak my mind. You see, when I am busy thinking things out, I don't notice what is going on around me. When I begin to speak, I get more information. It's an exchange. It doesn't matter who the person is, I can put what is in me outside where I can look at it—and maybe even get a reflection from the other person. Just by speaking I can break out of my self-made prison. I feel that I am seeing a tiny portion of truth."

After her first medical tests, Ruby reported that the doctor asked her to come back for additional exploration. "It makes me think that I am feeling the truth about death," she said at that time. "There's something very precious about that. All sorts of funny little moments. When I woke up this morning I thought about watering my plants. Oh no, I thought, if I'm going to die they can die. Then I thought, oh no, they don't have to die. My death is not their death."

Facing the possibility of her own death and leaving a vibrant world behind helped Ruby to discover that being alive offered her choices that she had never believed she had. Her fears in the past had had to do with personal survival. She now began to realize that in the long run, personal survival is a vain hope. Sooner or later we come to a time when we cannot survive as individuals, nor can we continue to cling to the ego we so carefully developed. We face the truth that the last battle is one we will and must lose. Because we have learned that it can happen to us from one day to the next, it becomes pointless to remain too attached to anything. If we can be cut off at any moment, why should we postpone what is important to us? Why should we postpone doing and being what we know we are here on this earth to do and to be? Why should we enmesh ourselves in obligations that serve no one, and that stand between our ego and the true nature of our being? Why should we not plunge fully into the life that is given to us as a gift for however long or short it may be? When dying no longer holds any terror, it becomes easier to walk lightly through one's life. Whatever comes to us in the way of material goods, friendship, or affection, lasts only a little while. If you know, as a result of your practice, that you can let it go, you will also be able to cherish it without anxiety while it is in your presence.

The Practice of Attending to the Body

> There is only one temple in the world
> and that is the human body.
> Nothing is more sacred than that noble form.
> NOVALIS, "Aphorisms"

Inner work begins with the body, whether we recognize this fact or not. For without the cooperation of the body, there can be little human functioning, and much of what we think or feel or sense or know depends upon the condition of the body. Letting go is part of the practice here, too. It is necessary to become aware that we are not our bodies. The body is the place where we live, but our essence is more than the physical body. I find it difficult to conceptualize body as separate from mind or soul. I agree with William Blake when he says in *The Marriage of Heaven and Hell*, "Man has no Body distinct from his Soul; for that call'd Body is a portion of Soul discern'd by the five senses, the chief inlets of Soul in this age. Energy is the only life, and is from the Body; and Reason is the bound or outward circumference of Energy" (1957, p. 149).

The vitality of the body empowers everything we do. Some tend to think of the body as something belonging to them, and that they are wrapped up in their personal bags of skin, with clear boundaries. This is not to be confused with what is outside of us, the "not-I." But the fact of the matter is that individuals are not independent entities at all. If we could close ourselves off from our environment we would quickly cease to live, for the breath that is in a continuous interchange with the air around us would cease its rhythmic flow in and out, in and out. Nor could we survive without food and drink, or without the hundreds of people who collectively grow, process, and transport what we need for even a simple meal. The body is dependent for its effective functioning upon everything that comes into it, and it needs also to dispose of what it does not require. As an organic system it relies upon and responds to its environment, and adapts to it.

One of the most effective ways of gaining a sense of harmony between the body and the worlds in which we live is through attention to our breathing. Long a part of meditation practice, paying close attention to breathing allows us to feel the internal rhythm that is continuously moving within us, without our knowledge most of the time, functioning with the necessary precision to keep us in a life-supporting relationship with the air that circulates within and without our beings. How deeply we breathe can be seen as symbolic of how deeply we partake of the breath of life—are we fully in it or do we just inhale enough to keep us alive? Do we allow the mysterious substance called the breath to flow freely through us or do we hold onto it as though it belonged to us? Do we recognize that since ancient times the breath has been identified with the life-giving spirit, and wind with the power of creation? Through the breath we know ourselves to be one with the rest of the universe; when this flow ceases, our individual lives are cut off from the growth process and we begin to decay. Breathing, then, is intercourse with the universe, with all of life. It keeps the body alive, and provides the substance in which the insubstantial can dwell. It is good to pay attention to this process; it lets us know where we are in the larger scheme of things.

One hears people talking about "the body/mind problem" as though there were a dichotomy between the body and the brain. Physicians have been known to say, "I can't find anything wrong [meaning, in your body]. It must be in your mind." Do people still need to be reminded that the headbone is connected to the neckbone? That the brain is a part of the body, and that mind and soul can only function in and through the physical body? It goes without saying that attention to proper nutrition, exercise, sufficient rest, and relaxation are absolutely necessary. Taking good care of the body is another way of sweeping the temple.

In some respects the body is like a machine. If it is kept in good condition, it can be driven to take us where we want to go. But it can also be seen as an organism, an aggregation of compatible systems that work together in a harmonious fashion most of the time, and that is capable of accommodating itself to changing circumstances. Even from a mechanistic viewpoint, it would have to be admitted that the body is an extremely intelligent "machine."

We need to treat the body as a whole, as well as a part of a larger system that is the human organism with all its functions. These include the intellectual functions associated with mind and the spiritual functions associated with soul. The free circulation of our vital energy comes about when we are able to relax bodily tensions and breathe fully, and this helps to integrate the physical, mental, and spiritual aspects of consciousness.

Listening to the precise messages of the body is an essential practice. It involves tuning into the subtle variations in feelings, cultivating the ability to pick up cues from variations in muscle tone, from blocks that inhibit free movement, from small discomforts. The body/mind is a repository of all the experiences a person has had since the moment of conception. The traces of every experience remain in the body in some form and can exert a subtle influence on feelings and behavior. If we consider mind and soul as part of the total organism, we would have to include also the collective unconscious, from which is drawn our information about the limitless invisible world.

It is unlikely that in the normal course of events the total history of this organism will ever be untangled, nor is it necessary to do so. It is an easier and more reasonable expectation that we get to know our bodies by paying attention to their needs. Health is a natural state. We tend to remain healthy most of the time when we do not abuse the body, but notice instead what it is saying to us. Tension builds up when we are unaware that we are straining or pushing ourselves or doing something about which we do not feel at peace. A destructive process may get started as a result and it may then become habitual. We hold onto something we would be better off releasing. We may *know* what the something is but it is difficult to put into words, so the body substitutes certain characteristic ways of expressing it nonverbally. Some of the ways in which it may express its discomforts are through backaches, headaches, postural problems, feelings of high excitation, anxiety, boredom, depression, or impotence. Body consciousness means asking the body what it needs: rest, exercise, play, sex, music, dance? It will let you know. Nonverbal expressions of the whole person can manifest through the body, mind, and soul. Each aspect interacts with the others; each aspect can enhance or depress the others. When any part of the human organism is out of balance, the whole suffers. Therefore, it would seem that moderation would be a wise rule to follow, with the goal of keeping the body functioning as well as possible. This requires that we pay close attention to what we do, for what we do is what can make us whole, can give us hope, and can lift us out of the limitations that would otherwise be imposed upon us by ignorance and insensitivity.

There is something wrong when individuals abuse their bodies by taking in substances that destroy that sensitivity or distort awareness. The body is not a toy, given to us for our amusement. Although it surely gives us pleasure, especially when it is well-functioning and in good condition, we must bear in mind that it is a complicated and highly articulated system; it is the only one we have; and our lives depend on it. So we must tune our consciousness to the body, even as we realize that this is only one aspect of our being. Without that body, that visible mass of flesh and blood, we simply would not exist. But if consciousness is limited to the visible world alone and one sees only through the eye of the ego, one is blind to the wider vision of what could be if we used all the strength and all the consciousness with which we are endowed. That blindness to the mystery of what is in this world beyond what is apparent leaves a great unacknowledged emptiness in the heart, longing to be filled. The possibility of filling that void with a magical substance that will make everything seem better than it is, may be the seductive hope that leads many people to subject their bodies to destructive excesses. Easy solutions and instant gratification do not provide the answer to long-standing problems. Finally, it is the way we live, every hour of every day, that determines the quality of our lives in the moment and in the future.

The Practice of Introspection and Expression

Psychoanalytic theory is rooted in the necessity of bringing to consciousness and to expression what is within the person, what the person knows and may have forgotten or repressed. But the psychoanalytic setting may pose a difficulty in itself. One of its key assumptions is that whatever is important in the analysand's life will be brought into the analytic setting and there reenacted with the analyst. The mantle of the parent or other significant person in early childhood is placed on the shoulders of the analyst. The consulting room becomes the staging ground for reliving the original situation in a new way, and it is hoped that with the guidance of the analyst new insights will be obtained. This process goes a long way toward furthering the awareness of individuals with respect to aspects of their life experiences in the visible world. The appearance of the parents in some disguised form and/or projected onto the analyst may explain some things on the level that relates to the individual's life experiences, but it hardly touches the archetypal level. The mysteries of the psyche that cannot be known because they belong to the unknowable tend to be something of an embarrassment to the traditional psychoanalyst. The childlike relationships of trust that we have more than likely forgotten or repressed may well turn out to be our connection with the numinous, the power of light, the grandeur of the unknown God. Whatever fear a child may have of parents or other human beings is dwarfed by the fear of the Nameless, and the anxiety accompanying it that we cannot control our destinies, no matter what "they" tell us. So learning to withdraw the projections we make upon the people we know (beginning with the analyst, if we happen to be in treatment) is only a prologue to what is really important. It is not even the first act. It prepares the way for the understanding of what is real, beneath the surface. It is a way of approaching the important and ever-present question: Who am I? Once an individual can respond to this question with some sense of personal authenticity, it becomes possible to act in the world in consonance with who one truly is. The telling part of any psychotherapeutic endeavor, of any relationship for that matter, and also of any intellectual or spiritual discipline, is what happens *after* the insights have occurred.

The Practice of Attending to Dreams

One of the important contributions of psychoanalysis has been the value attached to dreams, first by Freud and subsequently by many who followed him. Few people today doubt that dreams convey some sort of meaning, even if they do not understand these phantasms of the night. Much has been said and written about the interpretation of dreams. Jung suggested that dreams tend to compensate the conscious attitude and that therefore they may provide information that is not otherwise accessible to us. During the day when we are actively going about our business, consciousness selectively focuses on what is important and necessary to the enterprise of the moment. It represses or shoves aside much that we do not have the time or inclination to deal with immediately. These unexamined observations remain in the background of consciousness, sometimes only until we drop our guard in the blissful trustfulness of sleep, that night or sometimes many nights or weeks later. But these contents that are incompatible with consciousness will at some point gather enough energy to press through into the awareness of the sleeping person in the form of a dream. Often they carry with them the energy or the emotional charge of the original impression, but they have cryptic ways of expressing that charge, through images and symbols.

In beginning to attend to a dream, notice where the strongest feelings are, and what elements in the dream stand out as most impressive. What does the setting suggest? How do the characters in the dream reflect aspects of your own being that may be unfamiliar to you? And, finally, what is the role of the "dream-ego," the person who represents you in the dream? When you have discovered something about yourself that you did not know before, you will have gained a measure of understanding of your dream. Feel your way into the dream, and know that it offers you a glimpse of the invisible world within yourself. And if you will take the trouble to record your dreams regularly in a notebook each day when you waken, you will develop a history of your journey on the path of the invisible way.

The Practice of Gnosis and Creativity

To *know* is important. I am speaking of the sense that comes about through inner knowing, gnosis. It is the way Adam *knew* his wife after he ate of the apple, not before. To know in this sense means to wake up. It is the end of innocence. Jung put it well when he said, "He who looks outside, dreams; he who looks within, awakens." To be awake is to be up and doing, not drifting in the slumber of ignorance or indolence. For one who would know the invisible world, it is not sufficient to retreat into a state where insight may come, although this may be a necessary first step. Insights may take a long time to finally appear. When they do, they must be distilled and assimilated into our very being as nourishment for the soul. It is necessary to discriminate which of these insights can be put to use and which are better eliminated, so that what remains is energy-giving and life-giving, and works toward the purpose for which we have been put on this earth.

I cannot help but relate this to my own process as I write. I take up my pen—or perhaps I sit down before my word processor—with only a vague idea of what I intend to say. It may have been simmering in the cauldron of my thoughts for a few minutes, or days, or weeks, or years. It is shape-shifting chaos like the patterns of water in a river as it approaches a sharp drop in the contour of its bed; it is the vortices in the swiftly-running stream. But the moment when I actually begin to write—when I commit my thoughts to ink and paper or to letters of light shining from a cathode ray tube—the stream of consciousness begins to take shape. It acquires discipline and boundaries. It proceeds in a more or less orderly fashion. It gains coherence. It begins to give expression to the meaning that I only vaguely felt before. Now it comes to life. The exciting and surprising thing is that what I see before me is new to me; it is not necessarily what I intended before I sat down to write. It begins to have a pattern of its own. I wonder if my feelings are anything like what the new scientists felt when they came upon the concept of chaotic systems. I find that the process of writing, instead of letting my thoughts run down and run out like entropy approaching equilibrium, actually generates more thought.

Lines of an old poem float in from a distant memory: "Behind him lay the gray Azores, before him only boundless seas." This is how I feel as I reflect that behind me lie the insights of my past, before me the mysteries of the boundless ocean of the unconscious, waiting to be cleaved by the prow of my soul-ship. What a powerful male symbol that is—the prow of a ship separating the waves as it pushes through, plunging deep, feeling the great sea all around rising and falling, and leaving a splendid white froth in its wake. But there's a female symbol as well, for *she* is the sea, the enveloping mystery, the water that embraces this planet, the water that surrounded us before we were born, the watery womb from which life came forth.

What is happening is that the androgynous power of creation, symbolized by the union of ship and sea, is using a human being as its instrument of expression. Never mind that we live as males or as females in the visible world. When we enter the invisible world we can leave our sexual roles behind, as it is said by the living Jesus in the Gospel of Thomas: "When you make the male and the female one and the same, so that the male not be male nor the female . . . then will you enter the Kingdom" (Robinson 1988, p. 129). "When you disrobe without being ashamed, and take up your garments and place them under your feet as the little children and tread on them, then you will see the son of the living one and you shall not fear" (p. 130). "The living Jesus" in the Gospel of Thomas needs to be understood as that personification, or that avatar,[14] of the Divine that is present on earth either as an incarnate form or as an idea, but that has neither beginning nor end, as contrasted with the historical Jesus. This eternal being has been called "the Cosmic Christ" (see Matthew Fox's *The Coming of the Cosmic Christ*, 1988), but might just as well be Buddha or a bodhisattva,[15] or any of the sacred images that bridge the gap between the worlds. Their purpose is to provide guidance and help for us as we contemplate the Presence that we cannot name but that we long for and seek.

To have this knowledge, then, this gnosis of the androgynous nature of creation, is not a matter of insight or intellect alone. It requires

---

14. In Hinduism, a manifestation of the Divine who appears in the world in human form.
15. In Buddhism, a saintly person who refuses to ascend as a Buddha into Nirvana, but remains instead on earth to relieve suffering and to guide others in their search for enlightenment.

a certain amount of both, to be sure, but far more important is the practice that leads to the transformation of the ego from an end in itself to an instrument of the higher Self, an open door through which the alien and unknown God may become manifest.

The Practice of Meditation

John Blofeld, the late, great Taoist scholar who lived in China for many years, once told me about his life in Thailand, where he had taken refuge after the Chinese Cultural Revolution made it impossible for anyone to study the ancient Chinese culture in its native setting. Blofeld settled in a little house on the outskirts of Bangkok, where he made a small meditation garden and assigned the room next to it for his writing. As the years passed, the city grew up around his house and on all sides old buildings were demolished and new factories and office buildings were built in their places. Clouds of dust and the constant racket of air hammers and steel upon steel filled the atmosphere from early morning until late at night. I looked at the gentle blue-eyed Englishman in his navy blue Chinese-style jacket and asked him how he managed to meditate and concentrate in such a noisy, busy place. "It's not difficult," he replied. "I simply incorporate the sounds into my meditation. It becomes a kind of rhythm. It doesn't disturb my peace and quiet at all." I recognized that the quiet place, the sacred place, has to be within the person first of all. The external setting is important, but secondary.

Tibetan meditation master Soygal Rinpoche suggests that the Western problem-solving approach provokes the psyche and the emotions. Meditation quiets the emotions so that the depths of spirit can come through. According to Soygal, Tibetans say, "When the shit is dry, keep it dry." He, too, recommends that a special retreat space be set aside for meditation whenever that is possible. He stresses the importance of the environment in which the inner work takes place. Meditation is essentially training the mind. It offers three tools that help us penetrate to the invisible world.

The first tool consists of *listening and hearing*. This requires one to be free of distractions, not so easily achieved in this world of diversions, amusements, confusion, and anxiety. Yet it is not only possible, but there is also a hunger for it. Meditation requires the perfecting of attention. To attain this it is often helpful to focus the mind on something specific. Focusing the attention, however, is not by far all there is to meditation. Listening must be accompanied by hearing—and hearing is the taking into oneself and finding meaning in the sound. Seeing must be accompanied by insight, the taking in of the vision and finding its intrinsic meaning for an individual.

This requires the second tool, *reflection and contemplation*. For the visually minded, there are images designed to draw the attention to a central point. Tibetan mandalas, designs based on a circle with the focal point at the center, have been used for centuries for this purpose. So have Tibetan thankas, religious paintings in which a central figure receives the energy of the viewer and concentrates it. There may be other figures or designs on the thankas, but all of them are only temporary resting places on the way to the center. From the other side of the world come the brightly colored yarn paintings of the Huichol Indians of Mexico. These primitive images always include a *nierika* or circular hole that, when the attention is centered, leads the gaze of the viewer from the visible world into the invisible one. For those more attuned to sounds, the East Indian culture makes use of the mantra, a sacred sound with a certain quality of resonance that when repeated over and over leads to a dissolution of distractions and an auditory connection with the sacred. The chanting one hears in the Orthodox Jewish synagogue or the Gregorian chants of the Christian monastic tradition perform the same function. Prayer that depends on reflecting upon the invisible world and the Greatness that is coexistent with it, and contemplating one's relationship with it, is surely a form of meditation.

The third tool is *wisdom and activation*. It is not enough simply to know. One must bring that knowing into the world in a way that is in harmony with one's life-style and the situation in which one finds oneself. For some, the activation of wisdom takes place in the course of everyday activities, at work, at home, in teaching one's children. For others the activation occurs in a more public and dramatic way.

Amid Clatter, Monks Calmly Sift Sand

Not long ago, a picture appeared in *The New York Times* of three robed Buddhist monks kneeling on the pavement before the American Museum of Natural History in Manhattan. They were engaged in an unusual occupation that drew the attention of curious passersby. Kneeling on pillows under a pagodalike structure, they were carefully sifting grains of colored sand from what appeared to be a tiny tea strainer. For six weeks they would spend each day sifting incredibly fine grains of sand into an intricate pattern that, when it was done, would represent "the abode of the gods." All around them the visitors

stood and watched in rapt attention—even, perhaps, in silent meditation. The monks called their mandala "The Wheel of Time," and
while they worked they invoked the blessings of the 722 deities. The
circles, the largest of which was seven feet in diameter, protected the
many-chambered palace, and from the outer edge inward represented
fire, water, earth, and wind. Within the smallest circle, a dozen gateways led deeper into the palace—three from each direction, symbolizing body, speech, and, finally, mind.

"For artists of such a mandala," the Venerable Samten, one of four
attendants to the Dalai Lama, said in his gentle singsong voice, "the
process is a purification of negativism in the mind and the accumulation of positive potential that will benefit them toward enlightenment
in this life and in future lives. For those who simply come to see the
mandala, it is not only art, but a blessing for their inner peace and for
peace around the world. It will be manifest throughout the universe"
(Hevesi 1988).

If there was any trace of conflict about the Kalachakra mandala, it
surrounded the question of what should become of it. Museum officials
with their Western acquisitive attitudes wondered whether it should
be preserved. It is in the Tibetan tradition that upon completion—in
remembrance of the transitory nature of earthly things—a mandala is
swept away and its sand poured into a river.

The Universal Element of the Practices

What is the universal element that makes all these practices valuable? The practices take the sacred ideas and thought forms and enact
them in the visible world. We may follow one path or another, but it
is important that we not become attached to any one particular path
and view it as the "only" path or the "right" path. Every path is a
roadway that begins in the invisible world within and extends to the
invisible world without. Like the day, this road begins in darkness and
ends in darkness, and it is the same darkness.

If we have learned something about the invisible world, if some of
its mysteries have been revealed to us, then the meaning of our discovery is expressed in the way we manifest it. If we feel that our values
are good and true, then they are worthy of being put into practice and
tested. How we live our lives in the small details is a demonstration
of universal ideas. It is in the way we live day by day, hour by hour,
minute by minute that we make our mark upon this world. Like col-

ored grains of sand, wayfarers on the path may pause to take their places in the mandala of peaceful harmony for the little while that they are here, before being swept into the flowing stream.

11

Finding the Marvelous
in the Mundane

We have seen that there are many tools we can use to gain access to the invisible world. It is not necessary to go to the ends of the earth to find this place, for it is everywhere, all about us as well as within us. It is in the garden or in the park, in the vacant lot or the desert, wherever the miracle of new life sprouts from a tiny seed that has lain dormant through the dry season or the winter. It is in the sudden appearance of a cluster of fungi on the trunk of a tree after a week of rain. It is at home in the pleasure of wiping the dust off the furniture and revealing the surface beneath, in the preparation of a meal that makes a celebration of the earth's bounty. It is in the way you talk to your children, the way you greet your beloved, recognizing the love that surrounds you and, by extension, the love that streams out from you toward all beings. Knowing that it is all one, the visible and the invisible, enables you to bring the marvelous into the smallest acts of your daily life, thereby sacralizing every act. Knowing that the invisible world is filled with unlimited energy (one could almost say that it *is* energy) makes it unnecessary to hold fast to everything that you possess. The more you draw upon the source, the more energy is available to you; it enriches you without ever being itself diminished.

Those who live with the knowledge that they are able to draw upon this unlimited energy are not afraid to imagine the impossible, to create the original thing or idea that gives wings to their thoughts. They know they have nothing to lose, for there is an inexhaustible supply at the source. Yet not everyone can accept this. It appears that not everyone is able to become permeable to the invisible resources that surround us all. It seems to have something to do with a process of spiritual evolution, a developmental process much like the intellectual development of a person from birth to maturity. The spiritual dimension of evolution has as its focus the relationship between the unknown Source of all energy, all creativity, and its manifestations in the world of flesh and blood. People who are spiritually evolved see themselves as instruments of the living spirit. They experience that they are somehow called to do a certain work, to manifest an intention of which they have become aware, and they commit themselves to respond to that call.

The people I have chosen to follow through their dreams and insights are committed in some way to "see through" the visible world. They wouldn't necessarily put it that way, but when their awareness of a whole world beneath the surfaces of things is acknowledged, they feel at home. They know exactly what the ancient Chinese philosopher Chuang Tsu meant when he said, "Great Knowledge is all-encompassing; small knowledge is limited" (1974 translation, p. 22). But to approach Great Knowledge it is necessary that consciousness be open to discovering the inner opposites—for example, Logos and Eros—and to bringing them into harmony. Seeking the conjunction of the opposites is the basic theme of inner work. Only when this is purposefully addressed can one gain access to Great Knowledge.

A Time for Silence

Whoever finds the way to the invisible world does it in his or her own unique manner. True, there are guides who can offer helpful advice and much has been written and spoken about "the path," but still we come upon it, sometimes even blunder upon it, according to our own nature and in our own time. The Logos person approaches from a base of knowledge and reasons from that, trying to remain as objective as possible. How things really are and how things work are of major concern to this individual. The Eros person seeks to find the way through relationships and the feelings they engender. Such a person tends to take a mythical approach, one that endows people and objects with the capacity to exert a tremendous amount of influence. I have already discussed Jung's way of personifying these influences in the form of archetypal images such as the shadow, the trickster, the wise elder, and the divine child, to name a few. These inner images are projected onto persons and events, and one then holds feelings or beliefs like these: she is wise, he can help me, better not ruffle the feathers of this one, that one has the power to ruin my reputation, this situation is dangerous, that event can lead only to disappointment, the wind is cruel, accidents happen no matter how careful you are, if you want to belong you have to play by the rules, nuclear energy can only be destructive, the people of X nation are bent on destroying us, if only I could be with this person I would be content, and so on.

Ruby had become aware of her dependence upon other people for recognition and respect. She had this trait in common with most Eros people. Much of her life was taken up with business meetings, public performances, and social events. Her popularity brought her many requests for her presence on various occasions. People wanted her to perform; they wanted to spend time with her; they asked her for advice; they gave her advice; to the point where the pleasure she derived from these relationships began to be overshadowed by the excessive demands on her time and energy that she felt people were making. She came in one day saying that she wanted desperately to get away from everyone and see what it was like to sit in silence.

I said to her, "Why not?" I saw she was terrified at the prospect, yet the welling up of tears told me that something in her wanted it very much. She said that her husband was going away on a business trip for a week or so and her son would be in summer camp, and that she was thinking of going off somewhere by herself. "Where do you think you will find silence?" I asked her. She bowed her head and said nothing. Minutes passed, or so it seemed, before she looked up at me, putting her hand over her heart. I knew her answer, "in here," did not have to be put into words, and so did she. The recognition of one's inner wisdom is quite important for an Eros person.

What Ruby finally decided was that she would let it be known among her friends and associates that she would be "away" for that week. In reality she would put her telephone on the answering machine, stock up her refrigerator, and stay at home. Of course, she could have gone off to the desert and done a great meditation like the desert fathers. But then the place would have taken on the power that Eros people are only too willing to attribute to something outside of themselves. No, home was to be the place, where nothing was different from what it had ever been, and where any change in consciousness would have to come from the place where the potential had always been, inside.

I met with Ruby once well into that week, and again at the end of it. The first time, Ruby unloaded all her complaints about how she had messed up her life. She complained about how much her friends took out of her, and about how much work it was to maintain a household with all the details for which she was responsible. She complained about the many concessions she had to make in her work life to be well liked and successful. She recited the litany of ways in which she had made "practical" choices, choices for relationships that often were not especially helpful, and how she had neglected her creative life and her spiritual life.

Joseph Wheelwright, a wise and funny old man who is also a Jungian analyst, once said that many times during analytic sessions he had to wrap his foot around the leg of the chair to keep himself from sounding off with a brilliant but unnecessary opinion. This was just such a moment for me. I restrained myself from giving the obvious advice, and instead commiserated with Ruby about how terrible everything was and how, indeed, she had taken many wrong roads and it was amazing that she had survived as well as she had. I could see a faint shadow of shame or embarrassment creeping over her face, as though she might want to say, "Well, it's not *that* bad"—but she didn't admit it. What she did say was, "I guess I have to go back and think about it some more."

After a week of not seeing anyone or talking to anyone, Ruby returned to my office. She was in good spirits and, I felt, solidly grounded. I asked her how things were going and what she had been up to.

She indicated that she felt good about what had been happening: "I've been working in my garden a lot. I got so lonesome I started talking to the plants. And you know what? They talked back to me!" I knew from the twinkle in her eye that she was all right. "It started out that I would take a little piece of the garden and look at each plant very carefully, thinking, now what do you want? What do you need? Then I asked those questions aloud. The plants told me, not using words exactly, but they showed me where they were cramped so they could not spread out their roots, where they were overburdened with too much foliage, where they felt out of shape and wanted pruning, where they were ripe and ready to be harvested, which were hungry and which were thirsty, and which were ready to be plucked up and discarded and which only needed to rest for a time."

I suggested that Ruby was seeing things from a different point of view. "Yes, from down on my knees," she laughed. "I guess that means something, though. I have been looking at just what's there in front of me, not at what I think about it or at what someone has to say about it. I see it for what it is. I guess that's new for me. Maybe that's why I am feeling good. Plants don't criticize or compliment you. They just respond naturally to what you do for them. I like that."

I reminded her that every plant has its own way of being. Since it is true to itself, people know what they can expect of it. Each produces what it is meant to produce: rosebushes produce roses and tomato plants produce tomatoes. Ruby was quick to add, "If you care for them in the way that they need to be tended. Water and fertilizer and bug spray."

"All that and lots of patience. You have to cultivate plants just the way you have to cultivate consciousness. There isn't any measure of just how long plants take to ripen and mature. Every species of plant has its own maturation timetable. It doesn't do any good to lift them up by the roots to see how they are doing. They *know* how to grow. The gardener's main jobs are to provide growing space, stimulate the process with nutrients, and get out of the way."

Ruby saw the parallel. "That's what you do, isn't it? Being an analyst is something like being a gardener. I think I understand. All of those outer things that I have depended on for so long, are not quite as necessary as I thought. Nice, within limits, but I've been behaving as if my life totally depended upon them."

She had also been behaving as though their lives totally depended upon her. But just as with plants, one cannot make another person do something or not do something that is against that person's nature. Perhaps one can help, a little. But one cannot make another person happy. One cannot make another person unhappy. Another person cannot make us happy or unhappy. We do it to ourselves. A beloved person dies, either from natural causes or in some other way. One way of looking at it is to accept it rationally: it happened, that is the way things are. Of course one feels bad about it, one goes through the normal process of grieving, and in due time one pulls oneself together and goes on with one's life. Or possibly the spirit or soul or essence remains with the bereaved, to communicate and comfort, or to receive the feelings that were never expressed to him and her and now can be said to the ever-present memory. Another way is to see that person as part of one's own life, and the loss as the annihilation of a part of oneself that can never be replaced. Life will never be the same without that person. People who feel this way will ask, when there is a death or an unusual occurrence, "Why does this happen to me?" They rail against their god, as if this were a personal affront.

Ruby thought that there must be a better way. "When a plant dies I feel sorry, but it is not that overwhelming feeling of being deserted that I have when I lose a friend. It's just that this one plant, this one life is gone, but Life still goes on."

I reminded her: there is "a time to be born and a time to die; a time to plant and a time to pluck up what is planted. A time to kill and a time to heal; a time to break down and a time to build up" (Eccles. 3:2–3), and I asked her, "What is being broken down here?"

"Rigid attitudes. What I've discovered by spending so much time alone is that what I do, I do to myself. There is no one around who makes me do anything. If I don't accomplish what I set out to do, it's on my own head. There is no one to criticize. The negative ideas I have about myself all come from me, no one else. When I feel good about something, it is not because I have pleased someone, not because I have performed well. It is because I am doing what I am here to do. The other night I heard Joseph Campbell being interviewed on television. He said that the thing to do with your life is to 'follow your bliss.' He said you should do the things that really make you happy, the things that allow you to enjoy whatever talents or interests are yours. I liked the sound of that. And yet, isn't it awfully narcissistic? I mean, aren't we supposed to do for others, not just for ourselves? I was taught to put myself last, not first. That other people mattered more than I did. Now I'm not sure. I have come to know myself a whole lot better in the past week. I like this person who I am."

I asked her how it would be when her husband and son came home and she began her regular activities again, when she picked up the calls on her answering machine and found out who had been looking for her. She said that something was different now for her. It was all part of her inner work. While she was alone she was tempted to answer the phone the first few times it rang. "But I didn't. I didn't even monitor the messages. Then I thought, why not pull out the plug so I won't even hear the ringing? But it came to me that it is important *to hear* the ringing, and to make the conscious choice to answer or not to answer. To take responsibility for creating the silent space for myself if that was what I really wanted. So I let it ring, and each time I said to myself, there's always the choice. Every morning when I'd wake up I'd remember that what I do I do through my own choice. Then I'd have this dialogue—it's easy enough when there is no one around, no one to object. Of course you can live your life as you need to. But wait until other people are making demands. And then I'd remember, I have a choice. This doesn't mean I have to disregard other people, that I have to become withdrawn and self-centered. But I have the possibility of choosing how and when I will respond to their needs or requests. Or not respond."

It sounded to me as though Ruby intended not to be ruled any longer by outer circumstance or other people. I asked her how she would keep them from taking over her life. "How will you reserve time and space for yourself to do the inner work?"

Ruby recognized the issue with which she now had to contend. "In my relational life, friends and family make demands of time and of self. Then there's my creative work, my inner work, and that's hard to do when there are so many distractions. Yet I don't want to lose all my friends, or abuse them. It seems to me that my task now is to reconcile these parts of myself."

I wanted to show her the importance of establishing her own priorities to make space in her life, sacred space. "When you look at the whole picture, your life and its meaning, it is easier to make the choices that are necessary. Take, for example, the choices you make in the outer world—whom you will see and how you will spend your time. When there is something that needs to be done and it can be done by any number of people, you can choose to let another person do it. When it is something that needs to be done and only you can do it, then probably you will want to do it. It will be *yours* to do."

Ruby understood that the choices she made today did not bind her for all time. Every morning the choices must be made again. If she made a wrong choice, the next day would provide an opportunity for a new choice. Suddenly she was able to see how open-ended life really is. "It's a great life!" she announced.

It is a great life when one can empty oneself enough to receive Great Knowledge. Ruby had made an important transition in her capacity to enjoy relationships on terms that allowed her to express her own reality freely. Paradoxically, this had come about through withdrawing from relationships and experiencing the value of aloneness consciously chosen. This issue was not dealt with once and for all through this particular episode, but it became a model for handling similar inner conflicts that would arise in the future. The facility was developing, and would be reinforced every time Ruby was faced with the necessity of determining her priorities with respect to how she would spend her time. She had asked herself, in which world will I live? And the answer had come to her, you will live in both, as suits your needs.

Another Culture

Laurel, too, found her way into the invisible world in her own unique manner. As a research scientist, she worked in a disciplined intellectual environment where high value is placed on carefully reasoned judgments. She also had considerable insight into the invisible world, and what she "saw" there was often incompatible with the customs and demands of her professional activities. She had been coping with the dissonance that this split created by compartmentalizing these very different aspects of her life. One day she brought in the following dream:

> I am brought to a strange place, strange in terms of its culture. Others have been brought here with me. We are unclear as to why we have been brought here and what our role is to be. The people who live here raise little furry animals. Other larger animals control the little ones by putting them in their mouths to transport them. Although no one has been cruel to us, we are all bewildered because we have no idea why we are here, and concerned because it is also evident that we just can't leave. I notice that the little animals are both male and female—that is, they each have humanlike genitals of both sexes, and I realize that this culture has bred them that way to increase their breeding options.
>
> One of our group is rushing down a stairway when he severely bumps into a member of the opposite sex from the other culture. (We appear to be male.) He is arrested because he has inadvertently killed this person. The penalty, as determined by the consensus of that culture, is that he must die. He objects, but he is given a card prescribing, in poetry, a "dismemberment ritual" that he is to perform. He is, or has become, a complicated assemblage of bolts, nuts, screws, etc. The dismemberment consists of his unscrewing and unbolting himself until he is all in separate parts. Although he isn't thrilled about it, he participates in his own demise. In effect, he sacrifices the preeminent intellectual approach to life. Those of us who are new to this place are saddened by the taking apart of this person. I still can't figure out this strange culture, as they are saddened by the event as well.

Important as the content of a dream may be, it is often the feeling tone that makes it possible to discern the meaning, for experience always carries with it a certain valence that lends it importance or value.

With this in mind, I asked Laurel what she was feeling in the dream. She replied, "I felt sad but bloodless. I was thinking about the man dismembering himself as me, the part that is sterile intellect. In this new culture, intellect has no place. Feeling is important here. The man should have known not to go careening down the staircase. He has no sensitivity to the human condition. This sensitivity is what *I* need to develop more fully."

Clearly, Laurel was recognizing and coming to terms with the unsatisfying nature of a purely Logos approach. Her dream was showing her another way. I asked her what she thought this strange new culture represented. She said, "Since my experience with the Greatness, my perceptions have changed. And with changed perceptions, my experiences have changed. It is as though I were on one floor, got on an elevator, and now I am on another floor."

"The other floor, is that the strange new culture?"

"Yes. I don't know what the rules are in this new culture. The total intellectual approach is not so valued here. More important is sensitivity toward others."

I proposed that it was as though the culture in which Laurel ordinarily lived was primarily a Logos culture. The new culture depicted in the dream was an Eros culture. I asked her, "What happens to the man who dismembers himself?"

"He is just a heap of nuts and bolts."

I told Laurel that this reminded me of the differences between "heaps and wholes" that Ervin Laszlo, the systems theorist, talks about in his book *The Systems View of the World* (1972). If you have a collection of bricks and stones and pipes and wires, you have several heaps. But if they are all put together into a harmonious unit so that they function in a proper relationship, each part meshing into every other part, you have a house. That is a whole. A whole has something more than the heap or heaps: it has integrity. It is more than the sum of its parts. But when something is awry with the whole, you may have to take it apart, create a heap, and then go on to fix what is wrong and reassemble the parts, perhaps in a somewhat different way from before.

Laurel replied that it's all very well to talk about dismemberment, but when you are the one who has to be dismembered, you encounter tremendous resistance.

Knowing that inner conflicts often give rise to amazing dreams, I asked her, "Why do you suppose you were having this dream just now?"

"I'm trying to find a resting place between a certain elitism and the compassion that I feel. My elitism sometimes goes beyond the bounds of reason. When it does, I tend to create a world out of total intellect. The good news is that I sometimes become aware of it, and then it all falls apart. What do you see as the difference between projection and perception?"

I replied that a movie projector projects a picture on a screen and the sound track projects voices so that we enter into the drama and for a time are witnessing "real life" that *seems* to be coming from the screen. Just so, we project the images of our own minds upon the people we know and the world we live in. Perception involves recognizing this tendency and finding out how much is "I" and how much is "not I" and separating the two, so that what is perceived is not contaminated, or is minimally contaminated, with what we bring to it. If Laurel could remember this difference, she would be clearer about her perceptions. I reminded her also that her dream was dealing with the Logos/Eros conflict. Logos is exemplified in the highest degree by Buddha, Christ, and God—whole, remote, complete in themselves. Eros is exemplified by the bodhisattva, Mary Magdalene, the Holy Sophia. These find their meaning in their relationship to people.

Laurel was seeing clearly now how little meaning Logos has by itself. "What gives Logos its true meaning," she said, "is Eros. Both are needed. But the integration of Eros in me is sporadic, erratic. I perceive one of my roles to be communicating the results of my work, but my readership is a highly intellectual, specialized group of people. You are really good at making complex ideas simple without trivializing them. That is the task I need to undertake. It seems to me my dream is suggesting that my Logos has to be dismembered because it is so powerful."

I thought her dream also suggested a bringing together of the opposites. The furry little animals have both male and female genitals. In that culture there are both men and women, but they are breeding the little animals to be androgynous. That makes the creatures more creative; it increases their options.

Laurel agreed, and took this idea further. "You're saying that they are creating androgyny in that culture. At the moment the androgynous beings are little and vulnerable. Androgyny is a factor in that culture. I know that I'm moving in that direction, but it's extremely hard to do. Since I had the experience of the trap door, the incline has become much steeper. It's more difficult to climb up the hill. I have had to let go of my burdens, my preconceived ideas. Now I have more choices—not in all situations, but it is a general pattern."

I asked her how she knew that things were changing for her. She said, "It's nothing dramatic, nothing I can point to and say 'I did it!' It comes out in funny little things, and it surprises me. Like this little game I always was playing. I resented the high cost of parking and so I would always drive around looking for a place where I might get by without paying. Then suddenly I stopped doing it. Not that I made a conscious decision, but rather it was an unconscious shift. I just found myself saying, 'It's not worth the energy. It's not important. It's silly to be so involved with myself.' The unconscious is changing."

It is hard to imagine how threatening such a dream could be to a person like Laurel, whose self-concept was based upon her adequacy in the world in which she lived, the Logos-valuing part of society, where she excelled. Knowing that she also had other ways of knowing was one thing, but actually being transported, as the dream portrayed, into another land that frowned upon her style of calculated activity that was driven resolutely toward its own goals, was quite another thing. Here she was persona non grata, and had to pay the price for being different. As the dream suggested, it was not *she* who had to be dismembered, for *she* was male now, as were all the members of her group. I understood this to mean that she had gone from using her feminine sensibilities to using her masculine sensibilities; in other words, she tended to function either out of one half of her being or out of the other, but not both together. To blend the two and use the mode that was appropriate to the situation would be androgynous, but she had not appreciated the full importance of androgyny, yet.

The members of the strange culture did value androgyny. They were breeding creatures that were both male and female. It was not that they were undifferentiated—like so many people in *this* culture whose energy is neither clearly male nor clearly female. In the new culture, the animals that were being cultivated were *both*—that is, they each had humanlike genitals of both sexes. I understood the genitals as symbolizing opposite ways of being, of knowing, and of behaving, so that the androgynous genitalia would suggest that these creatures were whole or complete in themselves, possessing a creative potential of a different order from that of any one-sided individual.

The brusque, careless, masculine member could not survive in the culture that bred "androgynes," and so the death penalty was mandated. But how was it presented? Not in cold, rational, legalistic terms, as a death penalty would be pronounced in our culture, but in poetry!

Poetry speaks a mythological language; it doesn't build a case for itself, but comes straight to essence. "Dismember yourself" was the clear and direct message. What did this mean? I suggested that the dismemberment signified a process of taking apart all the old attitudes, the old ways of being, the old thought processes, and sacrificing them. How appropriate that these should be represented as bolts, nuts, and screws! And when the complicated machinery of a person has been dismembered, well, what then? No wonder the dream was shattering! The dreamer could not figure out this strange culture that was saddened by the sacrifice that had to be made. I could not help but believe that this symbolized the sacrifices that would be required before the re-membering process could begin.

■

"No bird soars too high if he soars with his own wings."
BLAKE, *The Marriage of Heaven and Hell*

Laurel's and Ruby's inner work brought each of them to an appreciation of how they relate to both the visible and the invisible worlds. They did the work themselves, and I do not claim any credit for it. It is a part of my own inner work to explore the edges of the unknown territory and I am glad when my own journey affords me an opportunity to walk with a companion along the way. I learn at least as much from these companions as they from me. The dialogues that take place in my consulting room are one way in which the inner work gets uttered, or one could say "outered." The insights enable persons to see the world in a different way, and consequently to live differently in it. They know that fate is not working for them or against them, but that fate is a description of life as it is. The life process in itself is neutral; one could even see it as meaningless, except as we discover the meaning hidden in it.

12

The Unfolding of the Invisible World

To see a World in a Grain of Sand
And a Heaven in a Wild Flower,
Hold Infinity in the palm of your hand
And Eternity in an hour.

BLAKE, "Auguries of Innocence"

As human beings evolve, the level of consciousness of the culture in which they live also evolves. Individual development entails the enlargement of the person's consciousness through the inclusion of material from the environment, the personal unconscious, and the collective unconscious. The development of cultures is a result of the increasing sophistication of the collective consciousness. This occurs in response to the contributions of individuals who, as they evolve personally, reflect their insights back to the society in which they live.

In the early stages of an individual's life or of a culture's formation, people are most immediately concerned with how to satisfy their elemental needs for survival. When they learn how to do this and there is time left over, individuals can develop their mental capacities and adapt to or change their surroundings. Developments in the culture come about, reflecting the growing intellectual faculties of its members. Both survival needs and the increasing complexity of cultures have as their objectives managing and manipulating the visible world. This is what has been occupying so-called "civilized" people over the past several millennia. As technology becomes more efficient, these objectives are accomplished more and more rapidly and effectively, but in principle they have not appreciably changed.

How Can We Transcend Our Concern for Personal Survival?

This requires a breakthrough to another level of consciousness, making it possible to see the visible world from a totally different perspective. In order to accomplish this, it is necessary to move to a point outside the system. It is as though we were used to seeing the world from some standpoint on our planet or from maps drawn from this or that specific place. We are used to observing the situations in which we are directly involved, or those we learn about from the people who are in the midst of them, through our various sophisticated modes of communication. But now in the last quarter of our century, we can see the visible world from outside the system, as an astronaut sees it from the surface of the moon or from outer space. We are at the point of pushing through to that other level of consciousness that parallels what is happening today in our own culture. Like some of the new scientists, we have glimpsed this level many times before and have been astounded by it. But always the everyday issues tend to crowd in, placing limits upon our explorations. Now, it appears that this no longer must be true. Many people in the world today are experiencing a shift in priorities. Many people are eager and ready to further explore the unmapped territories that first made their presence known through the knowledge of the heart.

How Can We Gain Access to the Invisible World?

This question has always been a subject of reflection and contemplation, but more and more it occupies people today. Do we accomplish it through a step-by-step ascent from lower states to a more spiritual condition through prayer or by doing good works? Or is the possibility of obtaining a higher state of consciousness something that is given to us by the grace of God, or by fortuitous circumstance, or through faith in the saving power of a Redeemer? This has been debated loud and long, and to my mind it is as fruitless a discussion as the old nature versus nurture controversy. There is no way to confirm for certain what is the source of spiritual growth or the wisdom of gnosis. In all seriousness, how much does it really matter? Today it is generally recognized that whatever an individual—or even a plant, for that matter—achieves in this world depends to some degree upon initial endowment—that is, upon genetic endowment. In the inorganic sciences, we have come to see that the events that occur are profoundly influenced by "initial conditions," or what was there at the beginning. Yet the beginning point does not wholly determine the outcome, either in the animal, vegetable, or mineral kingdoms. The body/mind/soul complex that empowers the human organism from birth is profoundly influenced by forces acting upon it from the outside. Still, we find even today when we examine various psychological perspectives or world views that traces of the old debate remain.

The Appearance of the Invisible World

Ken Wilber, in systematizing his transpersonal view of human development in *The Atman Project* (1980), defines a series of hierarchical stages and substages of consciousness. He says that these levels of development are all "enfolded within the organism from its beginning."[16] We begin our lives at the lowest level of the prepersonal stage, the substage Wilber calls the pleromatic self. Here the newborn's subjective and objective worlds are completely merged—there is no sense of self and other. Wilber takes the word *pleromatic* from old alchemical and gnostic writings, and interprets it as meaning that condition in which "the self and the *material* cosmos [Wilber's emphasis] are undifferentiated" (p. 7). He makes an important point of the notion that the lack of differentiation in the pleromatic stage is characteristic of the time when the individual is in a primitive state, deeply embedded in an archaic stage of evolution and focused on the physical body and instincts, especially those instincts pressing toward food and survival.[17] Passing through successive stages, the individual experiences the unfolding of consciousness, moving from the sensibilities that are mostly concerned with the needs of the physical body and their satisfactions in the material world; to the personal or mental-egoic stages, dominated by the ego and its functions in the intellectual (Logos) and the social (Eros) realms; to the transpersonal stages, where spiritual values dominate consciousness. At the higher end of Wilber's progression, the "ultimate" stage that few, admittedly, ever approach, is a total merging with the "only God in absolute Mystery and radical Unknowing." This ultimate stage corresponds closely to what the Gnostics

16. Note the parallel with David Bohm's "implicate order/explicate order," discussed in chapter 5.
17. This is a very different concept of the pleroma from that of the gnostic literature, where the pleroma represents the "fullness" of the divine or invisible world with all its many regions, called aeons. In the gnostic literature, the pleroma is the realm of the unknown God (Rudolph 1983, p. 67).

called the pleroma. According to Wilber, there is something inexorable about this movement through a series of psychospiritual transforma- tions. It is all there, at least *in potentia*, in every person, and the as- cension to the higher stages is somehow developmentally preordained.

Wilber writes:

Now this unfolding or manifesting of successively higher modes *appears* to the psychologist as the emergence of the higher "from" the lower—and many try to so define it: the ego is said to come *from* the id, the mind is said to come "from" conditioned body reflexes, the soul is said to come "from" the instincts, man is said to come "from" amoebas. In fact, the higher comes "after" the lower, and *separates itself out of* the lower, but it does not come *from* the lower. It is now common knowledge that in each stage in development or evolution, elements emerge that *cannot* be accounted for solely in terms that preceded it. . . . The higher modes can emerge because, and only because, they were enfolded, as potential, in the lower modes to begin with, and they simply crystallize out and differentiate from the lower modes as evolution proceeds. (pp. 174–175)

"Simply" indeed! I have found nothing either simple or inexorable about the process of coming to consciousness. It is hard work. It takes a long time and not everyone has the determination for it. Only those who are sufficiently attentive to be able to hear themselves called, who listen to what is asked of them, and who are willing to commit them- selves to following their secret inner knowledge, can set aside igno- rance and come to a realization of the larger truths that are enveloped in mystery.

Election to the Invisible World

Wilber's position can be compared to the gnostic view of the struc- ture of consciousness. Gnostic anthropology speaks of the division of people into classes, not stages. Stages imply a movement from lower to higher or from simpler to more complex. Classes are conditions in being; they have coherence and identity. One is in such and such a class because that is where one is, and also because that is who one is by virtue of one's essential nature. The first- and second-century Gnostics conceived of three classes of people. The first was called the *hylic* class, deriving from the Greek word *hyle*, meaning matter, fleshly, or earthly. The second was called *psychic*, and referred to the soul or mind—two concepts that were not differentiated in those days but that together referred to thinking and feeling (Logos and Eros) in this world. The third state or class was the *pneumatic*, *pneuma* being the Greek word for air, wind, or spirit. Wind is synonymous with spirit, as in "The Spirit of God hovered over the waters." (Gen. 1:2, RSV). The people in this class are aware not only of their temporal aspect but also of their eternal aspect, and of the relationship between them. Here is how the three classes are described in the gnostic document "On the Origin of the World" (Robinson 1988): "There are . . . three men, and also his posterities unto the consummation of the world: the spirit-endowed of eternity, and the soul-endowed, and the earthly" (p. 186).

And my old friend William Blake, whose lifelong struggle was against the tyranny of Reason, also writes in *Milton* of what he calls the three classes of mortal men:

> Here the Three Classes of Mortal Men take their fix'd destinations,
> And hence they overspread the Nations of the whole Earth,
> and hence
> The Web of Life is woven & the tender sinews of life created
> And the Three Classes of Men regulated. . . .
> The first, The Elect from before the foundation of the World!
> The second, The Redeem'd: The Third, The Reprobate & form'd
> To destruction from the mother's womb . . .
>
> (1957, p. 486)

The question this kind of statement raises is whether we are by our very nature destined to remain in the "class" in which we were born or whether we, as individual human beings, have the capacity to overcome the obstacles that hold us back and evolve to higher states. Some of the new evolutionary theorists have encouraging things to say about the latter possibility.

Evolving Toward the Invisible World

The view of the invisible world held by Erich Jantsch, systems theorist, philosopher, and interdisciplinary scholar in human and cultural evolution, is farther from the enfolded/developmental concept of Wilber and closer to the gnostic view of three distinct modes of apprehension that characterize the approaches of different classes of people. In *Design for Evolution* (1975), he writes:

Human life is movement. It is movement not by and for itself, but within a dynamic world, within movements of a higher order. On the one hand, these higher-order movements constitute the life of human systems—of relations, organizations, communities, institutions, nations and cultures, of the entire human world. For human systems, no less than individuals, have a life of their own, a life which is characterized and enhanced by human qualities and capabilities. In our Western world we have almost come to forget this since we started to draw organismic and mechanistic analogies for the interpretation of human systems. But on the other hand, human life is also embedded in the higher-order movement of nature, of an all-pervading flow of life and evolution which generates and energizes the lives of human beings and, through them, the lives of human systems. This we have forgotten to such an extent that, in order to remember and comprehend our own nature, we search in the myths of old and extinct cultures and in the depths of the subconscious—to emerge with but the vague contours of a remote reflection, an elusive memory from earlier phases of mankind's psychosocial evolution. (p. 5)

Jantsch suggests a tripartite structure of consciousness that is still another variation on what seems to be an archetypal theme. He calls the three ways of approaching the world (or worlds) "modes of inquiry." The three modes of inquiry are designated as the *rational*, the *mythological*, and the *evolutionary*.

The rational approach is basically a mechanistic system. Related to the Newtonian paradigm in physics, it assumes a separation between the observer and the observed. The basic organizing principle is logic, the results of inquiry are expressed in structural or quantitative terms, and the dynamic aspects are seen as change.

From our perspective, the rational approach is the approach of the developing ego that sees itself as central in the personality and the point from which the world takes its definition. This approach is concerned primarily with the material world. Attention to body and mind are both regarded as important, but not necessarily interconnected or interdependent. It is an approach in which individuals are primarily interested in their effect upon the material world (if they are extraverts) or the effect of the material world upon them (if they are introverts). This mode of inquiry closely parallels that of the gnostic hylic class.

The mythological approach, in Jantsch's terms, is basically an intellectual and psychological system. From this perspective, one sees a world built largely on subjective qualities and their interactions. "The weather can be good or bad, the sky friendly or threatening, a breeze strong or gentle, trees whisper and forests murmur, the sea rages or is calm; space and time are commodities which can be gained, saved or wasted, and so on," writes Jantsch. "Our daily life is a series of interactions with objects that seem to treat us with friendliness or malevolence" (p. 87). The world makes "demands" upon the person who holds this view. Interrelationships with the social fabric, including communications, roles and expectations, are major concerns to individuals using this mode.

This mode of inquiry corresponds to a more highly developed ego-consciousness than that which is limited to the purely rational domain. The ego that uses the mythological approach is a social ego, no longer entirely focused upon itself. This mode is similar to Wilber's mental-egoic stage. With this mode of inquiry, one is able to see how events cause and influence one another, and how the individual is related to events in a wider world. Rather than seeking change for its own sake, people using this mode are more concerned with process, with how people are transformed through what they do. Mind and soul experience and express thoughts and feeling in both Logos and Eros modes, although usually not at the same time. People using this mode would roughly correspond to the gnostic class of psychics.

Jantsch's evolutionary level mode of inquiry incorporates the values of the rational approach and the mythological approach, and goes beyond them. This mode is concerned primarily with *purpose*: Where am I going? How am I and my world evolving? It corresponds to the lower transpersonal stages in Wilber's scheme; but Jantsch, unlike Wilber, attaches no special value to transcending the visible world. Instead, he suggests the importance of being able to know and experience the invisible world, at the same time that one values everyday reality.

On the cover of Jantsch's book *Design for Evolution* is an ambiguous photograph of an organism complete in itself, it seems to me, with an outside and an inside delineated in soft sepia tones. It could be an abstraction of a shell, or perhaps a flower separated from its stem and leaves, or a smooth piece of marble with a hollowed-out cleft. The author uses this to illustrate how the subject/object relationship is depicted when the different modes of inquiry are applied. He writes:

Most people to whom I showed this picture felt obliged to try the rational approach, with vastly different explanations ranging from "a surface of ice" to "a duck taking off." How irrelevant scientific truth appears here! A young and sensitive friend felt frightened, or even hurt, by the picture—it struck her like an open wound, the pain of which she felt in herself. Taking the mythological approach, she established a very personal relationship with the quality of form brought about by an arbitrary event. But the artist calls her photograph "Rising to the Sixth Chakra"—which, in the Hindu scheme of the seven chakras or levels of consciousness, stands for wisdom, represented by the "third eye." In an evolutionary approach to inquiry, human and natural movement flow together, physical and spiritual meaning become aspects of the same overall motion. In this mood, one may see a flame, a symbol of life, striving toward light—or, rather, the reflection of the divine light which we touch in wisdom. (p. 91)

Finding the Way

It seems to me that the three classes, stages, or modes can be understood in terms of their manner of accessing the visible and invisible worlds. The first group of people use primarily the old paradigm manner of coming to know. They can recognize objects in a material world as discrete, finite, and quantifiable. They regard effects as related to some prior cause that is, at least theoretically, definable. The second group is more concerned with relationships, based on the "I-and-other" relationship, which can take any form from "I and Thou" to "Us and Them." Their concern is with the relationships between subject and object, where one is always either influencing a situation or being influenced by it. The third group is far more difficult to describe because its members live on the edge of the Great Mystery. Sometimes they are even able to enter into the flow of that life energy that they may not *understand* intellectually but can *know* with the "knowledge of the heart."

I do not see that any of these three classes of people is better or worse than any other. A society needs them all, for each one performs certain necessary functions for the whole organism that is society, and if any were absent the social order would suffer greatly for it. There is undoubtedly a need for the practical, commonsense attitude that is able to deal with the demands of the material world and function effectively in the midst of situations that other people might find threatening personally or destructive to society. The problem solvers, the organizers and planners, make it possible to live in the material world. And it must go without saying that most of us function in the context of this class a good deal of the time. The second group, focused as it tends to be on relationships both personal and human on the one hand and abstract or technical on the other, provides the grease that makes the machinery of a complex society go around. The third group of people must spend much of their time functioning out of one or the other of the first two modes, and this is necessary. That they are aware that there is another way of being, and not only aware but active in seeking it out, is not necessarily obvious to people who are not sensitive at this level. Many members of this third group are somewhat isolated in their spiritual lives, although more and more, they are finding other people who are of a similar persuasion. It is this special opening of consciousness that makes them feel different, and sometimes even a little "crazy," because their concept of the worlds is not what most other people imagine to be rational. As I work analytically with people who are moving and shifting between the second and the third groups, I often notice they have a great deal of resistance to entering the mysterious and incomprehensible space, and at the same time a fascination for the numinosum that emanates from there.

The question will surely be asked, Are there really three classes of people—some doomed to lead their lives in the hard struggle to survive; others actively moving to develop their mental resources so that they can achieve personal and economic security and a measure of control over the (visible) world in which they live; and a third group whose greatest interest is in how it all fits together: the known, the unknown, and the unknowable? I have a difficult time with the question myself, because I am unwilling to categorize people on the basis of where their interests or attention may be at a given moment. I prefer to think that the species *homo sapiens* is aptly named for the wisdom inherent in each individual that might be realized if all the necessary conditions were ripe for it.

What I am suggesting is that the higher stages of evolution are not too far from anyone who feels called to proceed on the perilous path that leads into the unknown reaches of the human potential. On the other hand, the more primitive aspects of human development—the desperate fear of not surviving that leads people to the defensive stance that can swiftly turn into aggression—are not very far from us either. Nor is the middle stage, the personal stage in which we identify ourselves as individuals and in which we are bent on the development of an ego that can cope successfully with the intricacies of life on the planet at the end of the twentieth century.

I believe that the "three classes of mortal men," as Blake put it, exist in each of us, at least *in potentia*. Wilber has suggested that the process of psychospiritual growth proceeds step by step through many stages. The only barriers to breaking through from one stage to the next reside within ourselves. At this moment the name Tony Sutich comes to mind. Sutich was the leading philosopher-psychologist and inspiration behind the original formulation of transpersonal psychology in the 1960s. Wasted away by a degenerative disease so that he could not move any muscle below his neck, he required assistance to meet his most elementary needs. Yet he continued to serve as a gifted therapist, able to bring healing to others, if not to his own body. He gathered around him some of the foremost thinkers in his field, and encouraged them to conceptualize with him the new discipline that came to be known as transpersonal psychology. Despite what might appear to be unsurmountable barriers, Sutich demonstrated the indomitable power of the human spirit. Examples such as his and that of physicist Stephen Hawking demonstrate that it is possible to live in the prepersonal stage of consciousness where one is largely dependent on others, in the world dominated by ego where personal identity is paramount, and in the world beyond ego—all at one time. Where people exert the major part of their energies is an individual matter, consciously or unconsciously determined. To move beyond the arena of the known, however, requires some major changes in consciousness. These are evolutionary changes, as Jantsch suggests, and humanity is in the process of evolving.

Changing Perceptions, Attitudes, and Behavior

Having once seen through the visible world, we must make the leap of faith to enter into and to experience the world of mystery. This brings about a changed perception, the essence of which is a recognition that knowledge (information) and wisdom (gnosis or the awareness of the indwelling spirit) both exist, and that both are real. Still, a change of perception or a change in attitude is of little value unless it brings with it a change of behavior. In our culture, knowledge has been overvalued and wisdom undervalued. Wisdom comes into being largely through gaining access to the invisible world. That world has been called by many names: the unconscious, the Kingdom of the Spirit, heaven and hell and purgatory, Eden, the world beyond the senses.

Esoteric though it sounds, all that is required to perceive that world is a change of focus from the foreground of consciousness to its background. The courage of one's convictions is needed to shift the viewpoint, if only temporarily, from seeing oneself as central in the universe to seeing oneself as a grain of sand on the beach. It is helpful to acknowledge the long-held traditions that support this point of view, especially the esoteric branches of the Judeo-Christian culture to which we are heir, including the contemplative and monastic orders, mysticism in Christianity, Kabbalah in Judaism, and the Sufi tradition in Islam.

Every human contact is altered in the light of seeing through the visible world. New modes of behavior are relatively simple to enact once the basic underlying concepts are grasped, yet they can be tremendously powerful. It becomes no longer necessary to prevail, to win a conflict, to persuade another of one's own point of view. "It is not necessary," as a Hindu sage once said, "to tell another person that he is drinking from a glass of foul water. What is needed is only to place a glass of clean water beside his glass." Behavior that exemplifies the conviction of a unitary world in which every act has its far-reaching consequences, is transformative behavior. It influences everyone it touches. Although we are finite beings, we participate in life, which is infinite, having neither beginning nor end; and although in this lifetime we reside in a finite space, our experience of life in the wider sense is nonlocal. The invisible world permeates the visible world like radio waves or television signals in the atmosphere. It makes itself known wherever there are instruments tuned to receive it.

To the degree that we can bring this wider consciousness to our perceptions, we gain the capability to alter the shape of both of the worlds we inhabit. When we consider the form and consciousness of Paleolithic man and compare even his skeletal form with that of contemporary man, we can see that Stone Age man was a far-from-completed specimen of humanity. We may be as distant from what we can someday become, as early man was from where we are now. But today there is a difference. With dizzying rapidity we have been gaining speed and momentum in the visible world through industry, technology, and access to information. What is needed now is a commensurate gain of speed and momentum in the other world; else our lack of vision will lead us ever more swiftly toward annihilation.

13

The Perilous Path

I would be remiss if I did not sound a warning concerning the dangers associated with a radical change of consciousness. Just at the time when you are ready to move toward the new way of being, the terror often strikes. Part of it is panic over the prospect of giving up the security of the familiar, of relinquishing old habits, of letting go of old relationships and even of your hard-won self-image. You will probably ask: Do I possess the necessary courage, the stamina, that is needed to walk this path? If I release the attachment to an identity that no longer serves me, will something better take its place? And if, by some happy miracle, I emerge from the terror transformed into a truer, more coherent self, will I still be recognized by friends as a friend and by my lover as a lover? Or will an estrangement occur between me and the others? And then the final, fateful doubt: What if I go through all this only to find nothing there, only emptiness? These terrors are the last struggle of the archons to maintain their negative powers over those who would eat the fruit of the Tree of Knowledge.

Whoever seeks to enter the invisible world must travel on a perilous path, as William Blake knew when he wrote in *The Marriage of Heaven and Hell*:

Once meek, and in a perilous path,
The just man kept his course along
The vale of death.
Roses are planted where thorns grow,
And on the barren heath
Sing the honey bees.
Then the perilous path was planted
And a river and a spring

On every cliff and tomb,
And the bleached bones
Red clay brought forth.
Till the villain left the paths of ease,
To walk in perilous paths, and drive
The just man into barren climes.

(1957, p. 148)

Trusting the Unconscious

It was no accident that I chose to write on William Blake for the thesis that was required as part of my analytic training. I wanted a subject that would allow me to try to penetrate the mind of someone who was in touch with the invisible world, and I knew from my long connection with Blake that he was more at home in the countries of the imagination—"Beulah . . . the place where the contrarieties are equally true . . . the lovely Shadow where no dispute can come" and "Great Golgonooza, free from the four iron pillars of Satan's Throne (Temperance, Prudence, Justice, Fortitude, the four pillars of tyranny)"; "Albion upon the Rock of Ages" and the "Three Heavens of Ulro . . . where the Seven Eyes of God walk round"—than he was in the streets of London. I had been struggling through Blake for many years, and now I desired to see whether the maps of the collective unconscious as laid out by Jung could be used to clear a pathway into Blake's world. I did not know how to approach this task, given the vast amounts of material in the writings of both Blake and Jung, since each writer's work is difficult to reach through the exercise of the rational mind alone. I had put the old pre-Zurich life behind me and had laid myself open and vulnerable to an entirely new and unpredictable existence on my return to my own country. To make matters worse, I was under the pressure of a severe time limitation. I had entered the training program late and now circumstances made it urgent that I return to the United States in less than six months, whether or not I had completed my training. But how to finish in time?

I was feeling like Psyche, who, in seeking to reunite with her lost lover, the god Amor, incurs the wrath of his mother, Aphrodite. As Erich Neumann tells it in *Amor and Psyche* (1956), the goddess, determined to prevent Psyche from achieving her goal, sets a series of insurmountable tasks for her. The first—to sort out a huge mound of barley, millet, poppy seed, peas, lentils, and beans—reminded me of my own training. Obviously, Aphrodite thinks the task of sorting out this huge muddle of seeds is impossible to perform. The seeds represent that creative principle associated with the masculine that when united with the feminine receptivity of Earth can bring into being an orderly process of growth and development. Psyche cannot do it alone, to be sure, but she gets help from an army of ants, who represent that unconscious element that enables her to select, sift, correlate, and evaluate what lies before her—in short, the Logos activity.

I saw this as my task also, for I was getting ready to move out of the sanctuary of my own analysis where I could think or dream or say whatever emerged from the unconscious, and to enter the professional world outside, where it was necessary that orderly thought processes prevail. Although I recalled the myth while I was feeling so incapable of my task, I did not remember who had started me on this path in the first place. It is only now as I attempt to pull together the strands of the fabric of my life that I realize that the parable of the ant with which I began this book came from the same unconscious anthill that produced the help I needed to solve the problem I faced toward the end of my analytic training.

It occurred in the middle of the night, when the body sleeps and the unconscious wakens. Lying in the quiet darkness of my room, I found myself ruminating about my thesis. Then gradually my random thoughts began to take shape, crowding out my fears and fantasies of failure. I saw an outline take form step by step, the major headings and, in between, the lesser topics, all neatly ordered in logical progression. I thought to myself, I'd better write this down, for I'll surely forget it when I wake up, so I reached for the pen and yellow-lined pad next to my bed that I kept there to record my dreams. As I began to write, the outline filled out in perfect sequence, with all of my ideas in place where they belonged. It was quite detailed, and it flowed from my pen without the slightest hesitation. When I came to the end of it I felt happy and relieved. I put the pad down and went back to sleep. In the morning I woke up with the feeling that I had had the most wonderful dream, but unfortunately I could not recall it. I reached for my yellow pad, thinking that if I were to begin to write something, anything, perhaps it would come back to me. When I looked at the pad—here I want to say and I will, "Lo and behold!"—the outline was there. I had written it in my own hand, and it was absolutely right just as it was. No corrections were needed. What spirit had moved me in the night I did not know, but I did know that I would carry through and complete my journey. I typed the outline and presented it the next day as my thesis proposal. It was accepted by my committee. The writing went along with very little difficulty and was completed on schedule. I had survived the uprooting of my life in the States, the shaking experiences of my personal analysis, and my four years in Zurich, which for me was another country in more ways than one.

I knew what Jung had meant when asked about his own experience of the Self. He said that he could only endure the amazing numinosity because he had dropped to the bottom of Hell and could go no farther. Jung, too, was aware of the peril. Of all psychologists, he alone talks about the Self as a partly conscious, partly unconscious aspect of the individual, and the connecting rod to the mysterious Other. If that connection is not fostered, supported, and maintained, we risk falling into the abyss of ignorance and chaos. And most of the time we do not even know that we have fallen into it! Therefore, if life is to have coherence and meaning in the widest sense, it is necessary to discover this connection, or rediscover it if we have lost the sense of it. Without it we cannot move freely back and forth between the visible and invisible worlds.

Laurel knew the peril also when she spoke to me about her sense of responsibility in the presence of so great an energy. Her actual words were, "It's very, very perilous. I have this partnership with the Self. If I did not trust the Self, my own connection with the divine mystery, I don't know how I could handle what moves in and through me."

When Laurel shared with me her awe and trepidation, I reminded her, "The fear of the Lord is a necessary part of the individuation process in which you are engaged. You know the story that is told about Moses when he went up to the mountain of the Lord, how he hid himself in the cleft of a rock so that he might be shielded from the light as the Glory of God passed by. Because of this awe, he was allowed to survive. Selene, the vain woman of the Greek myth who had been impregnated by Zeus, insisted that her immortal lover show himself to her friends to prove that he had been with her, as she had said. 'You promised me whatever I desired, when you lay with me,' she reminded him. Zeus acceded to her wish despite his better judgment, but Selene—no longer protected by awe—was consumed in the fiery heat of his presence."

When I reminded Laurel of these mythological events, they enabled her to see her own obsession with the Greatness in a clearer perspective. She saw that most religions offer symbols that mediate between the human being and the divine—symbols such as the Virgin Mary, the saints, the Hindu pantheon, the Olympian family of the ancient Greeks. Many people need them as "transitional objects," something to hold onto in the face of overwhelming power. But Laurel felt that her own experience did not come in symbolic form. "It's as though I have transcended the symbols," she told me.

"Here I find a difficulty," I said to Laurel. "We are forced to use metaphors and symbols because some experiences defy literal description. But we must be careful, I think, not to confuse the metaphor and symbol with what it is attempting to convey. Some mythologists fall in love with the symbol and stop there. They interpret it in a general way, as a sort of image that represents some aspect of that mysterious entity, 'the human condition.' They worship the symbol for its own sake. This is probably what you are resisting. But others, like Jung, can honor the symbol and yet *see through* the symbol into the experience."

"Perhaps that is why I feel closer to Jung than to the others," she answered. "If I had to put myself into some kind of lineage, it would not be among the contemplatives, but among people who have *stood their ground*, like the biblical Job. I once dreamed of a little child named Job. I *know* what Job felt like. I *know* what Jonah went through when God told him to go to Nineveh and prophesy, and he didn't want to do it. I *know* how the prophets must have felt when the voice of God ordered them to speak out against the wrongdoing of the people. They'd hear God, and say, 'What? Me?' I know how important it is to keep evil in the forefront of consciousness. That doesn't mean I have to fight evil all the time. But by standing firmly in front of it, I may be able to change it a little." Laurel could see why, when people have an experience of the *Mysterium Tremendum,* they might arrogate that power to themselves. She was learning that it is the responsibility of conscious people to find out what powers belong to them, and what powers they cannot rightly claim as their own. She recognized that acquiring this discrimination was part of her task here on earth.

The Peril of Pride

For those who choose this path there is, first of all, the danger of hubris. It comes in the form of the feeling that because one has been able to pierce the veils of the visible world, one has achieved a certain superiority over others who have not embarked upon this enterprise. Hubris does not expand the vision; it narrows it. Such people may come to feel that they are able, or even obliged, to teach or impose this knowledge upon others. It cannot be taught, but people can, if they will, learn it for themselves. There is an even more serious risk, that of feeling that when one has discovered a way to a wider vision, this knowledge can now be used for personal advantage. Sooner or later this attitude leads to disaster.

The case study narrated by Jung in his doctoral dissertation provides a good example. He describes how a young woman with psychic gifts received much acclaim because of her special ability to access hidden knowledge. People came every week to séances where she would transmit messages from people who had died, or from times before her own birth. Today we would call her a trance medium or a channel. After a time there were some occasions when people were gathered around her, that her "gifts" would not appear on demand. The young woman, afraid of losing her reputation, began to fabricate her presentations. Of course, she was eventually exposed, and both she and her purported special abilities were thoroughly discredited.

Every twist and turn of the perilous path brings its dangers and delights, its phantasms of the night and mysterious caves too deep and dark to penetrate very far. Mystics and sages have always said that this path is not for everyone, only those who are strongly motivated from within. Consequently, the truly wise have not made themselves easily accessible to guide the soul traveler. One has to seek diligently to find the right guides for the journey, learning in the process to tell the genuine from the spurious. The seeker must be prepared in body, mind, and spirit to undergo the ordeals and struggles that will have to be faced. This is one reason why tradition demands that no one shall be allowed to study the Kabbalah who has not reached the age of forty-five. By that time the aspiring student should have acquired enough life experience in the material world to keep grounded, while facing the mysteries of the invisible world. Other mystical traditions require initiations, trials, and tests to prove the individual's strength and commitment to a way that may require confronting the dark shadows of despair, misery, and the fear of madness, as well as the blinding light of sudden illumination.

Struggling with the Opposites

When a person stands at the threshold of the invisible world, a great desire to go forward arises. This conscious desire to know what others do not know and to discover secrets, hidden things that have not been recognized before, sets off a tremendous resistance on the part of the unconscious. Every complex in the person is activated, as if the unconscious were determined to undermine any intrusion into its secret and unknown territory. One is pulled this way and that, between the eagerness to delve into the mystery and the comfort of staying with what is known and secure. Fantasies race through the mind as though to seduce the person into throwing away all caution and leaping into the abyss. It is a time when great circumspection is needed.

William Blake, in *The Marriage of Heaven and Hell*, describes how he is tempted by an "angel" who comes to him and enters into a dialogue with him:

"O pitiable foolish young man! O horrible! O dreadful state! consider the hot burning dungeon thou are preparing for thyself to all eternity, to which thou art going in such career." I said: "Perhaps you will be willing to shew me my eternal lot, & we will contemplate together upon it, and see whether your lot or mine is most desirable." So he took me thro' a stable & thro' a church and down into the churchvault, at the end of which was a mill: thro' the mill we went and came to a cave: down the winding cavern we groped our tedious way, till a void boundless as a nether sky appear'd beneath us, and we held by the roots of trees and hung over this immensity; but I said, "if you please, we will commit ourselves to this void, and see whether providence is here also: if you will not, I will . . ." So I remained with him, sitting in the twisted root of an oak; he was suspended in a fungus, which hung with the head downward into the deep. (1957, pp. 155–56)

The greatest danger occurs when one has seen the abyss that separates the inner opposites and sets about to bridge that space. One's energy is fully occupied in the mental and emotional struggles between the side of ego-consciousness and the lesser known shadow side, or in the conflict between the inner opposites of the masculine and the feminine, or in the battle between oneself and the tribal gods with their repeated demands for fealty, devotion, and sacrifice. When at last the struggle begins to be seen for what it is, *the fruitless effort to maintain the illusion of one's own importance*, something marvelous yet terrifying can happen. Energy formerly bound up in the clash between the opposites is now suddenly freed. The person feels possessed of the capacity to do anything he or she wishes to do. It was at such a time that Blake confronted the angel and demanded to look into the void that is eternity. Yet for all his grandiosity, the poet wound his foot into the roots of trees before looking into the face of the abyss. Wisely, he remained attached to the material world, even while attempting to venture beyond it. Even this staunch defender of Imagination knew when it was time to call upon Reason for support!

Jung, writing in *Two Essays in Analytical Psychology* (1928/1966), warns of the danger that is likely to come upon us just when the warring opposites in our own nature that have plagued us for years appear to have come together in some sort of truce. Veil upon veil has been stripped away. With each rending of the curtains that separate the known, the knowable, and the unknowable, a glimpse appears of what lies beyond human consciousness. Insight occurs as the result of a great deal of inner work. A part of what had been so murky before, now seems suddenly clear. A sense of deepening understanding grows, and at a certain point one feels a powerful sense of relief.

This is just the time to be watchful for the appearance of the "mana personality," Jung cautions. *Mana* is a Polynesian word for a special kind of magical power that enables its holder to perform wonders. When people who have been working on resolving their inner opposites begin to experience a great influx of energy, they may start to feel a certain possessiveness about it. They may feel, "I am strong. I can do wonderful things that other people cannot do. I'm not afraid of anything. Nor do I care what other people think. I have a mission to perform in life and no one is going to stop me." These are the secret thoughts that arise, and although they may not be shared with anyone they can be projected into the world as prophetic statements or as political or military conquests. Mana personalities range from Hitler to cult leader Jim Jones, from petty tyrants who manage offices to rock stars who are followed around by their groupies. These people all project charisma, that magical personal quality of leadership that arouses enthusiasm and popular support. As long as the individual who is gripped by the mana personality archetype believes that the power belongs to him or her, the situation can be more hazardous than wildfire.

A Touch of Magic

Let us remember that the soul nature of the individual—that is, the aspect of the person that relates to the invisible world—is rarely if ever apparent to the casual observer. But it surely exists and it finds its voice in the company of people who can be trusted to hear, respect, and understand it. A result of the inner work, when it has been effective, is that the unrecognized or neglected aspect of the psyche assumes a new role. What was formerly a tendency to favor one side of the personality now opens to receive its opposite. This was true for each of the women whom we have been following. Over the months as Ruby and Laurel were dealing with disparate aspects of their psyches, some of their tensions were being resolved. Each woman, in her own way, felt a release of power, and each had to deal with magical feelings that gave rise to concern.

Ruby's primary mode of inquiry (in Jantsch's term) was mythological in that she tended to endow each person and each object in nature with qualities and capabilities that could exert a profound influence upon her. At a certain point it appeared to me that Ruby was approaching the culmination of the work of bringing her relationships into a better balance through integrating some of the Logos potential into her predominantly Eros nature. Now she was able to see clearly that her urgent wish to relate to people needed to be tempered by more awareness of the role each person played in her life, and whether or not the relationship brought meaning and harmony into her life and into that of the other person.

Some weeks after Ruby's silent retreat in her own home, she entered a new creative phase. She had been taking her work out into the world more joyfully than she had been able to do for a very long time. There was a real difference in her life, as she described it: "I didn't understand that if I took my inner vision seriously, that I would be changed. It does not stand in a separate place from my everyday life. I had to bring this vision into the world I live in, into my work, and into all the necessary tasks that would make it possible for my creative activity to be seen in the world. I could not see this from the place where I stood a few months ago."

Ruby had allowed herself to go deep inside, to introvert. Now she could see that this in itself was not the solution. It served as a way to change her standpoint, but it was not the beginning and end of it. Nevertheless, in the process she had discovered another aspect of herself—an introvert who feared extraversion. She could see now that even though relationships were very important to her, she was at heart an introvert. The shadow lay in the extraverted side. That side was relatively unconscious most of the time. It managed her; she did not have control over it. That is why extraversion had always given her so much trouble. It was a great surprise to Ruby when she discovered that. I said to her, "You have confronted that extraverted shadow, the one who couldn't have an easy, natural way of going about relationships. Eros was with you all right, but it had a shadowy quality. It compromised your freedom to express yourself because you were always feeling bound by the opinions of others—or by your fear of those opinions. It required your willingness to go into yourself in silence and solitude to be able to encounter that shadowy part of yourself. The dark powers in the world, that you felt were demanding your time and attention and sucking you dry, are no longer frightful strangers to you. You have finally come to make peace with them. You have let them teach you."

Ruby added to this the information that she had acquired a sort of inner teacher. "I find myself thinking about Merlin lately—the old magician who traveled back and forth between the mysterious realm of the Druid priests and priestesses and the court of King Arthur, where the love and loyalty to Christ and King were bringing about a new order. The old wizard who, they say, could walk about unseen, is somehow in my thoughts today. In him the old order and the new could be reconciled. I find myself thinking about magic and alchemy, for these are secret ways of bringing about transformation. This also puts me in mind of witchcraft."

I asked her what she meant by witchcraft. She replied, "Witchcraft is the magic that has to do with studying the *web*. Perceiving the relationship of all the parts, the connections. Where to touch, where to push a little, where to enter, where to intervene. It's seeing the whole first of all. Then the rest is relativized, it all relates to the entirety. The web consists of the barely visible fibers that make a single pattern of your life, not just bits and pieces here and there."

I reminded her that the original problem, the key problem with which we had to deal, was her relationships. She acknowledged that she had been at the mercy of her relationships. "I was submerged under them. Now there's a shift in the positioning of it all. It has to do with saying no. Before, I saw it as when I would say no to someone it was like putting a curse on that person, negating that person . . . an insult at the very least. But now, here's the paradox—to say no does not mean the end of a relationship. I have to view it as a particular kind of relationship; it puts you in a different place in the web. You're still in the relationship, but your priorities are different. Now when I say no it is a part of something bigger. The no is acceptable. I used to feel that my no was too powerful to be borne by the world. I don't have that feeling any longer."

I asked her whether it had occurred to her that by saying no to something she might be saying yes to something else.

"No, it didn't. But of course you're right. The no is part of a larger yes. It has to do with the ordering of images. There is always something beyond, something of greater value. I have the feeling that I am held, protected, valued simply for what I am. I used to spend so much of my time feeling that if I didn't kill myself with effort, I would fail. But now I see that these images are given to me. Rose. Wind. Stars. Mountains. Merlin. All I've had to do is just live and be open to what came. Nothing that springs from my creative impulse is impossible. Now I want to move into the space where I believe things are possible and that there are gifts."

I affirmed her feeling that there is a space that is rich with possibilities. I was thinking of the invisible world, the source of creativity in human beings. Whatever comes from that place needs to be manifested in the visible world. I reminded Ruby that in fairy tales you always have the mundane tasks to work with in the world, as well as in the inner world. Psyche had to sort out the different grains from a huge pile. She had to do it in the here and now. The regular world can be a sacred space. Ruby could see that. It was clear that she was bringing together the inspiration and the practice. She had learned to sweep the temple.

Beyond the Mountains Lie the Stars

Laurel was undergoing some important changes also, though not without a struggle. From time to time she would feel out of touch with many of the people she knew. One day she brought in the following very short dream:

> Roger tells me that we are related to or descended from Amelia Earhart.

I asked her what Roger and Amelia Earhart had in common.

"About the only thing I can think of is that they are both dead. Roger was a cousin of mine, a fine person, but unknown. Amelia Earhart was a very courageous woman explorer, and very well known. But she was only one in a long line of women who did the unusual, the marvelous, from Socrates' Diotima to Edwina Mountbatten, who explored the Himalayas. They are all, all, gone, after a brief period of time on this earth."

"You also are an explorer, Laurel," I said.

She replied that the kind of exploration she was concerned with had to do with inner exploration. I was not so sure. Rather, it seemed to me that her task was the integration of the outer with the inner.

When I suggested this to her she agreed. "Yes, that sounds right. But why is it so very difficult?"

"Because you are beginning now to bring your outer life more into conformity with your inner life. That means changing your outer life. And your outer life is reasonably comfortable. It supplies many of your basic needs and you enjoy relationships with old friends and with your own family. All that has to be subject to change. Jesus, speaking for the authority of the divine principle, demanded, according to the Gospel of Thomas, 'Whoever does not hate his father and his mother will not be able to be a disciple to Me, and whoever does not hate his brethren and his sisters and does not take up his cross in My way will not me worthy of Me.' This seems to say that yes, this path is difficult, very difficult, for one who is single-purposed. Many sacrifices will be asked. No wonder you are suffering. It would be much easier if you could just skip over the abyss from here to the other side, without causing pain and without feeling pain. The inner divine principle does not say it will be accomplished without great pain and difficulty. But there is Something on the other side of the abyss."

Laurel knew this very well. "What keeps me going is that I feel that I have this Greatness in me. It leads me on. I have a feeling of destiny, I feel that I am somehow special."

"Special? It doesn't matter," I said. "Like Amelia Earhart and like Roger, we only are here for a little while; then we go. Special or not, we become as the dust, as grains of sand on the ocean beach."

"Then is all of this about recognizing the Greatness a gigantic inflation? Is my ego puffed up, and am I not really so special? I suppose I have been extremely arrogant."

I asked her how she saw herself as arrogant.

"For one thing, I associate myself with Job. I see my suffering as something visited upon me by an unkind god. But then, I realize that I don't have to carry the burden of that god."

"What god are you talking about?"

"That's just where I am so confused. I feel that I am incarnating 'God,' but what god am I incarnating?"

She seemed to feel that the god she was experiencing as being so hard, so demanding, was a false god or a secondary god. When I asked her about this she was unsure of herself. She expressed the fear that she might have the capacity to corrupt the Greatness. When I inquired as to where this fear might be coming from, she made a significant admission: "I seem to understand people's problems. They sense this and they are always seeking my advice. I'm flattered when my opinion is asked. But then I notice that I am interested in expressing my own opinions. I'm not dependent on the approval of others."

"So it is your ego that you believe has the capacity to corrupt the Greatness?"

"My ego is in partnership with the Self. That is why I feel it is so powerful."

"And you're concerned that this is inflation! Well, perhaps. Inflation is born out of arrogance, and you feel that you may be arrogant. But let's trace this back to see where arrogance comes from. I think it is a product of narcissism. By narcissism I am thinking of a disorder typified by an almost obsessive idea that one is right and that one's needs and wants have to be paid special attention to—ought to be catered to both by oneself and by others. Narcissism is neurotic when it controls the person who is suffering from it, rather than the other way around. Going backward another step, narcissism is an extreme degree of confidence in oneself, confidence that one is on the right track. It makes it possible for the person to commit to follow a certain path regardless of the obstacles that get in the way. Going back still further, we come to humility, the shadow side of narcissism. It is the recognition of one's limitations as well as one's capacities. Now we are getting to something."

Here Laurel broke in, excited by what she was hearing. "Humility, yes. That's the part I've been missing. Humility is the key! I know this is true! Say more about humility."

I said that to begin with, it is necessary to understand that a relationship with the Self is not the same as a relationship with God. The Self—at least in the way Jung understood it—is our god-concept, the idea of God that we can only conceptualize; but a concept is not the real thing. We can come to know the Self, but we cannot know God, not the God that we envision as the unknowable reality who stands behind all god-concepts. Laurel had thought that everything was included in the Self, totally harmonized into a single unity. But, as I explained to her, that is not what integration means. If you have black people and white people, to integrate them in a room doesn't mean that you have brown people. You still have black people and white people, but they understand each other and can function together in a harmonious relationship, respecting whatever differences they might have. The differences remain, but the way of looking at them changes. There is intercourse between the opposites. This understanding, and acting upon this understanding, is what brings about the integration of the opposites.

Laurel appeared to be more concerned than before. "Even so, when I see what is possible, I am afraid. This Greatness I feel is so mammoth. I'm afraid of being overwhelmed by it."

Here I observed what appeared to be the last desperate stand of unconscious resistance as it begins to realize that its cause is all but lost. Now came the moment to press forward against that resistance. I had to challenge her "arrogance." "This Greatness that you feel is in you—maybe it's the other way around. Maybe it is *you* who are in the Greatness. Maybe you are just another grain of sand on the beach by the ocean, the boundary place between the land, which we know and which could represent the ego, and the ocean, which extends all around the earth and is deeper than we can imagine."

Laurel paused for a long time, deep in thought. I could almost see the shift taking place in her. She lifted her head, straightened her spine, and her body appeared looser and freer. She looked directly at me with brighter eyes and a new intensity. At last she spoke. "The Greatness is not in me. I am in the Greatness. What a relief! I don't have to carry it. I only have to be there for it, to let it express itself through me. So maybe it isn't arrogance after all. It feels more like being aware of my destiny, what I'm here on this earth for. To live out my own personal destiny."

"Yes. Perhaps that is what manifestation is about. The power manifests through you. You serve as a conduit for it. You are one of those who become aware of the presence of the Source of Wisdom and who open themselves to it, and let it touch them. You are not separate from this Source. Neither have you any control over it. You have the privilege of choosing to serve it. This is to have gnosis, the knowledge of the heart. Like Beethoven, like Mozart, like Amelia Earhart, and like Roger."

Laurel nodded. "Humility is the key. I need to remember that. That's the part that's been missing. Humility is the key, I know it now."

■

Some time had passed since the last dialogue. Laurel was nearing the completion of her research project. She had been able to formulate her ideas in a cogent and logical way. They fit together and seemed to point to some extraordinary conclusions. She explained exactly how she had come to the discoveries she had made. She had developed a methodology to test her hypotheses and carried it out. Her results supported her hypotheses, and she was able to justify the validity of her original thesis. She had even begun to develop the tools needed to apply her theory to practical problems. But all along the route she had been plagued by a recalcitrant inner voice that periodically would cry out, "No, it can't be done!" From her strong ego position, Laurel stubbornly continued to answer back: "But it has to be done!" At a certain point all this changed. Laurel had a dream that portended a transformation:

> I've taken out a book about Jack London and I find a coffeehouse where I can read it. On my way out I meet an old former professor of mine. He stops me and expresses an interest in the book I am carrying. He opens it and tells me things like, "Here's the part about the wild horses," and "Did you know Jack London and his wife dug up the same dinosaur several times?" He then writes his name down along with the names of several people who are experts on Jack London so that I can contact them should I become interested in further information. I leave.

I asked her about the professor. Did she know him? She told me that he had been a very important older man in her life, a real "wise old man," a mentor. Since I believe that everything in a dream has a specific meaning, I questioned her about the dinosaur.

"He's something obsolete. He's no longer able to function in the world we live in. Like outworn ideas that are no longer applicable."

"Do you think some of the ideas that you are 'digging up over and over again' may no longer be applicable?"

Laurel considered this thoughtfully before responding, "Yes. Oh, yes. The old tape. That says that some of the work I have been doing stretches out beyond my field of expertise. That says that I have no business doing it. And yet I want to do it. Something else is telling me that I'm on the right track."

I wondered if that could be the professor's message. Could he represent a wise person who was an aspect of her, and who appeared in her dream to remind her that some of the ideas that were holding her back were like dinosaurs? That she dug them up over and over again, never recognizing that they were the same old thing, the same old complexes speaking to her once again? Was it the dinosaur persuading her that she ought to limit what she was doing to the tired old conventions that everyone else in her field adopts? Yet those were the very same conventions that, as she had explained to me, had kept her field from progressing in ways that she had recognized as essential.

Laurel asked, "Is the dream saying I can go ahead and follow my inner sense of what is possible? That I can proceed, even though what

I am doing goes beyond what has been done before? That I can solve the problems that no one has been able to solve before? What a monumental task! I don't think I know enough. I'm setting myself up for failure."

I agreed that she was doing that. But no one can succeed without risking failure. "You are climbing, climbing the Himalayas. You go up and up and you reach a very high peak. It would be sufficient to rest there, get your bearings, consolidate your position. But no, you look over the ridge and see yet a higher mountain. You want to climb them all. It's as though you want to know *everything*. But you can go just so far, and then you must rest. You must absorb it. You have already learned a great deal from those who have gone before you. Yet you have only pushed the edge of understanding a little bit farther. Perhaps it's enough for right now. Whatever you do, remember this: someone will come along one day and supersede you. Someone will go beyond you, no matter how far you go."

Laurel said softly, "I have been too ambitious."

"You thought that you could climb the highest mountain, that the end was in sight. You reached a peak only to discover that another mountain range lay before you. You've been a brave pioneer. That is one way to look at it. Another way is that you are but a link in a chain of seekers, and that many have preceded you and many others will follow. The end is not in sight. The end is *insight*."

"There are places I can never go. I see that now. But I can see beyond the place where I stand."

I asked her, "What do you see?"

She replied, "Beyond the mountains lie the stars."

The Dance

The work of coming to self-knowledge continues for Ruby and Laurel. Ruby, who began with a diminished sense of self and a strong need of being affirmed by others, discovered depths within her that she could plumb only in solitude. By withdrawing for a time, she learned that also in her was the seed of Logos, germinating and yearning to flower. *Yearning* is a word akin to Eros, for it means to desire greatly. Ruby's Eros desired greatly the "other" within her that had gotten submerged while she was growing up and being socialized and conditioned for her place in the visible world. Laurel, on the other hand, having suffered abuse in early childhood, had buried her wounded Eros and grown up fiercely independent and well defended against any possible injury. She had controlled, or tried to control, every relationship in which she was involved. Yet she, too, was yearning; she was seeking the spontaneous, lighthearted childhood she had never experienced. The nearly impossible role of the mountain climber was a challenge for the developing Eros aspect of Laurel. Her Eros aspect wanted to say something like this: "I am very small and when I see the greatness of the stars I can only gaze in silent wonder." She had to let this happen.

So it is, I believe, with all of us. All of us have something of Ruby in us, and also something of Laurel. Eros seeks the clear light of Logos, and Logos seeks the receptivity and compassion of Eros. Always, in each person, the one seeks the other, and our nature strives for a dynamic balance. A saying of the old Gnostics is fitting here: "Yea, and we all dance the dance. He who danceth not, knoweth not what is being done."

14

The Two in the One

Are There Really Two Worlds?

I was flying over northern India from the desert of Jodhpur in the west toward New Delhi. For quite a while as I looked down all I could see were the parched fields below. Then suddenly all this changed and I was over hundreds of acres of country that had recently been flooded by torrential rains. In neither place could any crops grow, and the inhabitants of each area were suffering terribly from famine and disease. Though they could not see it from the ground, it was clear from the air that if some way could be found to distribute the excess water to places where water was insufficient, there would be enough for everyone to drink and the land would yield enough fruit and grain to feed its people. It made me think that too many people are short-sighted, observing only what is before their faces. Too much attention is paid to relieving our own suffering, and not enough to discovering the cause of all suffering. I thought again of how badly we need an Archimedean point somewhere outside the system from which to view the system in which we are embedded.

And then I remembered that we have such a view. It is the view that struck with wonder all who watched on television as men first walked on the moon. Space travel is taken for granted today, but not so long ago people could scarcely believe that human beings might someday break through the limits of earth's gravity. On that memorable day, we saw with breathless ecstasy the pictures sent back from the moon of our little planet turning round and round in the sky. We saw what no person had ever seen before, that in reality there are no national boundaries. They are only transitory constructs, lines drawn by human hands on a paper map. There is only land area and water area, partly hidden under a translucent veil of clouds. We saw that one land flows into another and that all the oceans are one ocean that embraces all the land. We saw that whatever threatens one part of the globe threatens all of it, and whatever heals one of its wounds must bring succor to all of it. We recognized it. We knew it, in the deepest sense. But the knowledge was too great for most of us, so we let it slip through our fingers. We were like the ant who watched me as I turned the doorknob and opened the back door. We saw it; we marvelled. But it was too much for us, and so we went back to our anthills to live as before.

Two Out of One

We begin life as an embryo in a state of unity with the mother. Consciousness, if it exists at all, is minimal at this stage of development. Soon after birth, the umbilical cord is cut and the primordial oneness becomes a duality. Duality is the condition of consciousness. As soon as we think any thought at all, we differentiate what is from what is not, beginning with what is "I" and what is "not-I." We differentiate our worlds: what is the nature of the world we see, and what is not? With respect to relationships, we soon learn to discern to whom we can properly relate, and to whom we cannot.

I had a friend once who told me, "You are one of us." I didn't know exactly what he meant, but I took the remark to mean that I was a person he cared about. I took it as a compliment at the time, but now I see it differently. What he meant came from a viewpoint that many people share. They see the world as divided into various groupings based on social class, education, lineage, manners, race, religion, and so on. They separate people into three categories—those who are acceptable, those who are not really acceptable but ought to be tolerated, and those whose existence can easily be overlooked. From the dualism of infancy there is a progression to a fragmented view of society. After some careful winnowing out, precious few remain "one of us," and most do not.

In the spiritual innocence of childhood, we are likely to feel ourselves to be in a state of oneness with the god of our fathers and mothers. He (typically male in our culture although female in some others) is everywhere, watches all that we do, and protects us from harm. As we are taught to believe, he performs miracles and wonders for those who have perfect faith in him. But, as we have seen, for most people at some point this guileless trust breaks down and we experience a separation between the divine and the merely human.

The divine is not necessarily depreciated, but rather it tends to be relegated to another world, the invisible world. We attempt to communicate with it and we hope or expect that it will communicate with us through various intermediaries or saints or avatars who manifest the will and intention of the Source, but are in themselves part human and part divine. We have seen how this dualism that eventually becomes fragmentation is reflected in our society. The rational is separated from the spiritual and the imaginal. Orthodox religions are wary of such heresies as gnosis, old and new, and the classic scientific method continues to hang on in disciplines where it does not belong. While the new scientists with their cosmic perspectives are just beginning to be heard by the better-educated people in our society, at the same time data are produced showing that illiteracy continues to be an increasingly urgent problem in these United States. We talk of a holistic paradigm, but there are paradoxes on every side. The Kingdom of the Spirit founders when it is isolated from the world of flesh and blood.

In biblical times, prophets proclaimed apocalyptic visions of the horrors that would precede the end of the world. Today, as we approach the next millennium, those of us who were adults before the Second World War have seen evil and destruction that the ancient apocalyptists never imagined. I remember the outrage everyone felt when we first found out about the mass murders in the Nazi concentration camps. I, for one, could not understand what would make decent, civilized people commit the unspeakable atrocities that took place. The camps are empty now, and serve as memorials for the dead. Today we still hear about them, and I suspect it is primarily because the Jews of many countries, including our own, who felt the inhumanity most keenly, are determined not to allow the public to forget, and rightly so. Yet we in the United States bear a share of the guilt for our reluctance to open our doors to the refugees from Germany and Eastern Europe. While ships sailed from port to port looking for haven, we eased our consciences by sending money to Israel to help with the resettlement of the refugees. The unfortunate survivors of the concentration camps were really "not our problem."

There is more to be said in an apocalyptic tone. It is painful to recall the sins and errors of the past, yet, if we forget, we will have to learn all over again that humanity is one and when any part of it suffers, the health of the whole is endangered. Almost every modern industrialized nation has a shadowy past in which it won its strength by exploiting or dominating weaker peoples. The world is filled with cruelty and inhumanity on every side, and we ourselves are hardly better than Germany or Japan or Australia or Russia or Chile or South Africa. We have only to remember Vietnam, Hiroshima, Nagasaki, and the Native Americans.

Today many people continue to hold the idea that the only way to insure peace is through weapons of war. We neglect the very sources of strength that would build a lasting peace: the physical and mental health of our people, the broad education of our children, the improvement of our environment, and compassionate help for those in need. Because so much of our energy is turned to destructive ends, our entire planetary system is being threatened with breakdown, stasis, collapse, or entropy.

Nevertheless, and despite all this doomsaying, hopes still persist for a messianic age to come in *this* world, the place where we live. Human beings are a stubborn lot and some vital forces are rising. On one side, we might observe that the universe is winding down. On the other, we could say that it is also winding up. If we stop short of the total annihilation of our planet, opportunities for redemption will be abundant. Imagine that instead of thinking of world surveillance from outer space as a "defense measure," we could see its potential for a cooperative effort on the part of many nations to observe and better understand the transnational currents in the air and on the seas. Imagine that the problems of the planet could be shared by all of its inhabitants. Much of the same technology designed for destruction could be used to bring about a better distribution of the world's resources and goods. In many places this is already beginning to happen. Much of what has been learned about nuclear energy is being put to peacetime uses, for producing cheap power, new developments in medicine, in agriculture, and in genetics, to name just a few of the areas.

We are born, and shortly thereafter we find ourselves in a world that appears to be in a state of chaos. Discipline is required to learn how to use the tools available to deal with the chaos. As we grow older, our discipline must become more rigorous if we are to make sense out of what we see around us. When we have learned to discipline ourselves and our desires, we begin to be able to make some order out of the chaos. When we have learned to follow the rules established by others, to organize, discriminate, and arrange our thoughts in logical order, we must inevitably come to the edge of knowledge, to the end of understanding, and hence to the end of perceived order. But then we are in a very different state from the one we were in when we first set out to deal with chaos. We are not helpless before the chaos, the *Mysterium Tremendum*, but rather we have matured to a point where we can become a sort of junior partner with the unknown God, and we must remember that we are *junior*. We are, after all, made of the same stuff as the stars; we embody the same energy. We move in the same rhythms as all creation, because, after all, we are part of creation—we are *creatura*, as the old Gnostics used to say, in contrast to the *pleroma*, the Fullness that lies beyond our understanding.

We need to keep very much in our place, without hubris, but being open to the wise guidance offered to us. We need to be unafraid of accepting what we do not fully understand. When we are able to tolerate ambiguity, paradox, and mystery, we no longer need so desperately to find all the answers. We know that answers do not beget contentment, only additional questions. Therefore, we may continue to take a keen interest in exploring the mystery more and more deeply, but not as something we are compelled to attack tooth and nail. Rather, we attend to it through the gentle process of continuing attention, so that when our Divine Partner speaks, we will be listening and we will hear, when we are called we will come, and when requirements are set upon us we will fulfill them with a whole heart.

The Two in the One

The proper relationship of the two worlds—the visible and the invisible—is not that one triumphs over the other, nor that one discredits the other. People who favor the one are no more whole or psychologically mature than those who favor the other. The proper relationship of the one to the other is in a commitment to the process of bringing about an understanding between the two worlds. The psyche, as the organ of consciousness, needs to be made permeable on both sides— to the inner experience and to the impact of the environment. The vision of the existence that is possible needs to be realized in the world as it is now. Then the practical necessities of the visible world will permeate the ideal world. In this way, the world beyond the confines of rational thinking will be able to bring new and healing insights and behaviors to the visible world, while the visible world will provide the grounding needed for the other world so that it does not evaporate into the space of airy theories with little relevance to the everyday problems of normal human beings. Intimations of the invisible world may come in sudden flashes, but an ongoing awareness of it requires the careful and patiently cultivated process of inner work. If what we see is truly what is beyond the visible world, we will perceive it and experience it as harmony within and harmony without. Finally, we will know that the visible world and the invisible world are only *concepts* created by the intellect, the functions of which are to analyze, to discriminate, to reason, and to judge.

If we could even for a moment throw away our concepts and see with the inner eye through all the veils of conditioning, we would know that there is only one world, one indissoluble whole. We would see that all the creatures on earth are part of a single system. There is no preferred species; there is no preferred race. In the Eye of Wisdom we are all equals, participants in one coherent cosmic system. The world we experience as visible was never separate from the whole; it only seemed so. The separation was an illusion. There is no other place from which we came, except in the illusions cherished by the mind. There is no other place to which we must someday go. It is all here, all now, in its entirety. The future does not exist, and the past is already gone. What we do, we must do in this very moment. There is no other, no preferred moment. When we can accept what is before our eyes, accept it with whole heart, we no longer have anything to fear, anything to long for. All we need to set the world aright is here. We have only to see it.

References

Bakewell, C., 1907. *Sourcebook in Ancient Philosophy*. New York: Scribners.

Barnstone, W., ed. 1984. *The Other Bible*. San Francisco: Harper & Row.

Blake, W. 1957. *The Complete Writings of William Blake, with All the Variant Readings*. G. Keynes, ed. New York: Random House.

Blofeld, J. 1973. *The Secret and Sublime: Taoist Mysteries and Magic*. New York: E. P. Dutton.

Bohm, D. 1957. *Causality and Chance in Modern Physics*. London: Routledge & Kegan Paul.

———. 1980. *Wholeness and the Implicate Order*. London: Routledge & Kegan Paul.

Campbell, J. 1949. *The Hero with a Thousand Faces*. New York: Pantheon Books.

Chuang Tsu. 1974. *Inner Chapters*. G.-F. Feng and J. English, trans. New York: Random House.

Dart, J. 1988. *The Jesus of Heresy and History*. San Francisco: Harper & Row.

Darwin, C. 1952. *The Origin of Species by Means of Natural Selection*. Chicago: Great Books. Encyclopaedia Brittanica.

Davies, P. 1988. *The Cosmic Blueprint: New Discoveries in Nature's Creative Ability to Order the Universe*. New York: Simon & Schuster.

Doresse, J. 1960. *The Secret Books of the Egyptian Gnostics*. New York: Viking Press.

Eldredge, N., and S. J. Gould. 1972. "Punctuated Equilibria: An Alternative to Phylogenetic Gradualism." In *Models in Paleobiology*, edited by T. J. Schopf. San Francisco: Cooper.

Fitzgerald, E., trans. Undated. *Rubaiyat of Omar Khayyam*. New York: Thomas Y. Crowell.

Fox, M. 1988. *The Coming of the Cosmic Christ: The Healing of Mother Earth and the Birth of a Global Renaissance*. San Francisco: Harper & Row.

Freud, S. 1900/1938. "The Interpretation of Dreams." In *The Basic Writings of Sigmund Freud*, translated and edited by A. A. Brill. New York: Random House.

Gilchrist, A. 1863. *The Life of William Blake*. London: Macmillan.

Gleick, J. 1987. *Chaos*. New York: Viking.

Graves, R. 1955. *The Greek Myths*, Vol. II. New York: George Braziller.

Guillaumont, A., H. C. Puech, G. Quispel, W. Till, and A. Masih, trans. 1959. *The Gospel According to Thomas*. New York: Harper & Row.

Hamilton, E. 1969. *Mythology: Timeless Tales of Gods and Heroes*. Boston: Little, Brown.

Hawking, S. 1988. *A Brief History of Time: From the Big Bang to Black Holes*. New York: Bantam Books.

Hesse, H. 1969. *Magister Ludi (The Glass Bead Game)*. R. and C. Winston, trans. New York: Bantam.

Hevesi, D. July 9, 1988. "Amid Clatter, Monks Calmly Sift Sand." *New York Times*.

Hiltunen, S. 1988. "Initial Therapeutic Applications of Noh Theater in Drama Therapy." *Journal of Transpersonal Psychology* 20: p. 71.

Holy Bible. King James Version. Undated. London: Oxford University Press.

Holy Bible. Revised Standard Version. 1952. New York: Thomas Nelson & Sons.

Huxley, A. 1963. *The Doors of Perception*. New York: Harper & Row.

Inge, W. R. 1921. *The Philosophy of Plotinus*. London: Longmans, Green.

James, W. 1928. *The Varieties of Religious Experience*. New York: Longmans, Green & Co.

Jantsch, E. 1975. *Design for Evolution: Self-Organization and Planning in the Life of Human Systems*. New York: George Braziller.

Jung, C. G. 1902/1970. "On the Psychology and Pathology of So-Called Occult Phenomena." *Psychiatric Studies* (Collected Works, Vol. 1). Princeton: Princeton University Press.

———. 1906–30/1961. *Freud and Psychoanalysis* (Collected Works, Vol. 4). Princeton: Princeton University Press.

———. 1921/1971. *Psychological Types* (Collected Works, Vol. 6). Princeton: Princeton University Press.

———. 1928/1966. *Two Essays in Analytical Psychology* (Collected Works, Vol. 7). Princeton: Princeton University Press.

———. 1928/1969. *The Structure and Dynamics of the Psyche* (Collected Works, Vol. 8). Princeton: Princeton University Press.

———. 1936/1968. *The Archetypes and the Collective Unconscious* (Collected Works, Vol 9, i). Princeton: Princeton University Press.

———. 1951/1968. *Aion* (Collected Works, Vol. 9, ii). Princeton: Princeton University Press.

———. 1942/1954/1969. *Psychology and Religion: West and East* (Collected Works, Vol. 11). Princeton: Princeton University Press.

———. 1961. *Memories, Dreams, Reflections*. New York: Random House.

Kohlberg, L. 1964. "The Development of Moral Character and Ideology." In *Review of Child Development Research*, Vol. 1, edited by M. and L. Hoffman. New York: Russell Sage Foundation.

Kronig, R. 1960. "The Turning Point." In *Physics in the Twentieth Century: A Memorial Volume to Wolfgang Pauli*, edited by M. Fierz and V. F. Weisskopf. New York.

Kuhn, T. 1970. *The Structure of Scientific Revolutions*, 2nd ed. Chicago: University of Chicago Press.

Laing, R. 1968. *The Politics of Experience*. New York: Ballantine.

Lao Tsu. 1972. *Tao Te Ching*. G.-F. Feng and J. English, trans. New York: Random House.

Laszlo, E. 1972. *The Systems View of the World*. New York: George Braziller.

———. 1987. *Evolution: The Grand Synthesis*. New York: Random House.

Loevinger, J. 1966. "The Meaning and Measurement of Ego Development." *American Psychologist* 21:195–216.

Lovelock, J. 1988. *The Ages of Gaia: A Biography of Our Living Earth*. New York: W. W. Norton.

March, A., and I. M. Freeman. 1962. *New World of Physics*. New York: Random House.

Miller, R. 1984 and 1988 (revised). *The Gnostic Holy Eucharist Service*. Palo Alto, CA. Unpublished.

Moyne, J., and C. Barks. 1984. *Versions of Rumi*. Putney, VT: Threshold Books.

Neumann, E. 1956. *Amor and Psyche: The Psychic Development of the Feminine (A Commentary on the Tale by Apuleius)*. New York: Pantheon Books.

Novalis. 1798. "Aphorisms," from *Pollen and Fragments*. C. E. Passage, trans. In Robert Bly, *News of the Universe*, 1980. San Francisco: Sierra Club Books.

Pagels, E. 1979. *The Gnostic Gospels*. New York: Random House.

———. 1988. *Adam, Eve, and the Serpent*. New York: Random House.

Pagels, H. 1982. *The Cosmic Code: Quantum Physics as the Language of Nature*. New York: Simon & Schuster.

———. 1985. *Perfect Symmetry*. London: Joseph.

Piaget, J. 1951. *The Child's Conception of the World*. London: Humanities Press.

Planck, M. 1949. *Scientific Autobiography and Other Papers*. F. Gaynor, trans. New York.

Prigogine, I. 1980. *From Being to Becoming: Time and Complexity in the Physical Sciences*. San Francisco: Freeman.

Pulver, M. 1955. "The Round Dance and the Crucifixion According to the Acts of St. John." In *The Mysteries* (Papers from the Eranos Yearbooks). New York: Pantheon Press.

Robinson, J., gen. ed. 1988. *The Nag Hammadi Library*, 3rd rev. ed. San Francisco: Harper & Row.

Rudolph, K. 1983. *Gnosis*. San Francisco: Harper and Row.

Scholem, G. 1954. *Major Trends in Jewish Mysticism*. New York: Schocken Books.

———. 1971. *The Messianic Idea in Judaism*. New York: Schocken Books.

Schopenhauer, A. 1891/1928. "The Ages of Life" in *The Works of Schopenhauer*. Translated by T. B. Saunders, and edited by W. Durant. New York: Simon & Schuster.

Sheldrake, R. 1981. *A New Science of Life: The Hypothesis of Formative Causation*. London: Blond.

———. 1988. *The Presence of the Past: Morphic Resonance and the Habits of Nature*. New York: Random House.

Singer, J. 1972. *Boundaries of the Soul: The Practice of Jung's Psychology*. New York: Doubleday.

———. 1989. *Androgyny: The Opposites Within*. Boston: Sigo Press.

Snow, C. P. 1959. *The Two Cultures and the Scientific Revolution*. Cambridge, England: Cambridge University Press.

Weinberg, S. 1977. *The First Three Minutes*. New York: Basic Books.

Wilber, K. 1977. *The Spectrum of Consciousness*. Wheaton, IL: Theosophical Publishing House.

———. 1980. *The Atman Project: A Transpersonal View of Human Development*. Wheaton, IL: Theosophical Publishing House.

———. 1981. *Up From Eden*. New York: Anchor Press/Doubleday.

Zimmer, H. 1953. *Philosophies of India*. Edited by J. Campbell. New York: Pantheon Books.

Ziolkowski, T. 1965. *The Novels of Hermann Hesse*. Princeton: Princeton University Press.

Zohar. Five volumes. 1956. Translated by G. Sperling and M. Simon. London: Soncino Press.

Index